LEARNING . services

01209 722146

Duchy College Rosewarne
Learning Centre

This resource is to be returned on or before the last date
stamped below. To renew items please contact the Centre

Three Week Loan

Dahlias
A Colour Guide

Dahlias
A Colour Guide

Ted Collins

The Crowood Press

First Published in 2003 by
The Crowood Press Ltd
Ramsbury, Marlborough
Wiltshire SN8 2HR

www.crowood.com

British Library Cataloguing-in-Publication Data
A catalogue reference for this book is available from the British Library

ISBN 1 86126 582 4

Acknowledgements
We would like to thank the National Dahlia Society (NDS) and the American
Dahlia Society (ADS) for full access to, and use of, their classification guides.
   Photography is by the late Derek Hewlett MBE and the late Terry Gillam; also
David Reid. Thanks must also be given for information from Ron Hedge, the
honorary librarian at Wisley; D. Bates (NDS); Alan Fisher (ADS); and Keith
Hammett (NZDS).We are also grateful to the many nurseries that provided
details from their lists.

Typeface used: Sabon, main text; Helvetica, captions.

Typeset and designed by
D & N Publishing
Lowesden Business Park, Lambourn Woodlands, Berkshire.

Printed and bound by Craft Print International, Singapore

Contents

Introduction

The garden dahlia has a colour for every mood, a form for every situation, and a size for every occasion. It excels for garden use, cut flowers, flower arrangement and for show exhibition. With care the dahlia is easy to grow, providing perfect blooms wherever it is grown throughout the world, at the same time providing tubers for next year's growth. It overcomes the extremes of nature and the unwanted attentions of various pests to provide breath-taking displays in the garden, either individually or in concert with other species throughout late summer and autumn. Alternatively it can provide an endless supply of cut blooms, week in, week out, for use in the home, church or office. It can be tall, up to 2m (6ft) in height, or small at 30cm (12in); it can be time-consuming, or it will survive with little other than dead-heading: the choice is yours.

Origins

The dahlia is a long-established favourite with horticulturists. It belongs to the Compositae group of plants that includes other genera such as asters, helianthus and chrysanthemum – it is known as 'composite' because of the composite structure of the flower, each bloom consisting of a group of florets arranged on a flattish or domed disc at the extremity of the single stem. Each floret is complete, with individual reproductive organs.

Compositae is the largest group of flowering plant, with more than 14,000 species worldwide. Many of these are vegetables – for instance lettuce and artichoke – and there are also trees and shrubs, alpines and aquatics, as well as garden species. The dahlia belongs to the sub-group Heliantheae, along with *Helianthus* (sunflower), *Rudbeckia*, *Coreopsis* and *Cosmos*; however, it is different from these genera, as it produces root tubers and has inter-floret bracts. In the past the genus *Dahlia* contained twenty-seven species that grew in the wild in Central America, mainly Mexico and Guatemala. Currently work is being done genetically in New Zealand to produce new species, such as *D. australis*, by Dr Keith Hammett.

The cultivated garden dahlia *Dahlia × variabilis* is an herbaceous perennial, classified by the Royal Horticultural Society as H3, a half-hardy perennial. It is thought to be the result of hybridization between two wild species several hundred years ago, possibly on the semi-tropical mountain slopes of Mexico. Whilst it is accepted that one parent was *D. coccinea,* there is conjecture as to whether the other parent is *D. imperialis*, the tree dahlia, or *D. pinnata*, both purple-flowered species: there is no conclusive proof as to which it might be.

It *is* known, however, that interest in the dahlia in Europe commenced in about 1650, when reports of Compositae were published in Rome, in particular in the work of Francisco Hernandez, a Spaniard who had spent seven years in Mexico, from 1650; he had been funded by Philip II, the then king of Spain, and amongst other research had perhaps been looking for another New World rival for the potato. He discovered instead the dahlia, which because of the flowers' hollow stems, the Aztecs called 'acocotli' or 'cocoxchitl', meaning 'hollow pipes' or 'water tubes'; and because of their star shape, the single blooms were linked by the Aztecs to religious rituals associated with the sun.

Dahlia seed arrived in Europe some time prior to 1789, sent by the director of the Mexican botanical gardens,

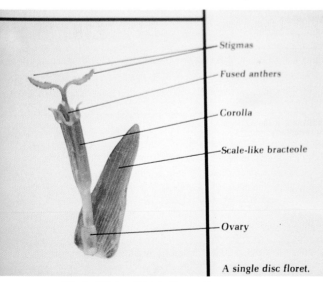

Stigmas

Fused anthers

Corolla

Scale-like bracteole

Ovary

A single disc floret.

Floret showing reproductive organs.

6

Levick's commander-in-chief, 1833.

Levick's beauty of Sheffield, 1834.

Vincent de Cervantes, to the Abbé Cavanilles, who worked at the botanical gardens of Madrid. Abbé Cavanilles published a report in 1791 based on the resulting plants, naming one species *Dahlia pinnata* in honour of the Swedish botanist Andreas Dahl, and two further species *Dahlia rosea* and *Dahlia cocchinea*. This report stirred the interest of horticulturists, though their requests for seed were unsuccessful.

Some of that seed was, however, acquired in 1798 by Lady Bute, the wife of the British ambassador to Spain, on behalf of Kew Gardens; some seed found its way to France in 1802 and some to Germany in the same year, where the leading botanist Professor Wildenow changed the name of the resulting plants to *Georgina* in honour of a Russian botanist, causing subsequent confusion in the horticultural world. It is from the resulting plants of these seeds distributed throughout Europe that the modern garden dahlia has evolved.

Natural genetic modification and pollination by insects changed the weak-stemmed, single-bloom *D. coccinea*, *D. rosea* and *D. pinnata* into *D. variabilis*; botanists subsequently improved on nature by further focused genetic modification. In the UK in 1816, double-flowered show and fancy varieties appeared, now called 'ball' varieties; other forms also developed, but because of

A promotional flyer from a early twentieth-century nursery.

the popularity of the show and fancy varieties, these were destroyed.

In Germany in 1850, Lilliput or Pompon varieties were developed, later to be improved in France into the Pompon of today; the name 'pompon' was derived from the name 'pompon' of French sailors' hats. Later in Germany peony-type dahlias evolved from flat petal, single varieties; these were also improved at this point in time by Dutch breeders. Eventually in Holland in 1872 the cactus varieties were obtained from one tuber received from Mexico. Finally in France in 1899 the Collorette varieties were discovered. This completed the range of modern garden varieties.

As early as 1836 the first dahlia register was published by the Horticultural Society of London (now the Royal Horticultural Society): this listed 700 varieties, such as Levick's Beauty of Sheffield, and Commander-in-Chief. In the nineteenth century nurserymen across Europe, such as Pape Bergaman and Quedunburg, were spurred on to produce new varieties, as horticultural shows then offered as much as 100 guineas as first prize money (as a yardstick, the average weekly wage was perhaps around £2 per week). Since that time both nurseries throughout the world and individual enthusiasts have produced a fantastic range of garden dahlias, some 50,000 individual varieties, each named after something or someone special to the raiser.

by frost. By watching a long-range weather forecast it may be that the frost can be prejudged and the plants cut just prior to the frost, because if you cut just before the plants are frosted they are easier to handle.

However good the cultivation, if a lot of dahlias are grown, pests and diseases will be contained within these cut plants as well as in the straw if this is used for mulching. This debris of old plants and mulch can be composted, however – though if this option is chosen, it has to be well done, and it may be that your local municipal authority can do this much more efficiently. What is important is that this material does not remain over the winter season in your garden untreated. If you want to compost your own, ensure

A plant cut down in early winter.

Propagation

When and where does dahlia growing begin? For most established beds of dahlias it must be with the tubers they contain. During the flowering season those plants that produced the best blooms, either in quantity or quality, should be especially marked, in order that future propagation is done from the 'best' plants (anyway, every plant should be labelled with its name in such a way that its progress can be followed from cutting to lifting).

It is usual to cut plants down when they have been blackened

Carefully lifting tubers to avoid damage.

8

Storing tubers over winter.

the wardrobe, or in a box in the garden shed – this used to be a favourite with dahlia lovers. Nowadays a more practical way of storing them is in the greenhouse or frame. When first lifted from the garden bed, the tubers, known as field tubers, are best laid upside down initially for, say, fourteen days so that any residual water can drain from the hollow main stem; sometimes the main stem is actually 'hollowed out' to ensure that residual water is lost.

The tubers should then be stored in trays of peat or vermiculite, or in between layers of straw or wood shavings. They should also be securely labelled to ensure that when you embark on propagating the following year, the plants are what you want. In early spring the tubers can be brought to life in readiness for propagation by spraying with warm water, and by providing additional heat, preferably from below, by way of soil cable, to about 65°F; the air temperature should be increased to about 55°F.

There are some varieties that are difficult to keep over winter as field tubers; with these, a few plants should be kept through the summer in 10 or 13cm (4 or 5in) pots, rather than planted in the dahlia bed – this forces the plant to produce compact tubers, from which propagation can take place.

that you build up, layer by layer, a compost heap that can breathe and that will break down all the vegetative material contained; using a compost tumbler and proprietary compost maker will also help.

Dahlias require protection against frost, and, once the top growth has been removed, there are two options. If you grow dahlias in Nova Scotia for example, with 25 degrees of frost or anything approaching that, dig the tubers up with a fork, being careful not to damage them; and if any damage does occur, cut off these tubers close to the crown. Store them in a frost-free place. In the UK and the USA, nine years out of ten it is possible to leave the tubers in position, provided 2–3cm (1in) of soil is drawn up over the crown; alternatively, straw, peat or similar materials can be used. Always take anti-slug precautions during the winter, according to conditions in your area.

Storing Tubers
Stored tubers will be better for future propagation purposes if you can prevent them from drying out, and there are as many ways of doing this as there are dahlia growers: wrapped in paper they may be placed under the bed or on top of

An example of a field tuber after lifting.

9

A chicken leg.

Creating Additional Plants

If you do not want too many plants from your field tubers, you can create additional plants by splitting the clump. To do this, select a 'green eye' on the crown, and cut it away with at least one tuber attached (the 'crown' being the part of the dahlia plant that was previously at, or just above, ground level). This can be done either with tubers lifted and stored, or with tubers left in the ground and lifted in the spring. These single-eyed tubers are known as

Taking cuttings.

'chicken legs', and they can be grown on in the greenhouse or, depending on climate, replanted in the garden bed. Alternatively the tubers – either as field tubers or as chicken legs – can be set up as previously described in a greenhouse and supplied with heat, preferably bottom heat, and moisture; the eyes will develop into shoots. It is important not to cut the tubers in half, as the feeding roots mainly emerge from the ends of the tubers. If the clump is too big, reduce the number of tubers by cutting them individually close to the crown.

When the shoot has two pairs of leaves or more, a cutting may be taken below the first leaf joint; use a sharp knife to do this. These 'cuttings' can then be rooted: using a proprietary hormone powder or gel, each one should be firmly placed – definitely firmly placed – in a rooting medium, when it will produce roots within ten to fourteen days. The original cut 'eye' will callous over, and normally two more green eyes will appear where the original eye was on the crown.

When rooted, the small plants should be potted on into individual 7cm (3in) (0.23ltr) pots containing a good potting mixture, either bought in, or of your own composition. There

Tubers sprouting.

Prepared cuttings

are many proprietary brands of compost-making chemicals available that will do this; then plants may be moved on into larger pots until planting out.

The dahlia is thus bountiful in supplying just the number of new plants you want from the old stock. It is even more bountiful in that once plants are established, leaf cuttings can be taken: this is done by removing a leaf complete with an axial bud; this often means removing a small portion of the stem and rooting this, as for a crown shoot. One three-paired leafed plant will provide six plants, with a good chance that the original plant will also grow on in due course. How-ever, Nature keeps the situation in check as it will be found that too much cutting in this way weakens the immune system of the resulting progeny. Thus moderation in propagation is no bad thing, because although it is possible to obtain hundreds of plants from one field tuber, doing so will increase the chance of virus infection.

The Flowering Season

During the flowering season you may find that one of your yellow-bloomed plants has produced a white bloom on one stem: this is a 'sport', and most of the axial buds should be treated as for leaf cuttings. Once secured as a small plant and over-wintered, the progeny from this plant or plants should be white, whilst the off-spring of the original plant remain yellow-bloomed. An example of this is Hillcrest Desire sporting to Sylvia's Desire, and then Jackie's Desire. Be careful, though: if all the blooms are white, you may have just mixed up the labels.

Dahlias can be grown satisfactorily from seed, topmix and many bedding varieties, and many wonderful double-flowered varieties have been achieved in this way. Unfortunately

Rooted cuttings.

11

An example of a sport where Hillcrest Desire became Sylvia's Desire and then Jackie's Desire.

with double-bloomed varieties, more than 95 per cent or more of seed-grown plants will produce single-flowered blooms, or double blooms of poor quality, and those saved will have to be grown for three or more years to be sure that your raising of them is worthwhile. However, anyone can produce his or her own seed, and this can be rewarding because no one knows what the end result will be.

Collect the seedheads in late autumn when they are fully ripe: the heads will feel plump to the touch, even though they will still look green. Allow to dry out completely in the greenhouse or in some frost-free place, by which time they will be brown and crisp.

Seed pods.

Ripe pod.

Remove the petals, blowing away unwanted parts; initially the seed will be green or light brown, but it will turn blackish and will harden, and it should then be stored. As with any perennial seed, sow from mid-spring onwards, in trays filled with almost any seed compost; cover lightly. Pot on as with any other plants.

Cultivation

Dahlias will grow in any soil, in any location. However, as with most flowers, they will grow that much better if good gardening practices are observed. For instance, as a species the dahlia is a lover of water, indeed

Seed pod opened.

it is almost greedy for it; but it will not thrive if its roots are waterlogged, so the soil needs to be well drained.

Next, for what use do you intend your dahlias? As part of a mixed bed, or on their own, as garden or cut flowers, or for exhibition purposes? Whatever their use, good ground preparation is essential. Where dahlias have been removed, or for a first-time bed, the traditional dig is to be recommended. For this, remove a spade's width of soil across the bed at one end, placing this soil adjacent to the opposite end. Break up the underlying soil, and rough dig the second row into the space left by the removed soil, and so on, incorporating well rotted garden compost or animal manure into the digging. If the bed is then left over the winter months, frost, rain and nature will complete the work. Garden dahlias do not require intensive double digging, as the roots for feeding and water intake are fine, extending in the top 15cm (6in) of soil, up to 1m (3ft) in radius from the tuber tip. In early spring apply a proprietary inorganic and or organic fertilizer, raking this into the soil – and then hoe, hoe, and hoe again, both before and after planting, to encourage those fine roots to grow and extend – though obviously, avoiding root damage as much as is possible.

A well grown plant.

Potting On and Planting Out

The dahlia requires room to grow at every stage, so be generous when you begin potting on. As planting-out time arrives, ideally your plants should be in 13cm (5in) (1.1ltr) diameter pots, they should have been given plenty of light and, about a month before planting out, should have been placed in a cold frame or where they are protected from frost and cold winds. Although 'hardened off', the plants should still be soft and vibrant; however, do not be afraid to discard 'early' plants if these have become over-tall or woody. Given reasonable weather, younger, more-compact plants will soon overtake their 'elders'.

Because of the way their fine roots spread, dahlia plants need to be spaced at generous intervals. To obtain exhibition standards, giant and large varieties need to be spaced 1m (3ft) apart, whilst most others need to be 60cm (2ft 6in) apart, except for bedding dahlias that need be only 30–45cm (12–18in). So mark out the distances before planting. If not growing for exhibition, still be as generous as possible with planting distances. Dig a hole large enough to contain all the root soil-ball of the plant, and so there is a slight depression left after planting; many garden centres supply specialized tools to make this an easy task when a large number of plants must be

Planting.

Mulching.

'Stopping'

Once a plant is well established, the growing centre of the plant should be removed. When this is done will depend on the type of season, the location of the garden, the dahlia variety, and the use you intend for the blooms. If growing for garden display it should be about a month after planting out; if growing for shows, six to eight weeks prior to the show date. If it is left unchecked, the centre stem will become dominant because of the plant hormone auxin produced in the stem tip: this promotes the growth of the stem, and when the stem stops growing, it suppresses the growth of side shoots. The effect of auxin reduces with time, but in order to obtain even-sized branches with even-sized blooms, it is necessary to 'stop' the plant at an early date, as indicated.

Unlike some species, 'stopping' the dahlia is not an exact science because of its luscious nature – meaning its ability to respond quickly in growth to heat and moisture. As

planted. Once *in situ*, support each plant with a cane for early protection – though garden varieties by their nature are generally more compact and require less support than exhibition types; in addition, by allowing more branches to grow, the plants tend to become self-supporting.

It helps the plant to become acclimatized if the soil of the rootball is quite wet before planting: never plant dry. One method is to soak each plant in a bucket of water containing a dose of systemic insecticide together with a compatible liquid fertilizer; allow each plant to drain back into the bucket before planting, and top up the bucket with insecticide and fertilizer from time to time. If the weather is dry, after a couple of days a good sprinkling of water is useful, and thereafter as the plants grow, a consistent regime of watering and hoeing is to be recommended.

As the plants grow, so to do the weeds, despite hoeing; as well as being unsightly, they compete for ground moisture, so a good mulching with straw or well-rotted animal manure or spent mushroom compost is required. It is important to ensure that your mulch is pest free. It is not unknown to import a whole colony or two of earwigs into your garden with bales of straw, so check these carefully before using them, and destroy any pests. Similarly the source of manure is important: zealous farmers may have used a herbicide that although harmless to animals, is harmful to your dahlias, with dire results. The mulch should be applied when the soil is extremely moist, so water if necessary; that goes for straw also, if used – it may be a good idea to soak bales in advance.

'Stopping' or pinching out the growing centre.

15

Removing side buds.

we have seen, 'stopping' encourages growth into the plant's lateral branches, rather than into the main or central stem. Each lateral branch will produce a terminal flower bud and lateral flower buds, as well as axial shoots that are each capable of providing further lateral branches. It follows that the more lateral branches and axial shoots on a plant, the more blooms will be provided – all of which will be perfectly good for the garden. These blooms will be smaller than blooms produced on plants where lateral branches have been reduced, axial shoots removed, and finally side buds removed.

Some varieties flower such that the main-stem bloom has a short stem; but if the main-stem bud is removed and the side bud retained, this will produce as good a bloom about ten days later, but with a longer stem. This is particularly useful for exhibition purposes, firstly to improve the bloom's appearance, but also to delay the bloom for the date required. As previously mentioned, however, nature requires a price for interference like this, and the resultant 'side' bloom will be smaller than a 'centre' bloom.

If growing giant varieties for exhibition, only three or four branches will be retained. Virtually all axial shoots will be removed, except for perhaps a couple of the latter, in case a 'sport' occurs. As a result, with the right variety, blooms can be obtained that are each 45cm (18in) across and 38cm (15in) in depth.

'Tying up'.

For medium varieties, five or six branches are normally retained, and for small varieties and miniatures, up to nine branches; but varieties vary, and only experience will govern what choice is made when debranching. With pompon dahlias, to obtain a fully spherical bloom the calyx or green outer covering must be removed as colour shows in the bloom, and with most varieties it is necessary to retain side buds until the last few days before the show.

Most garden dahlias are big, showy plants, and despite strong stems require support; the application of potash is valuable in ensuring a strong stem. The support needed will depend on why you are growing the dahlia: for garden or cut flowers, a strong central wooden support with some supplementary twine or raffia loops to the plant will be enough; for exhibition, mostly three canes are used, in a triangle with two or three loops at varying heights. Remember that the dahlia plant will become large, and will have either several large blooms or many smaller ones; so when wind and rains come, the plant has to support a considerable weight – therefore a measure of assistance will ensure that the plants and blooms remain upright. Exhibitors will go to considerable lengths to ensure this, with a range of covers to prevent rain and wind damaging the blooms.

Harvesting the Blooms

Having achieved excellent blooms on long stems, the gardener will want to remove these from the plant, whether for exhibition or decorative use. Using a sharp knife, the stem should be cut with a sloping cut just above a pair of leaves so that the leaf axial bud is left undamaged; it will then develop into the next branch complete with bloom, perhaps providing a bloom in about fourteen days. It is very important that the cut stem is placed almost immediately in water, and to this end always have water buckets close by when cutting. It is also very important to try to cut in the early morning or in the late afternoon, and never in full sun, otherwise back-petal wilt will follow; the blooms will recover, but the damage to the back petals will be visible. Once the blooms are cut and the stems placed in water, with large hollow-stemmed varieties it is advantageous to further cut or 'spike' the stem under water, thereby releasing air to ensure that water is taken up the stem to prevent petal droop.

Exhibiting Dahlias

Exhibiting dahlias is addictive, and to be a winner requires dedication, whether at village, area or national level: the higher the challenge, the more dedication is required, but the greater the thrill of the win, and particularly if it is

Cutting blooms.

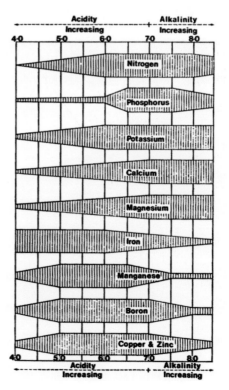

The pH scale and nutrients.

17

unexpected. Judges look for perfection in size, form and freshness, with no evidence of damage by either man or pest. Whole books can, and have been, dedicated to the subject, so a few words can only point the way. To begin with, it is important to accept that there will be successes and failures, so set out with an attainable target; it requires experience of varieties and types of dahlia to be able to produce winners. For example, some soils favour cactus types, others decorative types or pompons. Have your soil analysed: the result will not tell you the type of dahlia to grow, but you will know whether you have the right soil balance, namely neutral to pH7. Do not fight the soil. Also, be prepared to be ruthless: although you may think a variety is a winner, the judges may not, so be ready to ditch it after repeated failures.

Preventing Damage

As a guide, growing 100 dahlias to show standards requires a minimum of an hour's work every night for six weeks of the run into and during the flowering season – it cannot be fourteen hours once a week. To avoid weather damage, some form of cover is required during peak bloom time, for instance a framework of wood and plastic to cover a whole bed of flowers, or an umbrel-

Covers for protection from weather.

la or similar to protect individual blooms. Blooms must also be prevented from damaging each other, so it is important to cane the stems and tie back flowers as necessary.

Pest control is essential, and earwigs are the obvious cause of much damage. Good husbandry will help to reduce their numbers, in that these insects breed in late winter in dead leaves and similar debris: so take action in early spring using paraffin or similar, and with traps in pots with straw or paper. As the show season approaches, some exhibitors smear a 7–8cm (3in) band of Vaseline around each stem, about 15cm (6in) below the bloom once colour shows in the bud.

Having grown and cut the perfect bloom, do not throw away a winning chance by risking damage to it in transit. Have a system of carriage that prevents blooms moving against each other or against the vehicle. Similarly on arrival, survey the area for staging, and make sure that you reserve a firm surface for staging your blooms, safe from inadvertent damage by others – it happens! Alas some cheating occurs, too, but very little, as showing is an honourable occupation; but occasionally it does happen – a pompon bloom, say, is removed or added – so time for a last-minute check of all your exhibits is essential, even if only to replace maybe a wilted bloom.

Make sure you know the schedule requirements: many exhibitors are disqualified for showing an incorrect number of blooms, or incorrect types in exhibits.

Go fully equipped with sharp knife, tweezers, cotton buds and a small paintbrush, and don't be afraid to pull out damaged or dead petals, particularly rear petals – what the judge doesn't see won't cost you points.

Try not to get carried away by the buzz of the pre-show atmosphere. Join one or more local societies; and don't be afraid to ask questions – most exhibitors will be pleased to help. Finally, join your national society.

Pests and Disease

The dahlia is similar to many other species in that it is prone to attack by aphids, caterpillars, earwigs, molluscs, red spider mite and wasps. Aphids come as blackfly, greenfly and whitefly, all of which are clearly visible on plants at various times in their life cycle: greenfly early, whitefly in mid-life, and blackfly at plant maturity. Aphids can spread viruses, distort buds or compromise the development of florets; however, control is

Capsid bug damage.

relatively easy, requiring no more than a regular spray programme. Spray before aphids appear, and as recommended by the manufacturer of the spray, whether a contact or systemic type. The following pests will attack dahlias:

The capsid bug is a sap-sucking insect that attacks and distorts buds and the growing tips of leaves. Regular spraying will prevent and/or control this pest.

Caterpillars damage foliage and blooms. Again, a spraying programme is the answer. Regrettably there is no ecological solution, as with the demise of the caterpillar there is also the loss of the subsequent butterfly or moth.

Earwigs damage foliage or blooms – usually the best bloom you have ever grown. There is no easy cure, no magic spray: prevention is by good husbandry, specifically clearing up all debris so none is left lying around over winter, thereby removing the insects' breeding areas. Make traps of straw or paper in pots from which earwigs can be dropped into paraffin or hot water, hunting them down in the evening or at night and using finger and thumb to destroy them – though beware! – earwigs can nip. An empty washing-up liquid bottle makes an excellent vehicle for squirting paraffin into crevices that you know are sheltering earwigs.

Molluscs: Slugs and snails gnaw foliage and blooms causing similar damage to that wrought by caterpillars. Traps can be set under pots or old wood; also metaldehyde, in liquid or pellet form, can be used around plants. Use bird-, animal- and children-friendly versions, all of which are necessary for a happy garden.

Red spider mite is microscopic in size; individually they are usually brown in colour, but en masse they appear to be red. The first symptoms are a yellowing of the lower leaves, that eventually turn brown and crisp,

Slug damage.

19

Red spider.

with a steady progression onto higher leaves; if left untreated, the spiders eventually spin webs across the blooms. The effect of the infestation is to debilitate the plants.

The spiders can overwinter on tubers and/or surrounding trees and bushes; they thrive in hot, dry weather. One remedy is to spray the leaves profusely on both sides; otherwise – and more effectively – a proprietary insecticide should be used. It is important to spray at ten-day intervals because the mites lay eggs that hatch at ten-day intervals, so it is important to kill not just the mites but their descendants, too. It is essential to treat greenhouses and frames where tubers have been stored or set up, and also surrounding trees or wooden fencing. Unless especially required, infected plants are best destroyed.

Wasps are insects that live by boring into the stem of a plant: they thrive on the fleshy part, extracting sugar and using the stem tissue to line their nests. They will come back again and again to the same plant and the same stem, weakening it until it collapses; if it is a main stem this will destroy the plant. Control wasps by trapping them with sugar water in pots with a small entry hole.

Fungal Infection, Galls and Viruses
The dahlia is not exempt from diseases such as fungal infection, galls and viruses:

Fungal infections, one of which is 'Dahlia Smut', occur in humid conditions, to start with showing as a light green spot on the leaves: this spot increases in size, turning yellow, then brown, before dying. Infected

Dahlia smut.

spores splash up from the ground during rain or watering, so collect and burn any dead leaves, and use a proprietary fungicide on the plant and surrounding soil. You do not want this disease more than once.

Galls consist of wart-like growths that appear on the crown of the plant, and very rarely on leaves. The galls are caused by soil bacterium entering the plant tissue after damage has occurred, and they will spread, eventually producing shoots that look like cauliflower shoots. If growing this plant is important, remove the growth and grow on, but *do not propagate* from the damaged

20

Crown gall.

or cutting blooms. It is often advised to sterilize the blade between cuts, but in fact there is no fully effective sterilizer; all you can do is try to reduce the risk.

At the first sign of a suspected virus in the plant, destroy it: it doesn't matter if you paid a fortune for it, or if it has great sentimental value – you should destroy it, and remove it from your garden at once. Regrettably there is no cure at present, although in the year 2000 the American Dahlia Society embarked on a serious research programme for a cure. The signs of virus in plants are stunting and/or distorted and mottled yellowing of the leaves, and any plant so affected must be destroyed as soon as identified, as it is a danger to all other dahlias in its vicinity. Virus infection has dramatically reduced in recent years as growers have realized its seriousness, and that destruction is the only cure; all in all this has ensured better husbandry.

area. More realistically, lift and destroy the plant and tubers.

Viruses are a serious problem for dahlias: such disease can arrive in good-looking plants that you have bought, or in the pre-packed or otherwise purchased tuber. They can be spread when the sap of one of your dahlias is infected by a biting or sucking insect that has just bitten or sucked an already infected plant in your garden; or by insects that travel from someone else's garden. A contaminated knife can also transmit infection on the blade, whilst taking cuttings

There are several viruses: **dahlia mosaic** is the most common, appearing as mottled, distorted leaf patterns. **Cucumber mosaic** is another type of virus, with similar mottling of the leaves; the effect is stunting or dwarfing of the whole plant to perhaps a third of its normal height, and consequent distortion of blooms. **Spotted wilt virus** causes the plant to wilt and die.

Mosaic virus.

21

Stunt virus.

Virus plant.

Garden Use

Dahlias can be grown in the garden for summer bedding schemes in spectacular blocks of colour, using one variety in particular if it has a striking colour and contrasting foliage. Alternatively yellow- or pink-flowered dwarf bedding varieties can be combined effectively with Verbena Homestead Purple or silver-leafed *Cineraria maritima*.

A different combination is a contrasted tiered approach for block planting; this can be achieved using 30cm (12in) dwarf bedding varieties in the first row, 45cm (18in) varieties in the second row, and so on, up to, say, 60cm (2ft) in height. Using the A to Z section will help you spend many worthwhile winter hours planning such a bed, and many more during the flowering season enjoying the results.

In some areas a sub-tropical bedding scheme can be successfully achieved, again using dwarf bedding varieties of bright red, yellow or bronze flowers, to combine or contrast with the striking bronze or green leaves and lily-like flowers of the Cannas. Alternatively *Abutilon megapotamicum variegatum* or standard plants of heliotrope can be used as contrast plants, as can the castor-oil plant *Ricinus communis* with its rich green or bronze foliage that contrasts brilliantly with dahlias in a sub-tropical scheme.

Nowadays, however, most gardens contain borders of mixed hardy perennials, bulbs or half-hardy perennials in which dahlias serve as a focal point of colour and foliage texture. In the border the permanent framework is usually flowering or foliage-hardy shrubs, and dahlias blend or contrast with any number of types of shrub. For example, red dahlias work well with purple-leafed cotinus or berberis, and silver- or grey-leafed *Senecio*, the latter also working well with yellow dahlias.

Waterlily varieties can also be used effectively in mixed beds: for example, the pink varieties such as Gerrie Hoek, Pearl of Heemstede or Red Velvet work well with yellow rudbeckias, sedums and pink/purple-flowered *Liatris spicata*. Some of the taller varieties of waterlily, such as Taratahiti Ruby, can be used to striking effect at the back of the border.

Today, even without a garden in which to plant dahlias, they can still be enjoyed in pots or containers on a patio: using dwarf varieties either exclusively or with other species of a similar height, and either matching or of contrasting colour, success can be guaranteed provided good compost is used, and with adequate and regular watering.

The range of dahlias on offer is immense, so experiment: success is yours for the taking, and your bedding mix will be unique as well as rewarding.

Definitions

The garden dahlia is classified by the Royal Horticultural Society as 'h3', a half-hardy perennial, and all varieties listed hereinafter are h3. The varieties that follow in the A-to-Z list have been mainly selected from the current National Dahlia Society's (NDS) classified directory and the American Dahlia Society's (ADS) current classification and handbook of dahlias. Where possible, types, colours, usage, raiser, country of origin and

Petal types for classification.

year of introduction are provided, as well as the variety name.

There are many instances of differences between NDS and ADS classifications. In the main these arise from the difference in climatic conditions, the UK having a more temperate climate overall, as opposed to the USA's that is very varied, from a similarly temperate climate in the western seaboard, to the much hotter and drier conditions of the eastern states.

The NDS classified directory is issued every two years, and is produced by the classification committee. The main criterion for inclusion is that the cultivar listed must have been included in one supplier's catalogue during the previous three years. The classification of individual varieties is achieved by removing petals from about two-thirds the depth of the bloom. Over the years the groups included have been modified to accommodate the changes produced by breeders or growers of the dahlia to ensure that the best interests of the dahlia itself are achieved; such changes require the approval of the executive council.

The ADS handbook originates with the ADS classification committee, whose members are drawn from across the states. As well as the ADS, it incorporates the Central States Dahlia Society, the Federation of Northwest Dahlia Growers, the Midwest Dahlia Conference, the Pacific Northwest & Southwest Conferences, and the Southern States Dahlia Association. One of the criteria for initial inclusion in the ADS handbook is that the cultivar listed must have won two blue ribbons in the preceding year, and it must have won three blue ribbons in the last two consecutive years to remain listed (a blue ribbon is awarded for a class winner at a dahlia show). Alternatively a cultivar must have achieved an evaluated score of 85 or greater at an official trial ground or seedling bench. Points are awarded for bloom size, colour and form, together with an assessment of foliage.

For inclusion in the biennial NDS Classified Directory, the variety must be in at least one current UK trader's catalogue. Size definitions are set by the Royal Horticultural Society, colour definition is based upon the current RHS colour chart. Formation types are assessed independently by the ADS and NDS, that is decoratives, cactus, semi-cactus, etc. However, there are differences between the NDS and ADS assessments in as much as the ADS classification contains a wider range of groups. More comprehensive details follow.

For exhibition in the UK, judging rings are used that give a degree of tolerance, as blooms grow in size when cut and left in water. If a bloom does not pass cleanly through the ring, the whole exhibit is disqualified. This is not the case for ADS exhibiting. Unclassified varieties in the UK are judged as appertaining to the class type in which the exhibit is displayed. If in the opinion of the judges the exhibit does not conform, then it may be either disregarded or downpointed, as would under-sized blooms.

Various awards are presented to different categories of dahlia throughout the year. For instance, the NDS awards the Stredwick medal to the disbudded double cultivar gaining the most points during a season at trials held at the Royal Horticultural Show at Wisley Gardens in Surrey, judged by a joint NDS and RHS committee. The John Brown medal is awarded at the same trials to bedding dahlia varieties. The Harry Howarth medal is awarded at the NDS trials for exhibition varieties held in the Leeds City Council's Golden Acre Park, all cultivars being disbudded; the winner is the variety with the overall maximum quality and quantity of seasonal blooms.

The ADS awards are the Lynn B. Dudley, the Evie Gullickson and the Derrill Hart, all of which require a minimum of three scores over 85. The Lynn B. Dudley is for a fully double variety on the seedling bench; the Derrill Hart for a fully double in a trial garden; and the Evie Gullickson is for both seedling and trial bench, for open-centred varieties. The award goes to the highest scoring in each group. The Stanley Johnson medal is awarded to the cultivar with the highest number of 'higher awards' (other than best in class), such as best in show.

A History of Registration
As previously mentioned, in 1836 the London Horticultural Society issued a register of some 700 varieties. A century later, in the early 1960s, a series of conferences took place in Europe and the USA to organize a concise directory of dahlia varieties, hopefully to avoid duplication. As a result of this, in 1969 the Royal Horticultural Society issued the first international directory of dahlia varieties, and from time to time has issued

supplementary lists. No one knows the approximate total number of named varieties that have been produced and grown since 1836, but one source in the UK lists 27,000 named varieties, and in the USA another list stands at 44,000, each name on both lists individual, but some appearing on both. The RHS is responsible for classifying by size and providing colour charts, so that the NDS and the ADS can classify varieties by colour and size.

Size

The designated sizes for each category are as follows, although for competition the NDS allows an increase in size for each size classification. These increases are shown after the RHS size classification:
Giant-flowered: Usually over 250mm (10in).
Large-flowered: Usually between 200 and 250mm (8 and 9.8in) (up to 260mm/10.2in).
Medium-flowered: Usually between 150 and 200mm (6 and 8in) (up to 220mm/8.6in).
Small-flowered: Usually between 100 and 150mm (4 and 6in) (up to 170mm/6.7in).
Miniature-flowered, except ball: Not usually exceeding 100mm (4in) (up to 115mm/4.5in).
Pompon-flowered: Not exceeding 50mm (1.96in) (up to 52mm/2in).
Miniature-flowered ball: Usually between 50mm (1.96in) up to 100mm (4in) (up to 115mm/4.5in).

Form

Single-Flowered
NDS: Single dahlias have blooms with a single outer ray of florets that may overlap, the centre forming a disc.
ADS: Single and mignon, open-centred dahlias with a single row of uniform, evenly spaced, ray florets in a flat plane surrounding the disc.

Anemone-Flowered
NDS: Blooms with one or more outer rings of generally flattened ray florets surrounding a dense group of tubular florets, and showing no disc.
ADS: Anemone dahlias with one or more rows of ray florets surrounding a centre of elongated tubular disc florets. The disc florets should be fully developed and present a domed pincushion appearance.

Collerette (NDS); Collarette (ADS)

NDS: Blooms with a single outer ring of generally flat ray florets that may overlap, with a ring of small florets (the collar), the centre forming a disc.

ADS: Open-centred dahlias with a single row of uniform, evenly spaced, compound ray florets in a flat plane surrounding the disc. The petaloids surrounding the disc are less than one half the length of the ray florets.

Waterlily

NDS: Fully double blooms characterized by broad and generally sparse ray florets that are straight, or slightly involuted along their length, giving the flower a shallow appearance. The depth should be less than half the diameter of the bloom.

ADS: Blooms should be fully double and symmetrical, the side view should be flat to saucer shape in arrangement, and the layer of florets should be openly faced to give a delicate appearance; the centre should be closed and dome-shaped, breaking gradually to four to seven rows of fully developed outer florets. The outer florets should be broad and slightly cupped; the preferred bloom position, 45 degrees.

Decorative

NDS: Fully double blooms showing no disc. The ray florets are generally broad and flat, and may be involuted for no more than 75 per cent of their length (longitudinal axis) or slightly twisted; they are usually bluntly pointed.

ADS: *Formal decorative*: Ray florets flat, partially revoluted, partially involuted. Petals uniform and regularly arranged, tending to recurve towards the stem.

Informal Decorative: Ray florets twisted, curled or wavy, imparting a petal that is not flat. Petals may be partially revoluted, with their arrangement irregular.

Ball

NDS: Fully double blooms, ball-shaped or slightly flattened. The ray florets blunt or rounded at the tips, with margins spirally arranged and involuted for at least 75 per cent of the length of the florets.

ADS: Fully double flowers, ball-shaped or slightly flattened at the face, the ray florets blunt, rounded or indented, involuted for most of their length, fully involuted for about one half of their length; normally displayed in a spiral arrangement.

Pompon

NDS: Fully double spherical blooms of miniature size, with florets involuted for the whole of their length (longitudinal axis).

ADS: Fully double flowers to ball dahlias, but more globular and smaller in size; the ray florets involuted for the whole of their length, and fully involuted for more than half their length.

Cactus

NDS: Fully double blooms, the ray florets usually pointed, the majority narrow and revoluted for 50 per cent or more of their length (longitudinal axis) and either straight or incurving.

ADS: *Straight cactus*: Ray florets revoluted for more than one half their length: pointed, straight. Or recurved, radiating in all directions from the centre.

Incurved cactus: Ray florets revoluted for one half their length; pointed, with pronounced curvature of petals towards the centre of the flower head.

Semi-Cactus

NDS: Fully double blooms, the ray florets are usually pointed and revoluted for more than 25 per cent of their length, and less than 50 per cent of their length. Longitudinal axis, broad at base and either straight or incurving.

ADS: Ray florets, broad at base, straight or incurved, with ray florets revoluted for up to one half of their length.

Miscellaneous

NDS: Any dahlias that do not fall into one of the foregoing groups, e.g. orchid-flowered.

Stellar ADS: Fully double, breaking gradually from immature florets to fully developed outer florets. The outer florets should be narrow and involuted with a slight recurve to the stem. The less mature florets should possess the same narrow and partially involuted characteristics. The depth of the Stellar dahlia type should be from one half to two-thirds the diameter of the bloom, the greater depth being the ideal.

Lacinated ADS: The split or lacination should be in proportion to the ray floret length. There should be an overall twisting in the area of the split involuted or revoluted ray florets to give an overall fringe effect.

Peony ADS: Open-centred dahlia with two or more rows of ray florets surrounding the disc florets. Ray florets adjacent to the disc florets may be smaller, twisted and or curled.

Orchid ADS: Open-centred dahlias with a single row of uniform, evenly spaced ray florets in a flat plane surrounding the disc flowers. The ray florets are involuted for two-thirds or more of their length, and fully involuted for at least one-third of their length.

Novelty ADS: Have characteristics from the preceding classifications.

Open: Have a disc centre.

Fully Double: Will have a fully double centre.

Glossary, ADS

Blends: Two or more colours that gradually merge but are distinguishable from 2m (6ft). The short or immature ray florets comprising the central portion of the fully double flowers when at their prime stage.

Disc: A more or less flat, circular group of tubular florets that make up the central part of the flower head, visible in open-centred dahlias

Disc florets: Small tubular florets that make up the central part of the flower head, each with a pistil and stamens, but generally no other conspicuous flower parts.

Floret: One of the small flowers that collectively comprise the flower head.

Fully double: Flower heads with multiple rows of ray florets: the disc florets are immature and completely covered by central rays when the flower is at prime time.

Incurved: The ray florets curve forward along their length toward the face of the flower head.

Involuted: Margins of the ray florets roll forward along their longitudinal axis. When fully involuted, the margins touch or overlap so only the reverse of the floret is visible.

Lacinated: The ray florets are split: there should be a twisting in the area of the split, involuted ray florets, to give an overall fringed effect.

Margin: The edge of the ray florets and the area are adjacent.

Marginal rays: Fully developed ray florets that establish and determine the maximum diameter of a bloom: mature florets rather than immature central ray florets.

Petal: The common name for the conspicuously coloured part of a floret.

Ray florets: One of the broad, conspicuously coloured florets, the structure of which suggests a single petal of an ordinary bloom. These form the radiating border in the open-centred type of dahlia, or massed together, the flower head in fully double types.

Recurved: The ray florets curve backward along their length towards the stem.

Revoluted: The margins of the ray florets roll backwards along their longitudinal axis. When fully revoluted, the margins touch or overlap.

Straight: The ray florets have little or no curvature throughout their length.

Colours

The following colours are common to NDS and ADS:

White; yellow-orange; bronze; flame; pink; red; dark red; lavender; purple.

In addition, NDS link lilac or mauve with lavender; and Pink Wine or violet with purple. Blends, bicolour and variegated are included.

Also ADS lists dark pink, light blend and dark blend.

In addition some unclassified (NDS) and undisseminated (ADS) examples have been included where these appear to the author to be warranted to ensure a balanced view for the reader.

Suppliers

Where to purchase a variety may be found at the end of each entry, where the supplier is introduced by available data, for example, 'Swan Island'. Suppliers are listed alphabetically, also by country, after the A–Z of Varieties section. This data is based on 2002 listings; it should be recorded that most nurseries operate a minimum sales limit per year, which if not reached will mean the variety is then discarded. Also nurseries go out of business or are sold.

The Seasonal Calendar

Early Winter

- Cut down all plants to just above ground level soon after, or just before, the first frosts. Remove debris for composting or burning.
- Carefully lift the tubers; ensure the labels are firmly fixed.
- Store the tubers in a frost-free place; initially keep them upside down to assist drainage from their hollow stem.
- Try to keep the tuber from drying out.
- Check all heating appliances, including stand-by appliances.

Mid-Winter

- Start rough digging; obtain a soil test for fertility.
- Read the lists you will have received from nurseries, but only order what you really need. Check your supplies of labels, and order as necessary.
- Complete the cleaning of greenhouse frames, pots and so on.
- Remove dead leaves and general debris to limit earwig breeding.
- From time to time check the stored tubers for fungus infection; remove any affected parts, and treat with fungicide.

Late Winter/ Early Spring

- Set up tubers on a heated bench, removing any that are damaged or infected.
- As early shoots occur, take cuttings and root in pots or trays.
- Spray night and morning, and commence your spraying programme with insecticide.
- Towards the end of the period, if without a greenhouse lift field tubers, and carefully split the clump if additional plants are required.

Late Spring

- Place split tubers on a heated bench in the greenhouse or in a cold frame, to increase stock.
- Put well-developed plants into a cold frame to 'harden off'.
- Hoe carefully between plants to open up the topsoil and keep down weeds.

Early Summer

- Plant out when there is no further risk of frost.
- Remember to allow room between plants for the root run.
- Ensure that plants are well watered at this stage.
- Towards the end of this period mulch between plants.
- Finally, remove the growing centre i.e. 'stop' the plant.
- Start a feeding programme with a higher nitrogen content.

Mid- and Late Summer

- If intending to exhibit, remove branches as necessary, together with axial buds.
- Continue the feeding programme.
- Tie up plants as necessary.
- Keep up the routine of watering and spraying with insecticides.

Late Summer

- Continue disbudding for exhibition purposes, and tying up generally.
- Increase the watering programme to about 4.5ltr (1gal) per day for each plant.
- Check covers.
- Ensure that a plentiful stock of split canes for branch support is available.
- Growth is now rapid, so you will need to increase the time you spend with the dahlias.

Early Autumn

- Cut bloom after bloom.
- Change the feeding regime to include a feed with a higher potash content.
- Continue the spraying routine: it is at this time that this gets forgotten.
- Win or lose, enjoy the dahlia shows. Note what wins, and grow that next year; and look out for new varieties.

Mid- to Late Autumn

- Plants continue to decline, but remember to mark the 'best' plants from which to propagate next year.
- Decrease the watering.
- Purchase a supply of fungicide to spray or dust the tubers when they are lifted.
- Prepare storage space, and be ready to lift the tubers.

A–Z of Varieties

A

A. J.
Miniature ball (ADS); red exhibition variety; height 1.2m (4ft); originated by Clacks, USA in 1999. Available USA: Clacks.

A La Mode
Medium; formal decorative (ADS); bicolour orange and white; growing to a height of 1.1m (4ft). Excellent exhibition and garden variety with striking blooms; originated by Swan Island, USA, in 1993. Available USA: Capistrano, Connell's, Dahlia Dandies, Elkhorn, Swan Island; Canada: Ferncliff.

Abingdon Ace
Small decorative (NDS); red exhibition, a garden and cut flower dahlia; raised by C. Rance, UK, in 1992. Available UK: National.

Abridge Ben
Miniature decorative (unclassified); purple exhibition, garden and excellent cut flowers variety; height 0.9m (3ft); raised by Jack Kinns, UK, in 1986 – named after the family dog.

Abridge Natalie
A small waterlily (NDS) with pink and yellow blended blooms on strong stems; useful for exhibition, garden and cut bloom use; height 1.3m (4.5ft); raised by Jack Kinns, UK, in 1989. Available UK: National, P. & L.; USA: Connell's.

Abridge Taffy
A miniature decorative (NDS); a good, white, classic exhibition, garden and cut flower variety with blooms on long stems on a compact bush 1.2m (4ft) in height; raised by Jack Kinns, UK, in 1978. Available UK: Cruikshank, National, P. & L.; elsewhere: Jacks

Ad Lib
Giant cactus (ADS); variegated purple and red, exhibition variety; height 1.5m (4.5ft); raised by

Chambers, USA, in 2001. Available USA: SB Gardens.

Advance
Giant, informal decorative (ADS); light blends of yellow and pink, exhibition variety; height 1.2m (4ft) mid-season (USA); originated by Simon, USA, in 1990. Available USA: Elkhorn; Canada: Ferncliff.

Ailsa Bailey
Miniature formal decorative (ADS); dark pink, exhibition and garden variety; height 1.1m (3.5ft); long black stems; introduced R. Bailey, New Zealand, in 1994. Available USA: Dan's Dahlias; Canada: Ferncliff; elsewhere: Jacks.

Akita
Classified as a miscellaneous dahlia (NDS); blooms are red/yellow blends with large chrysanthemum petals, the tips of which turn inwards. Grows to 1.2m (4ft) in height; introduced by Konishi, Japan, 1988. Available UK: Abacus, National; elsewhere: Dgid, Engelhardt, Graines.

Akita No Hikari
Novelty (ADS); dark red, garden variety, 1.5m (5ft) in height; introduced Ohta, Japan, in 1981. Available USA: Alpen, Capistrano, Clacks, Dahlia Dandies, Dan's Dahlias, Mingus, SB Gardens.

Aksel Juul
Miniature formal decorative (ADS); bicolour purple and white, garden and exhibition variety; height 1.2m (4ft); originated by Juul, USA, in 1984. Available USA: Clacks.

Al Almand
Medium lacinated (ADS); orange, exhibition variety; originated by W. Almand, USA, in 1993. Available USA: Elkhorn.

Alan Melville
Collerette with red blooms and a yellow collar (unclassified);

an excellent garden variety; height 75cm (30in); introduced by M. Roberts, UK, in 1993. Wisley Award Garden Merit, Wisley (NDS) 1996.

Alden Snowlodge
Miniature straight cactus (ADS); white garden variety; height 0.9m (3ft); originated by Rossack, Australia, in 1990. Available USA: Clacks, Dan's Dahlias.

Alena Rose
A waterlily (ADS); light blends of lavender and white; prolific early cut-flower blooms on a 1.2m (4ft) high bush; originated by L. Connell, USA, in 2000. Available USA: Connell's.

Alfred C
Giant semi-cactus (ADS); orange exhibition variety, a prolific winner over many years; height 0.9m (3ft); originator W. Almand, USA, in 1974. Available USA: Arrowhead, Clacks, Hamilton, Mingus.

Alfred Grille
Medium, incurved (ADS); light blends yellow and pink, exhibition and cut flower variety; height 1.2m (4ft); introduced Severin, Germany, in 1965. Available USA: Dahlia Dandies, Elkhorn, Mingus; elsewhere: Wirth.

Ali Oop
Miniature formal decorative (ADS); red, cut flower variety; height 1.2m (4ft); prolific, with 10cm (4in) blooms that are very deep, almost forming a ball; originated by N. Gitt, USA, in 1995. Available USA: Swan Island.

Alicia Marie
A small, formal, decorative (unclassified); light yellow exhibition variety with blooms on a 1.2 (4ft) high bush (unclassified); originated by L. Connell, USA, in 2002. High-scoring seedling in Lynn B. Dudley (ADS) trials in 2001. Available USA: Connell's.

ABRIDGE BEN

ABRIDGE TAFFY

ALAN MELVILLE

ALFRED C

Aljo
A large semi-cactus (ADS) with dark pink blooms on strong stems; a tall grower, to 1.3m (5ft); raised in Holland, introduced in 1978. Available USA: Clacks, Connell's; elsewhere: Wirth.

All Triumph
Medium semi-cactus (ADS); pure white exhibition garden and cut flower variety; 0.9m (3ft); compact bush; originated USA in 1972. Available USA: Arrowhead, Dan's Dahlias, Frey's, Swan Island.

Allan Snowfire
Medium semi-cactus (ADS); white exhibition blooms on a 1.1m (3.5ft) bush; raised by R. Cook, UK, in 2001.

Allie Yellow
Medium formal decorative (ADS); yellow exhibition variety; height 1.2m (4ft); originated by Simon, USA, in 1996. Available USA: Mingus.

Allison
Small, lacinated cactus (ADS); yellow exhibition and cut flower variety; tall grower to 1.5m (5ft) in height, on medium-length stems; originator Nowotarski, USA, in 2000. Awarded Lynn B. Dudley medal (ADS), 1999. Available USA: Clacks!

Alloway Candy
A double orchid (NDS) or a stellar (ADS) variety; pink and white blends (NDS), or pink (ADS); growing to a height of 1.2m (4ft). Useful for garden and cut flower, and excellent for basket and floral artwork; introduced J. Stitt, New Zealand, in 1988. Available USA: Alpen, Clacks, Connell's, Dahlia Dandies, Dan's Dahlias, Elkhorn, SB Gardens, Sea-Tac.

Alloway Cottage
Medium decorative (NDS), medium formal decorative (ADS); light blend yellow and pink exhibition blooms on strong stems growing to a height of 1m (3.5ft); introduced by J. Stitt, New Zealand, 1970. Available UK: Halls, National, Oscroft, P. & L, Roberts, Tivey; USA: Alpen, Capistrano, Clacks; elsewhere: Engelhardt, Geerlings, Graines, Jacks, Wirth.

Alltami Classic
Medium decorative (NDS), medium formal decorative (ADS); yellow exhibition variety; height 1.2m (4ft); raised by H. Williams, UK, in 1980. Available UK: Halls, National; elsewhere: Jacks.

Alltami Ruby
Medium semi-cactus (NDS); red exhibition and garden variety; raised by H. Williams, UK, in 1984. Available UK: National; USA: Elkhorn.

Almand Climax
A giant decorative variety (NDS) of well formed lavender and white blends; an exhibition type growing to 1.2m (4ft) in height; raised by W. Almand, USA, in 1968. Award merit 1976 Wisley (NDS). Available UK: Cruikshank, National, Oscroft, Tivey; Canada: Ferncliff; elsewhere: Geerlings, Wirth.

Almand Delight
Medium lacinated cactus (ADS); yellow; originated by W. Almand, USA, in 1996. Available USA: Elkhorn.

Almand Joy
A large, formal, decorative (ADS); lavender and white sport of Almand Climax growing to a height of 1.2m (4ft); useful exhibition variety; introduced by W. Almand, USA, in 1968. Winner of the Derrill Hart medal. Available USA: Connell's, Elkhorn, Frey's, Hamilton, Sea-Tac, Swan Island; elsewhere: Engelhardt, Graines.

Almand Supreme
Giant semi-cactus (ADS); yellow exhibition variety; height 0.9m (3ft); originated by W. Almand, USA, in 1991. Available USA: Clacks, Elkhorn, Mingus, Sea-Tac.

Aloha
A medium semi-cactus (NDS), with yellow/red blended blooms; good garden and exhibition variety; raised by M. Geisert, USA, in 1986. Awarded the Lynn B. Dudley medal in 1985 (ADS). Available UK: Cruikshank, National, Scotts, Station House, Tivey; USA: Connell's; elsewhere: Dgid, Engelhardt, Graines, Wirth.

Alpen Blaze
Anemone (ADS); orange exhibition variety, 1.5m (4.5ft) in height; originated by W. McClaren, USA, in 1994. Available USA: Clacks, Dahlia Dandies; elsewhere: Konishi.

Alpen Bob
Large, informal decorative (ADS), with variegated lavender and purple blooms; for garden use and exhibition purposes; originated by W. McClaren in 1999. Awarded the Derrill Hart medal. Available USA: Arrowhead.

Alpen Cherub
Collarette (ADS); white, excellent exhibition and garden variety; grows to a height of 1.2m (4ft); introduced by W. McClaren, USA, in 1987. Available USA: Capistrano, Clacks, Connell's, Creekside, Dahlia Dandies, Dan's Dahlias; Canada: Ferncliff; elsewhere: Wirth.

Alpen Currant
Small cactus (ADS); dark red blooms for garden use; originated by W. McClaren, USA, in 1996. Awarded Lynn B. Dudley medal 1995 (ADS). Available USA: Alpen, Arrowhead, SB Gardens.

ALLAN SNOWFIRE

ALMAND CLIMAX

ALOHA

Alpen Flame
Miniature straight cactus (ADS); flame exhibition variety; height 0.9m (3ft); originated by W. McClaren, USA, in 1995. Available USA: Capistrano, Clacks, Dahlia Dandies.

Alpen Flathead
Collarette (ADS); purple, with variegated purple and white collar; garden variety; height 1.2m (4ft); originated by W. McClaren, USA, in 1997. Available USA: Capistrano, Dahlia Dandies.

Alpen Fury
Anemone (ADS); red, garden variety; height 1.5m (5ft); originated by W. McClaren, USA, in 1995. Available USA: Dan's Dahlias, SB Gardens; elsewhere: Konishi.

Alpen Imp
Orchid (ADS); pink, exhibition variety; height 1.5m (5ft); originated by W. McClaren, USA, in 2002. Available USA: Alpen.

Alpen Jewel
Medium, formal decorative (ADS); variegated purple and red, exhibition and cut flower variety; height 1.2m (4ft); originated by W. McClaren, USA, in 1991. Available USA: Creekside.

Alpen Lois
Collarette (ADS); light blends pink and yellow, exhibition variety; height 1.2m (4ft); originated by McClaren, USA, in 2001. Available USA: Dahlia Dandies.

Alpen Marjory
Miniature ball (ADS); variegated lavender, red and yellow garden variety; height 0.9m (3ft); originated by W. McClaren, USA, in 1986. Available USA: Clacks, Dahlia Dandies, Dan's Dahlias, SB Gardens.

Alpen Pearl
Anemone flowering variety (ADS); light blends pink and white blooms on a 1.2m (4ft) high bush; originated by W. McClaren, USA, in 1997. Available USA: Clacks, Connell's, Dahlia Dandies, Dan's Dahlias; elsewhere: Konishi.

Alpen Rhicky
Miniature cactus (NDS and ADS); red exhibition, garden and cut flower variety; height 1.2m (4ft); originator W. McClaren, USA, in 1992. Available USA: Alpen, SB Gardens.

Alpen Rocket
Orchid (ADS); red garden and exhibition variety 1.2m (4ft) in height; originated by W. McClaren, USA, in 2002. Available USA: Alpen.

Alpen Shadows
Single (ADS); bicolour dark red and lavender, garden and exhibition variety; 1.1m (3.5ft) high; plants originated by W. McClaren, USA, in 2000. Available USA: Alpen, Clacks.

Alpen Snowflake
Miniature semi-cactus (ADS); white garden variety; 0.9m (3ft) in height; originated by W. McClaren, USA, in 1991. Available USA: Capistrano, Clacks, Sea-Tac.

Alpen Splendor
Anemone (ADS); an orchid, dark pink with yellow and purple centre tubes; growing to a height of 1.1m (4ft); stands out against fimbriated foliage; originated by W. McClaren, USA, in 2000. Available USA: Alpen.

Alpen Steve
Small, informal, decorative (ADS); white exhibition and garden variety; 1.5m (5ft) in height; originated by W. McClaren, USA. Awarded Derrill Hart medal (ADS). Available USA: Alpen.

Alpen Velvet
Medium, formal, decorative (ADS); dark red garden variety; originated by W. McClaren, USA, in 1999. Available USA: Arrowhead, Capistrano.

Alpen Wonder
Orchid dahlia (ADS); pink blooms for garden use; originated by W. McClaren, USA. Awarded Derrill Hart medal 1989 (ADS). Available USA: Clacks.

Alsie
Small, informal, decorative (ADS); light blended yellow and pink blooms; garden variety; originated by Simmons, USA, in 1976. Awarded Derrill Hart medal (ADS).

Alta Bishop
Single (ADS); red and yellow garden variety; originated by Mason and Yano, USA, in 1967. Awarded Lynn B. Dudley medal (ADS) in 1968. Available USA: Dan's Dahlias.

Alva's Doris
Small cactus (NDS); with red blooms growing to a height of 0.9m (3ft); excellent for the garden; raised by V. Frost, New Zealand, in 1965. Award Merit Wisley 1970; award Garden Merit Wisley 1993 (NDS). Available UK: Aylett's, National.

Alva's Supreme
Giant decorative (NDS) or large informal decorative (ADS); a pure yellow; raised by V. Frost of New Zealand in 1956; for exhibition purposes; strong-growing stems to a height of 1.4m (4.5ft), with 38cm (15in) diameter blooms (UK); late flowering (UK); requires early start (UK January). Wisley Award Merit sported Cream Alva's (E. Machin, UK, 1990); Wisley Award Garden Merit 1995, White Alva's (J. Mills, UK); Wisley Award Garden Merit 1997. Available UK: Abacus, Cruikshank, Halls, National, Oscroft, P. & L., Station House, Tivey; USA: Dahlia Dandies, Elkhorn; Canada: Candahlia; elsewhere: Dgid, Wirth.

ALPEN FURY

ALPEN SNOWFLAKE

ALVA'S SUPREME

Amalfi
Medium semi-cactus
(unclassified); red garden
variety to a height of 1.2m
(4ft); originated Holland.
Available elsewhere: Turc.

Amaran Pentire
Small, semi-cactus (NDS);
yellow and orange exhibition
blooms; raised by R. Stevens,
UK, in 1994. Available UK:
National.

Amber Banker
Medium cactus (NDS); orange,
exhibition blooms, also useful
for garden; raised by P. Tivey,
UK, in 1982. Available UK:
National; elsewhere: Jacks.

Amber Festival
Small, decorative (NDS);
orange blended exhibition
blooms, useful for garden and
cut flowers; raised by D. Boyd,
UK, in 1999. Available UK:
Halls, JRG, National, Porter,
Pratt, Spencer, Station House,
Taylor; USA: Creekside;
elsewhere: Jacks.

Amberglow
Miniature ball (NDS and ADS);
bronze (NDS), orange (ADS);
excellent for use in the garden;
growing to a height of 0.9m
(3ft); also for exhibition work
(hard centred); introduced by
Cor Geerlings, Holland, in
1994. Available UK: Aylett's,
National, Oscroft, P. & L.,
Tivey; Canada: Candahlia;
elsewhere: Geerlings.

Amberley Emma
A tall, double-orchid variety
(unclassified); 1.4 m (5ft) in

height; pink and white,
excellent garden variety (back
of border); introduced in 1999.

Amberley Nicola
Small, decorative or formal
type (unclassified); free-
flowering lavender and white
blooms; excellent garden
variety; introduced in 1999.

Ambition
Small, lacinated cactus (ADS);
purple exhibition blooms, also
useful for garden and cut
flower use; on a 1.2m (4ft)
bush; introduced by Ballego,
Holland, in 1989. Available
USA: Mingus.

Amelia's Surprise
Large, decorative (NDS);
lavender and white blended
exhibition blooms; introduced
by T. Bailey, Australia, in 1976.
Available UK: National.

Amgard Coronet
Miniature decorative (NDS);
pink and yellow blends, useful
for exhibition work; height
1.2m (4ft); raised by D. Bates,
UK, in 1985. Available UK:
Abacus, Cruikshank, JRG,
National, Scotts, Station
House.

Amgard Delicate
Large, decorative (NDS), large
formal decorative (ADS);
pink/yellow blooms (NDS),
(ADS) deep blooms on a 1.1m
(3.5ft) bush; good for
exhibition purposes; raised D.
Bates, UK, and introduced in
1994. Available UK: National,
Oscroft; USA: Connell's;
elsewhere: Jacks.

Amilesweert
Medium semi-cactus
(unclassified); yellow and
orange blended garden and
exhibition variety; introduced
Holland in 1972; height 1.2m
(4ft). Award of Merit 1977
Wisley (NDS).

Amira
Small ball (NDS) or small
formal decorative (ADS);
purple blooms on strong stems,
growing to a height of 1.1m
(3.5ft); can be used for
exhibition, garden or cut
flower; introduced by Cor
Geerlings, Holland, in 1997.
Available UK: Abacus,
Cruikshank, Halls, Jones,
National, Oscroft, P. & L.,
Scotts, Tivey, Unwin;
elsewhere: Dgid.

Amorangi Joy
Incurved cactus (unclassified);
bright yellow; good stems on a
1.2m (4ft) bush; garden
variety; introduced by R.
Ingham, New Zealand, in
1990. Available USA:
Connell's.

Amorangi Pearl
Waterlily (ADS); yellow blooms
on a 1.2m (4ft) high bush.
Garden variety introduced by
R. Ingham, New Zealand, in
1986.

Amorus
Small, formal decorative
(unclassified); variegated
red/orange exhibition blooms
on long stems; originated by L.
Connell, in 2002. High-scoring
seedling Lynn B. Dudley trials
2001.

AMARAN PENTIRE

AMBER FESTIVAL

AMBERGLOW

AMELIA'S SURPRISE

AMGARD CORONET

AMGARD DELICATE

AMIRA

AMORANGI JOY

Amy Campbell
Formal, decorative (ADS);
bronze exhibition blooms and
garden use on powerful 1.4m
(5ft) bush; introduced by
Bruidegom, Holland, in 1999.
Available elsewhere: Jacks.

Amy K
Medium semi-cactus (ADS); a
tall grower to 1.6m (5ft); light
blends white and pink; good
all-round variety; introduced
by L. Connell, USA, in 1993.
Available USA: Clacks,
Connell's, Creekside, Dahlia
Dandies, Dan's Dahlias,
Elkhorn, Mingus; Canada:
Ferncliff; elsewhere: Jacks.

Amy's Star
Orchid variety (ADS); white
and purple garden blooms;
originated by H. Rissetto, USA,
in 1998. Awarded Lynn B.
Dudley medal 1997 (ADS).
Available USA: Alpen,
Capistrano, Clacks, Dahlia
Dandies; Canada: Ferncliff.

Andrea Clark
Medium decorative (NDS),
medium informal decorative
(ADS); yellow exhibition
blooms on a bush 1.2m (4ft)
in height; raised by J. Clark,
UK, in 1999. Available UK:
Clark, Cruikshank, Halls,
Oscroft, Porter, Pratt, Spencer,
Station House, Taylor.

Andrew David
A large, incurved cactus
(ADS); light blends pink and
yellow exhibition variety on a
0.9m (3ft) bush; introduced by
L. Connell, USA, in 1992.
Available USA: Clacks,
Connell's, Elkhorn.

Andrew Lockwood
Pompon (NDS and ADS);
lavender blooms of classic
exhibition formation, growing
to a height of 0.9m (3ft);
introduced by A. Lockwood,
UK, in 1960. Available UK:
National; elsewhere: Graines.

Andrew Magson
A vigorous medium or small
semi-cactus (NDS), or small
semi-cactus (ADS) with bright
red flowers; excellent for
exhibition, garden or cut
flower; height 1.2m (4ft);
raised by W. Mark, UK, in
1994. Award Garden Merit
Wisley (NDS). Available UK:
Cruikshank, Halls, National, P.
& L., Spencer.

Andrew Mitchell
Medium semi-cactus (NDS and
ADS); a striking red, good for
exhibition work; height 1.4m
(4.5ft); raised by L. Nicholson,
UK, in 1996. Available UK:
Abacus, Cruikshank, Halls,
National, P. & L., Porter; USA:
Arrowhead; elsewhere: Jacks.

Andriana
Large, lacinated (ADS); white,
exhibition variety; height 1.2m
(4ft); originated by Freitas,
USA, in 1987. Available USA:
Clacks, Elkhorn.

Andries Orange
Miniature semi-cactus (NDS);
orange blooms much used by
UK floral arrangers, also useful
as a prolific display flower in
the garden; grows to a height
of 1.1m (3.5ft); introduced by
Andries Holland in 1936.
Available UK: Butterfield,
National, Station House.

Angel Face
Small decorative (NDS);
red/white bicoloured garden and
cut flower variety; introduced
by Lammerse, Holland, in
1961. Available USA: Elkhorn.

Angel's Delight
Medium lacinated (ADS); light
blend, yellow and lavender,
growing to 1.3m (4.5ft); an eye-
catching variety. originated by
Clack, USA, in 2000; a seedling
of Kenora Lisa

Angel's Dust
A white waterlily (ADS);
originated by N. Gitts, USA, in

1997. Awarded the Derrill Hart
medal. Available USA: Frey's,
Swan Island.

Anglian Water
Miniature decorative (NDS);
purple blooms on plants growing
to a height of 1.1m (3.5ft);
blooms are useful for garden and
cut flower as well as exhibition
use; raised by Norman Lewis in
1991. Available UK: Halls,
National, P. & L., Pratt, Roberts;
USA: Connell's.

Angora
Fimbriated small decorative
(NDS) with white blooms; good
for the garden border; grows to
a height of 0.9m (3ft);
introduced by C. Piper, UK, in
1961. Award Merit Wisley 1962
(NDS). Available UK: National.

Anna
Medium informal decorative
(ADS); variegated white and
red; introduced by Gregersdal,
Denmark, in 1996. Available
USA: Elkhorn.

Anniversary Ball (synonym
Brookfield Enid)
Miniature ball (NDS); formal
blooms of pink blends; excellent
for garden or cut flower, can be
used for exhibition; grows to a
height of 0.9m (3ft); raised by
Gareth Rowlands, UK, in 1992.
Available UK: Aylett's, National.

Apache
Fimbriated medium semi-cactus
(NDS); a red variety (largish
blooms), useful for garden
work; grows to a height of
1.1m (3.5ft); introduced by
Bruidegom, Holland, in 1960.
Award Merit Wisley 1965
(NDS). Available UK: National;
elsewhere: Dgid.

Appenzell
Medium semi-cactus (NDS);
purple, garden and cut flower
variety; introduced by
Geerlings, Holland, in 1989.
Available UK: National, Tivey.

AMY K

ANDREA CLARK

ANDREW MAGSON

ANDREW MITCHELL

ANGLIAN WATER

APPENZELL

Apple Blossom
Medium cactus (NDS); pink
and white blended garden
variety; raised by Ballego,
Holland, in 1959. Available UK:
National; USA: Swan Island.

Apricot Beauty
Medium semi-cactus (NDS) of
orange blends; useful for
exhibition and garden; grows
to a height of 1.2m (4ft);
introduced by Cor Geerlings,
Holland, in 1962. Available
UK: National, Oscroft, P. & L.,
Spencer, Tivey; elsewhere:
Geerlings.

Apricot Honeymoon Dress
Small decorative (NDS); bronze
blended; exhibition, garden and
cut flower blooms on a 0.9m
(3ft) high bush; raised by M.
Hall, UK, in 1990. Available
UK: Abacus, National, Oscroft,
P. & L.

April Dawn
Medium informal decorative
(ADS); light blends, lavender
and white blooms; excellent
exhibition and garden variety
on a bush 1.2m (4ft) high;
originated by L. Connell, USA,
in 1984. Winner of Lynn B.
Dudley 1983, Derrill Hart and
Stanley Johnson medals (ADS).
Available USA: Clacks,
Connell's, Dan's Dahlias,
Elkhorn, Hamilton, SB
Gardens, Swan Island; Canada:
Candahlia; elsewhere: Jacks.

April Showers
Small, informal, decorative
(unclassified); lavender and
white blended garden blooms
on a 1.2m (4ft) bush; originated
by L. Connell, USA, in 2002.
Available USA: Connell's.

Arabian Night
Small decorative (NDS) or
miniature formal decorative
(ADS); red (NDS) or dark red
(ADS); for garden or cut flower
use; introduced by Weijers,

Holland, in 1951. Available
UK: Abacus, Blooms, Jager,
National; USA: Dan's Dahlias,
Elkhorn, Frey's, Sea-Tac;
elsewhere: Dgid.

Araluen Fire
Small straight cactus (ADS);
flame, exhibition and garden
variety; 1.2m (4ft) in height;
introduced Weijers, Holland, in
1987. Available Canada:
Ferncliff.

Aravis
Medium lacinated variety
(ADS); eye-catching dark pink
and yellow blends; firm-
stemmed; excellent exhibition
variety; 1.2m (4ft) high; raised
by L. Connell, USA, in 2002.
Available USA: Connell's.

Arc de Triumph
Medium decorative (NDS);
orange blooms; excellent
garden variety; raised by
Topsvoort, Holland, in 1950.
Available UK: National;
elsewhere: Geerlings, Turc.

Art Deco
A gallery range dahlia originated
by Adrian & Cees Verwer of
Holland (unclassified);
originated in 1999; a novelty
dahlia, double-centred, dark
blends, bronze/orange centre,
low height 25cm (1ft), suitable
for borders or patio pots. Award
Garden Merit, Wisley, and
awarded Wisley John Brown
medal. Available UK: National,
Proculture, Unwin; elsewhere:
Dgid, Graines, Konishi.

Art Fair
A gallery range, novelty dahlia,
originated by Adrian and Cees
Verwer of Holland in 1999
(unclassified); double-centred,
yellow blends; low height 25cm
(1ft), suitable for borders or
patio pots. Available UK: Jager,
National, Unwin; elsewhere:
Dgid, Graines.

Art Nouveau
A novelty, gallery dahlia,
introduced by Adrian and Cees
Verwer, Holland, in 1999
(unclassified); double-centred,
purple blended blooms; 25cm
(1ft) high, suitable for border
or patio use. Available UK:
Blooms, National, Proculture,
Unwin; elsewhere: Dgid.

Arthur Hills
A small cactus (NDS); bronze
blooms for exhibition, garden
and cut flower use; grows to a
height of 1.2m (4ft); raised by
Arthur Hills, UK, in 1985.
Award Garden Merit, Wisley
(NDS) in 1994.

Arthur's Delight
A giant decorative (NDS);
yellow exhibition blooms; raised
by G. Armstrong, UK, in 1992.
Available UK: National, P. & L.;
USA: Arrowhead, Clack.

Asahi Chohji
An anemone variety (NDS and
ADS); red and white bicolour,
excellent garden variety,
growing to a height of 1.2m
(4ft); introduced by Kyohno,
Japan, in 1962. Available UK:
National; USA: Clacks,
Connell's, Dan's Dahlias.

Ashley Marie
Miniature formal decorative
(ADS); dark pink, good
exhibition blooms on 1.2m
(4ft) high bush; originated by
Jerry Wittig, USA, 2001.

Aslan
A large semi-cactus variety
(unclassified); orange and pink
blooms; great depth on a 1.2m
(4ft) bush; originated by L.
Connell, USA, in 1992.

Astrid Siersen
Collarette (ADS); purple with
purple and white collar;
exhibition variety; originated
by Juul, USA, in 1983.
Available USA: Dan's Dahlias.

APRICOT BEAUTY

APRIL DAWN

ARTHUR HILLS

ARTHUR'S DELIGHT

ART DECO

ASAHI CHOHJI

ART FAIR

Athalie
Small cactus (NDS) or a small straight cactus (ADS); with dark pink blended blooms on strong stems; tall, growing to a height of 1.5m (5ft); excellent exhibition variety; raised by W. Dawes, UK, in 1974. Sported: lavender in 1991, Majestic in 1982, peach in 1986, salmon in 1988. Available UK: Jones, National, Oscroft, P. & L.; USA: Clacks, Sea-Tac.

Atilla
Small decorative (NDS); blended purple and red for exhibition and garden use; introduced in 1997. Available UK: National, Tivey; elsewhere: Dgid, Geerlings.

Audacity
Medium decorative (NDS) or informal decorative (ADS); bicolour red and white (NDS); light blends white and purple (ADS); excellent garden variety; originator Holicky, USA, in 1989. Available UK: Aylett's, National, P. & L.; USA: Mingus.

Audrey Grace
Small formal decorative (ADS); red exhibition, cut flower and garden variety; height 1.2m (4ft); originated by H. & R. Brown, USA, in 1995. Available USA: Arrowhead, Clacks, Connell's, SB Gardens: Canada: Ferncliff.

Aunt Norma
Large, incurved cactus (ADS); light blends white and lavender; garden and exhibition variety; originated by J. T. Thiermann, USA, in 1992. Available USA: Elkhorn.

Aunt Ruth
Small, incurved cactus (ADS); orange blooms; originated by Boley, USA, in 1998. Available USA: SB Gardens.

Aurora's Kiss
Miniature ball (NDS and ADS); red (NDS), dark red (ADS); excellent for exhibition and garden; grows to 1.1m (3.5ft); originator W. Holland, Canada,

in 1997. Available UK: Butterfield, Halls, National, P. & L., Pratt, Scotts; USA: Arrowhead, Clacks, Elkhorn; Canada: Ferncliff; elsewhere: Geerlings.

Aurwen's Violet
Pompon (NDS and ADS); purple exhibition and garden variety; 1.2m (4ft) in height; raised by R. G. Robert's, UK, in 1998. Available UK: Aylett's, Hall, National, P. & L., Pratt, Roberts; USA: Alpen, Clacks, Connell's, Creekside, SB Gardens.

Autay Chipper
Small formal exhibition decorative (ADS); with yellow blooms on medium-length stems; originator L. Miller, USA, in 2000. High-scoring seedling in Lynn B. Dudley trials 1999. Available Canada: Ferncliff.

Autumn Choice
Medium formal decorative (ADS); bronze blooms on a 1.2m (4ft) bush; exhibition and garden variety. Sport from Keith's Choice. Available elsewhere: Jacks.

Autumn Fire
Medium semi-cactus (unclassified); red and bronze blends; one-time excellent exhibition variety, growing to a height of 1.1m (3.5ft); introduced by Dobbie in 1960.

Avoca Salmon
Medium decorative (unclassified); salmon blooms; good for exhibition and garden use; 1.2m (4ft) in height; originated by Roger Turrell, UK, in 2001.

Ayers Snow Angel
Medium lacinated (ADS); white exhibition variety; originated by H. Ayers, USA, in 2002. Available USA: Clacks.

Aztec Gold
Large semi-cactus (ADS); yellow exhibition variety, 1.2m (4ft) in height; originated by Wyn, USA, in 2001. Available Canada: Ferncliff.

Azuma Kagami
Anemone (ADS); dark red garden variety; height 1.1m (3.5ft); originated Japan, in 1990. Available USA: Clacks, Dahlia Dandies.

B

B. J. Beauty
Medium decorative (NDS); white exhibition variety, 1.2m (4ft) in height, strong stems; tends to produce clock-faced blooms, but still a UK winner. Introduced by Terry Clarke, UK, 1976; named after Burton Joyce, a UK village. Available UK: Abacus, Aylett's, Clark, Cruikshank, Halls, JRG, National, Oscroft, P. & L., Porter, Scotts, Spencer, Station House, Taylor.

Babette
Small or miniature ball (NDS), small ball (ADS); purple exhibition blooms; grows to a height of 0.9m (3ft); introduced by C. Geerlings, Holland, in 1998. Available UK: Butterfield, Cruikshank, National, Oscroft, P. & L., Scotts, Spencer; elsewhere: Dgid, Geerlings.

Baby Dan
Small formal decorative (ADS); light blends red exhibition variety, early bloomer; height 1.2m (4ft); originated by Stevens, USA, 2001.

Bacchus
Medium semi-cactus (NDS); striking red garden and cut flower variety; 1.1m (3.5ft) in height; introduced by dahlia Maarse, Holland, in 1952. Award Merit Wisley, 1954 (NDS). Available UK: National.

Badger Pink
Medium semi-cactus (ADS); exhibition pink blooms on long stems; tall plants 1.5m (5ft) in height; originated by John Thiermann, USA, in 2002. Available USA: JT.

ATILLA

AUDACITY

AURORA'S KISS

AURWEN'S VIOLET

AUTUMN FIRE

AVOCA SALMON

B. J. BEAUTY

BABETTE

Badger Star
Large, straight cactus (ADS); light blends lavender and white-tipped exhibition blooms, on 1.1m (3.3ft) high plants; originated by John Thiermann, USA, in 2002. Available USA: JT.

Ballego's Glory
Medium decorative (NDS); a red and white-tipped, bicoloured, garden-type variety, growing to a height of 1.1m (3.5ft); introduced by Ballego, Holland, in 1932. Available UK: National; USA: Mingus; elsewhere: Geerlings.

Bambino
Lilliput single (NDS), mignon single (ADS); a dainty white and yellow blended garden variety, growing to a height of 75cm (18in); suitable for bedding or patio work. Introduced by Topsvoort, Holland, in 1955. Available UK: National; USA: Swan Island.

Banker
A medium cactus (NDS); a striking, tall red exhibition dahlia, growing to 1.2m (4ft) high; introduced by dahlia Bruidegom, Holland, in 1970. Produced Amber Banker, a sport from P. Tivey, UK, 1982. Available UK: National.

Bar Early Morn
Medium formal decorative (ADS); light blended pink and yellow exhibition and garden variety; height 1.2m (4ft); originated by D. Barnes, USA, 2002.

Barbara B
Giant informal decorative (ADS); tall, dark pink exhibition variety, 1.6m (6ft) in height; originated by Moore, USA, in 1991. Available USA: Creekside, Hamilton.

Barbara Z
Small lacinated (ADS); orange garden variety, 1.5m (5ft) in height; originated by

Zatkovich, USA, in 1988. Available USA: Creekside.

Barbara's Pastelle (synonym **Sunlight Pastelle)**
Medium semi-cactus (NDS); yellow-blended, long-stemmed exhibition blooms, plants 1.4m (4.5ft) high; raised by R. Nelson, UK, in 1997. Available UK: JRG, National, Oscroft, Porter, Station House.

Barbary Ball
Small ball (NDS), or ball (ADS); orange/pink blends (NDS), orange (ADS); for exhibition or garden use; grows 1.2m (4ft) high; raised by Barry Davies, UK, in 1991. Awarded Lynn B. Dudley medal in 1992 (ADS). Available UK: National; USA: Connell's, Dan's Dahlias, SB Gardens.

Barbary Banker
Miniature decorative (NDS), or miniature formal decorative (ADS); pink (NDS), or dark pink (ADS); on long-stemmed bush 1.1m (3.5ft) high; good garden or cut flower; raised by Barry Davies, UK, in 1988. Available UK: Aylett's, National, P. & L.; USA: Clacks, Connell's, Dan's Dahlias, Sea-Tac.

Barbary Bluebird
A purple miniature ball (ADS); exhibition variety, growing to 1.1m (3.5ft) high; raised by Barry Davies, UK, in 1996. Available USA: Hamilton; Canada: Candahlia; elsewhere: Jacks.

Barbary Carousel
Small ball (NDS), or ball (ADS); white lavender blends (NDS), or dark blended purple and white (ADS); exhibition, garden and cut flower variety; height 1.2m (4ft); raised by Barry Davies, UK, in 1990. Available UK: Abacus, National, Oscroft; USA: Clacks, Dan's Dahlias, Elkhorn.

Barbary Chevron
Medium decorative (NDS), or medium informal decorative (ADS); red exhibition variety growing to a height of 1.2m (4ft) on long stems; raised by Barry Davies, UK, in 1996. Available UK: National; Canada: Candahlia.

Barbary Dominion
Miniature decorative (NDS), or small formal decorative (ADS); pink variety useful for exhibition, garden or cut flower; grows to a height of 1.2m (4ft); raised by Barry Davies, UK, in 1989. Award Garden Merit Wisley (NDS). Available UK: National, Oscroft; USA: Alpen, Clacks, Creekside, Dahlia Dandies, Hamilton; elsewhere: Jacks.

Barbary Echo
Miniature ball (ADS); orange exhibition variety on a 1.2m (4ft) high bush; raised by B. Davis, UK, in 2000. Available USA: Connell's.

Barbary Esquire
Miniature formal decorative (ADS); dark red exhibition variety, 1.5m (5ft) in height; raised by Barry Davies, UK, in 1995. Awarded the Lynn B. Dudley medal in 1992 (ADS). Available USA: Arrowhead, Clacks, Connell's, Dan's Dahlias.

Barbary Flush
Miniature decorative (NDS); pink and yellow blends for exhibition, garden and cut flower; grows to a height of 1.2m (4ft); raised by Barry Davies, UK, in 1989.

Barbary Gateway
Medium decorative (NDS), medium formal decorative (ADS); bronze (NDS), light blends orange and yellow; exhibition variety, 1.2m (4ft) in height; raised by Barry Davies, UK, in 1996. Available UK: Scotts, Station House; elsewhere: Geerlings.

BARBARRY BLUEBIRD

BARBARRY CAROUSEL

BANKER

BARBARA'S PASTELLE

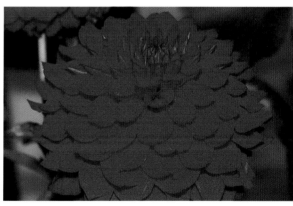

BARBARRY CHEVRON

BARBARRY BALL

BARBARRY GATEWAY

Barbarry Gem
Miniature ball (NDS and
ADS); purple (NDS) or dark
red (ADS); garden and cut
flower variety; 1.1m (3.5ft) in
height; raised by Barry Davies,
UK, in 1990. Awarded the
Lynn B. Dudley medal in 1990
(ADS). Available UK: National,
P. & L.; USA: Dan's Dahlias,
Elkhorn, Sea-Tac.

Barbarry Glamour
Miniature ball (ADS); dark
blends dark pink and purple;
exhibition variety; 1.5m (5ft) in
height, raised by Barry Davies,
UK, in 1991. Available USA:
Clacks, Dan's Dahlias,
Elkhorn.

Barbarry Indicator
Ball (ADS); lavender exhibition
and cut flower, reflexing back
to stem; height 1.2m (4ft);
raised by Barry Davies, UK, in
1989. Awarded the Lynn B.
Dudley medal in 1989 (ADS).

Barbarry Nationwide
Small formal decorative
(ADS); purple exhibition
variety, 1.2m (4ft) in height;
raised by Barry Davies, UK, in
2001. Awarded Lynn B.
Dudley medal 2000 (ADS).

Barbarry Oracle
Small decorative (NDS); purple
exhibition variety, growing to a
height of 1.2m (4ft); raised by
Barry Davies, UK, in 1991.
Available UK: Abacus, National.

Barbarry Pet
Miniature flowered, formal
decorative (ADS); purple
exhibition variety, 1.2m (4ft)
high; raised by Barry Davies,
UK, in 2001. Awarded the
Lynn B. Dudley medal (ADS).

Barbarry Pimpernel
Small decorative (NDS); red
exhibition variety, height 1.2m
(4ft); raised Barry Davies, UK, in
1992. Available UK: National.

Barbarry Pinky
Small decorative (NDS); pink-
flowered variety, 1.2m (4ft)
tall; exhibition and garden
variety; raised by Barry Davies,
UK, in 1991. Available UK:
National, P. & L.; USA:
Elkhorn.

Barbarry Pioneer
Small formal decorative
(unclassified); dark red
exhibition and garden-variety;
height 1.1m (3.5ft); raised by
Barry Davies, UK. Available
USA: Clacks.

Barbarry Prefect
Miniature ball (ADS); dark red
exhibition variety; raised by
Barry Davies, UK, in 2002.
Awarded the Lynn B. Dudley
medal (ADS).

Barbarry Pricket
Medium formal decorative
(ADS); purple garden and cut
flower variety, on a 1.2m (4ft)
high bush; raised by Barry
Davis, UK, in 2002. Available
USA: Connell's.

Barbarry Purple Glow
Medium formal decorative
(ADS); purple exhibition
variety, 1.2m (4ft) high; raised
by Barry Davies, UK, in 1992.
Available USA: Dan's Dahlias.

Barbarry Red Baron
Miniature decorative (ADS);
dark red exhibition variety;
raised by Barry Davies, UK, in
2002. Awarded the Lynn B.
Dudley medal (ADS).

Barbarry Red Dwarf
Miniature formal decorative
(ADS); dark red exhibition
variety; raised by Barry Davies,
UK, in 2000. Awarded the
Lynn B. Dudley medal in 1999
(ADS). Available USA:
Arrowhead.

Barbarry Salmon
Small formal decorative (ADS);
orange garden and exhibition
variety, 1.1m (3.5ft) in height;
raised by Barry Davies, UK, in
1989. Available USA:
Capistrano, Clacks, Elkhorn.

Barbarry Snowball
Medium formal decorative
(ADS); white variety growing to
a height of 1.2m (4ft); raised by
Barry Davies, UK, in 1996.

Barbarry Standard
Medium formal decorative
(ADS); dark red exhibition
variety, height 1.2m (4ft); raised
by Barry Davies, UK, in 1991.
Available USA: Dan's Dahlias.

Barbarry Summit
Medium formal decorative
(ADS); lavender exhibition
variety, height 1.2m (4ft); raised
by Barry Davies, UK, in 1992.
Available USA: Arrowhead.

Barbarry Yellow Cloud
Ball (ADS); yellow exhibition
variety; raised by Barry Davies,
UK, in 2000. Awarded the
Derrill Hart medal in 1999
(ADS).

Baret Joy
Large semi-cactus (NDS), or
medium semi-cactus (ADS);
white exhibition variety,
growing to 1.2m (4ft) high;
raised by J. Joyce, UK, in 1994.
Available UK: Abacus,
Cruikshank, Halls, National,
Oscroft, P. & L., Roberts.

Baron Bryce
Small informal decorative
(ADS); light blends pink and
yellow; raised by Ron Miner,
USA, in 2001.

Baron Evan
Medium informal decorative
(ADS); yellow blooms;
originated by Ron Miner, USA,
in 2000. Awarded the Derrill
Hart medal (ADS).

BARBARRY GEM

BARBARRY PIONEER

BARBARRY SNOWBALL

BARET JOY

BARBARRY PINKY

Baron Lindsey
Medium formal decorative
(ADS); exhibition pink blooms
on long stems, plants 1.2m
(4ft) high; originated by R.
Miner, USA, in 2001.

Bashful
Single (ADS); dark blends
purple and lavender; height
0.6m (2.5ft); prolific bloomer,
its incredible colour makes this
a useful garden variety;
originated by Swan Island,
USA, in 1999. Available USA:
Swan Island.

Bassingbourne Beauty
Small decorative (NDS); white
and pink blended exhibition,
garden and cut flower variety,
growing to a height of 1.1m
(3.5ft); raised by J. Scriven,
UK, in 1985. Available UK:
National, Oscroft.

Be a Sport
Novelty double centre (ADS);
variegated red and white
exhibition variety, exciting
sport of Candy Cane; height
1.2m (4ft), blooms 10cm (4in)
in diameter; originated by
Swan Island in 1984. Available
USA: Elkhorn, Mingus, Sea-
Tac, Swan Island.

Beatrice
Miniature ball (NDS); orange-
flowered exhibition, garden
and cut flower variety, growing
to a height of 1.2m (4ft);
introduced by Cor Geerlings,
Holland, in 1997. Available
UK: National, Oscroft, P. & L.,
Pratt, Tivey, Unwin; elsewhere:
Dgid, Geerlings, Wirth.

Bedford Blush
Medium formal decorative
(ADS); light blends white and
lavender, exhibition variety and
garden variety with 18cm (7in)
blooms on a 1.2m (4ft) high
bush; originated by Woznicki,
USA, in 1976. Available USA:
Elkhorn, Swan Island.

Bella S
Giant informal decorative
(ADS); lavender, exhibition

variety; height 0.9m (3ft);
originated by Strunz, USA, in
1995. Available USA: Clacks,
Creekside, Dahlia Dandies,
Elkhorn, Mingus; Canada:
Candahlia.

Belle of Barmera
Giant informal decorative
(ADS); dark pink exhibition
variety, early bloomer, 33cm
(13in) blooms on a bush;
height 1.1m (3.5ft); originated
by Simon, USA, in 1987.
Available USA: Clacks,
Mingus; Canada: Ferncliff.

Belle of the Ball
Large, fimbricated semi-cactus
(NDS), large purple lacinated
cactus (ADS); a striking
lavender-pink dahlia, excellent
for exhibition or garden use,
growing to 1.2m (4ft);
originated by Bob Surber, USA,
in 1995 (NDS). Available USA:
Clacks.

Ben Huston
Giant decorative (NDS), or giant
informal decorative (ADS);
orange blends (NDS), or bronze
(ADS); exhibition variety
blooms 30cm (12in) in diameter,
height 1.5m (5ft); originated by
Earl Huston, Canada, in 1985.
Available UK: Abacus,
Cruikshank, P.& L.; USA:
Arrowhead, Clacks, Dahlia
Dandies, Elkhorn, Hamilton,
Mingus; Canada: Ferncliff;
elsewhere: Engelhardt, Konishi.

Bernice Sunset
Small semi-cactus (NDS);
orange, exhibition variety;
1.2m (4ft) in height; raised by
Bob Korth, UK, in 1996.
Available UK: National.

Berwick Wood
Medium decorative (NDS),
medium informal decorative
(ADS); exhibition and garden
variety, growing to a height of
1.3m (4.5ft); raised by Roger
Turrell, UK, in 1989; early
bloomer (USA). Available UK:
Cruikshank, Halls, National, P.
& L., Roberts, Scotts, Station
House, Tivey; USA: Alpen,

Connell's, Dahlia Dandies,
Elkhorn; elsewhere: Jacks.

Bert Pitt
Small informal decorative
(ADS); bicoloured dark red and
white, garden variety 1.5m
(5.5ft) in height; originated by
Palminteri, USA, in 1974.
Available USA: Creekside,
Dahlia Dandies, Hamilton.

Beryl K
Medium lacinated (ADS); light
blends pink and yellow, garden
variety, prolific blooms on a
1.1m (3.5ft) plant; originated
by Phil Traff, USA, in 1995.
Available USA: Arrowhead,
Connell's, Elkhorn.

Betty Bowen
Small decorative (NDS); purple
blended exhibition, garden and
cut flower variety, growing to a
height of 1.2m (4ft); raised by
H. Keirby, UK, in 1983.
Available UK: JRG, National.

Beulah Ruth
Miniature formal decorative
(ADS); orange exhibition, cut
flower and exhibition variety
on a 1.1m (3.5ft) high bush;
introduced by Rodewald, USA,
in 1988. Awarded Lynn B.
Dudley medal, 1987 (ADS).
Available USA: Clacks,
Connell's.

Beverley F
Medium informal decorative
(ADS); orange exhibition and
garden variety; height 1.2m
(4ft); originated by Connell,
USA, in 2002. Available USA:
Connell's.

Big Bird
Large informal decorative
(ADS); yellow exhibition variety;
originated by Dabel, USA, in
1997. Available USA: Elkhorn.

Big Boy
Giant informal decorative
(ADS); flame exhibition variety;
height 1.4m (4.5ft); originated
by W. Almand, USA, in 1995.
Available USA: Dahlia Dandies,
Elkhorn, Mingus.

BEATRICE

BELLE OF THE BALL

BETTY BOWEN

Big Orange
Large informal decorative (ADS); orange variety; originated by Connell, USA, in 1993.

Bilbo Baggins
Small formal decorative (unclassified); magenta garden variety, tall grower 1.6m (5ft) high bush; early bloomer; originated Connell, USA, in 2002. Available USA: Connell's.

Bill Holmberg
Giant decorative (NDS); bronze blended exhibition variety, 1.1m (3.5ft) high; originated by M. Giesert, USA, in 1989. Available UK: Cruikshank, National, Oscroft, Tivey; USA: Clacks, Mingus; elsewhere: Geerlings, Wirth.

Bill's Place
Pompon (ADS); purple garden variety, height 1.2m (4ft); originated by Bonneywell, USA, in 1994. Available USA: Arrowhead, Dahlia Dandies.

Bingo
Miniature formal decorative (ADS); orange cut, excellent exhibition, garden and cut flower variety; height 1.2m (4ft); originated by Rodewell, USA in 1977. Available USA: Connell's.

Birchwood (synonymous Willo's Violet)
Pompon (NDS) exhibition variety; purple blends; raised by Gardiner, UK, in 1976.

Bird Nest
Large, incurved cactus (ADS); pink exhibition variety, height 1.2m (4ft); originated by Juul, USA, in 1990. Available USA: Clacks.

Bishop of Llandaff
Miscellaneous dahlia (NDS), or peony (ADS); a red (NDS), dark red (ADS), single petal surrounding an open centre, with yellow anthers and dark

foliage; grows to a height of 0.9m (3ft), very much for garden use; raised by I. Treseder, Wales, in 1928. Available UK: Abacus, Aylett's, Blooms, Cruikshank, Halls, Jager, Jones, JRG, National, Oscroft, Roberts, Scotts, Station House, Taylor, Tivey, Unwin, Winchester; USA: Sea-Tac, Swan Island; elsewhere: Dgid, Geerlings, Graines, Turc, Wirth.

Bitsa
Miniature ball (NDS); red exhibition variety; 1.1m (3.5ft) high, raised by Sid Hinchcliffe, UK, in 1979. Available UK: Cruikshank, National; USA: Dahlia Dandies, SB Gardens, Sea-Tac.

Black Narcissus
Medium lacinated (ADS); dark red, cut flower, variety height 1.5m (5ft); originated by Schissler, Canada, in 1956. Available USA: Connell's, Frey's, SB Gardens.

Blackberry Ripple
Medium semi-cactus (ADS); variegated lavender and purple, garden variety, height 1.2m (4ft); originated by Willoughby, Canada, in 1993. Available USA: Arrowhead, Dan's Dahlias, SB Gardens; elsewhere: Engelhardt.

Blended Beauty
Miniature cactus (ADS); dark blends, dark red and white exhibition variety; height 1.2m (4ft); originated by W. Almand, USA, in 1992. Awarded the Derrill Hart medal (ADS). Available USA: Clacks, Dan's Dahlias.

Bliss
Waterlily (ADS); light blends, yellow and pink, garden and cut flower variety; prolific blooms on strong stems, height 0.9m (3ft); originated by Phil Traff, USA, in 1992. Available USA: Alpen, Clacks, Connell's, Elkhorn, Swan Island.

Blithe Spirit
Large decorative (NDS); red and white bicolour garden variety, growing to 1.1m (3ft); introduced by dahlia Bruidegom, Holland, in 1962. Available UK: National; elsewhere: Engelhardt, Geerlings.

Bloomquist Hope
Medium semi-cactus (ADS); light blends, orange and yellow, garden and exhibition variety; height 1.2m (4ft); originated by Bloomquist, USA, in 2002.

Bloom's Amy
Miniature decorative (NDS), miniature formal decorative (ADS); white and lavender blends, 1.2m (4ft) high, exhibition and cut flower; originated by Bloom, USA, in 1987. Available UK: Halls, National; USA: Capistrano, Dahlia Dandies; elsewhere: Jacks.

Bloom's Centennial
Medium formal decorative (ADS); orange exhibition variety, 1.1m (3.5ft) in height; originated by Bloom, USA, in 1989. Awarded the Lynn B. Dudley medal (ADS). Available USA: Clacks.

Bloom's Graham
Small semi-cactus (ADS); purple cut flower variety; showy and prolific bloomer, height 1.1m (3.5ft); originated by Bloom, USA, in 1989. Available USA: Connell's, Elkhorn; Canada: Ferncliff.

Bloom's Irene
Waterlily (ADS); flame exhibition and cut flower variety, robust grower; height 1.4m (4.5ft); originated by Bloom, USA, in 1990. Available USA: Connell's, SB Gardens.

Bloom's Kehala
Waterlily (ADS); red blooms, tall grower 1.5m (5ft); good cut flower variety; originated by Bloom, USA, in 1997. Available USA: Connell's.

BIG ORANGE   BILL HOLMBERG

BISHOP OF LLANDAFF   BLISS

Bloom's Wildwood
Small incurved cactus (ADS);
yellow exhibition and garden
variety; originated by Bloom,
USA, in 1997. Available USA:
Connell's, Elkhorn.

Bloom's XL
Medium straight cactus (ADS);
striking dark red variety, prolific
bloomer on 1.2m (4ft) high
plant; originated by Bloom,
USA, in 1998. Awarded the
Lynn B. Dudley medal in 1997
(ADS). Available USA: Connell's.

Blossom
Miniature ball (NDS); lavender
and white variety, for garden
use; 1.1m (3.5ft) high;
introduced by dahlia Bruidegom,
Holland, in 1961. Available UK:
National.

Bob Fitzjohn
Giant semi-cactus (NDS);
bronze exhibition variety, 1.2m
(4ft) high; raised by David
Walker, UK, in 1985. Available
UK: National, P. & L.

Bobay
Medium semi-cactus (ADS);
light blends, yellow and
lavender exhibition variety;
height 1.2m (4ft); originated by
Gene Boeke, USA, in 1975.
Available USA: Creekside.

Bo-Lei
Medium lacinated (ADS);
lavender, exhibition variety,
height 1.5m (5ft); originated by
Gene Boeke, USA, in 1976.
Available USA: Creekside.

Bodacious
Giant informal decorative
(ADS); red exhibition variety,
height 1.2m (4ft); originated by
N. Gitts, USA, in 2002.
Awarded the Derrill Hart
medal (ADS). Available USA:
Swan Island.

Bokay
A small waterlily (NDS); pink,
for garden and cut flower use;
1.2m (4ft) high; raised by Terry
Clarke, UK. Available UK:
National; USA: Elkhorn;
elsewhere: Dgid.

Bonaventure
A giant decorative (NDS), giant
formal decorative (ADS); bronze
yellow blends (NDS), bronze
(ADS), of great exhibition use;
grows to 1.5m (5ft) high;
originated by Simon, USA, in
1982. Awarded the Lynn B.
Dudley (1981) and Derill Hart
medals (ADS). Available UK:
Cruikshank, Halls, National,
Oscroft, P. & L., Scotts, Station
House; USA: Alpen, Arrowhead,
Clacks, Creekside, Dahlia
Dandies, Dan's Dahlias, Elkhorn,
SB Gardens, Sea-Tac; Canada:
Ferncliff; elsewhere: Dgid.

Bonne Esperance
Lilliput single (NDS), mignon
single (ADS); a pink exhibition
and garden variety, 0.4m (16in)
high; introduced by Topsvoort,
Holland, in 1951. Available
UK: National, Station House;
USA: Clacks, Dahlia Dandies,
Dan's Dahlias, Swan Island.

Bonnie Jean
A small semi-cactus (ADS);
lavender exhibition variety,
height 1.2m (4ft); originated by
Franklin, USA, in 2000.
Awarded the Lynn B. Dudley
medal 1999 (ADS). Available
USA: Clacks, Creekside, Dahlia
Dandies; elsewhere: Konishi.

Bonny Blue
Small ball (NDS); lavender
garden variety, sometimes
known as 'Blue Danube'; raised
by Archer in 1920. Available
UK: National.

Border Princess
Dwarf bedder semi-cactus
(NDS); 1.1m (3.5ft) high;
orange/yellow blended, garden
and cut flower variety;

introduced by Lammers,
Holland, in 1964. Available
UK: National

Bowen (synonym **Small World**)
Pompon (NDS and ADS);
white exhibition, garden and
cut flower; introduced in 1966.
Available USA: Clacks, Dahlia
Dandies, SB Gardens.

Bracken Astra
Orchid (ADS); dark blends red
and yellow exhibition and
garden variety; height 0.9m
(3ft); introduced by Naumann,
Australia, in 1997. Available
USA: Clacks.

Bracken Ballerina
Waterlily (NDS and ADS); pink
(NDS), blends of pink and
white (ADS); excellent for
exhibition, garden and cut
flower; blooms on 1.1m (3.5ft)
long stems; raised by Naumann,
Australia, in 1988. Available
UK: Abacus, Aylett's, Halls,
Jones, National, Oscroft, P. &
L., Scotts, Station House; USA:
Alpen, Arrowhead, Connell's,
Dahlia Dandies, Dan's Dahlias,
Elkhorn, Mingus.

Bracken Triune
Waterlily (ADS); light blends
bronze and yellow, cut flower
and garden variety; height 1.2m
(4ft); raised by Naumann,
Australia, in 1992. Available
USA: Alpen, Dan's Dahlias.

Brackenhill Flame
Small red decorative (NDS);
good for exhibition, garden
and cut flower; 0.9m (3ft) high;
long stems. Raised by E.
Furness, UK, in 1995. Available
UK: Abacus, National.

Brandaris
Medium semi-cactus (NDS);
flame blended garden variety;
1.1m (3.5ft) high; introduced
by Topsvert, Holland, in 1950.
Award Merit Wisley, 1952
(NDS). Available UK: National.

BOB FITZJOHN

BONAVENTURE

BRACKENHILL FLAME

Brandy Bay
Formal decorative (ADS); dark blends orange and yellow, exhibition and garden variety; originated by Baldwin, USA, in 2001. Available USA: Arrowhead, Creekside.

Brassy
Waterlily (ADS); yellow garden variety, height 1.1m (3.5ft); introduced by Ballego, Holland, in 1971. Available USA: Dan's Dahlias.

Brian R
Medium decorative (NDS), formal decorative (ADS); lavender exhibition variety, 1.2m (4ft) high; good bloomer on strong stems. originated by Phil Traff, USA, in 1995. Awarded the Derrill Hart medal (ADS). Available UK: National, P. & L.; USA: Alpen, Connell's, Creekside, Dan's Dahlias, Mingus, SB Gardens; Canada: Candahlia.

Brian's Dream
Miniature decorative (unclassified); white, pink overlay, exhibition variety; 1.2m (4ft) in height; introduced by B. King, UK, in 2002. Available UK: Halls.

Brian's Sun
Peony (ADS); light blends orange and yellow, cut flower; 1.5m (5ft) in height; originated by S. Fry, USA, in 2001. Available USA: Frey's.

Bright Eyes
Star (ADS); purple garden and exhibition variety, 0.6m (2ft) in height; originated by Gill, USA, in 1981. Available USA: Clacks.

Bright Star
Small, straight cactus (ADS); orange cut flower (floral art) variety; 1.2m (4ft) in height; originated by Muller, South

Africa, in 1966. Available USA: Clacks, Dan's Dahlias, Frey's, Mingus, Sea-Tac, Swan Island.

Brio
Anemone dwarf bedder (NDS); flame and orange blooms on a garden variety bush 75cm (15in) high; introduced by Hippeastra, Holland, in 1965. Available elsewhere: Dgid; Graines.

Bristol Bugle
Miniature cactus (ADS); dark red exhibition variety, height 1.1m (3.5ft); originated by Dan and Kathy Franklin, USA, in 1997. Awarded the Lynn B. Dudley medal in 1996 (ADS). Available USA: Alpen, Dan's Dahlias; Canada: Ferncliff; elsewhere: Jacks.

Bristol Fleck
Small, formal decorative (ADS); variegated white and purple exhibition variety, 1.2m (4ft) in height; originated by Dan and Kathy Franklin, USA, in 2000. Available USA: Arrowhead, Elkhorn.

Bristol Snowflake
Small, straight cactus (ADS); white exhibition variety, 13cm (5in) blooms on a bush 1.5m (5ft) in height; originated by Dan and Kathy Franklin, USA, in 1998. Available Canada: Ferncliff.

Bristol Spartan
Medium formal decorative (ADS); dark red exhibition blooms on 1.2m (4ft) high bush; originated by Dan and Kathy Franklin, USA, in 2001.

Bristol Sunny
Miniature semi-cactus (ADS); yellow exhibition variety, prolific bloomer on strong stems, 1.54m (5ft) in height; originated by D. and K. Franklin, USA, in 2000. Available Canada: Ferncliff; elsewhere: Konishi.

Bristol Tangerine
Miniature formal decorative (ADS); orange garden variety, 0.9m (3ft) in height; originated by D. and K. Franklin, USA, in 2000. Available Canada: Ferncliff.

Brookfield Leah
Miniature ball (NDS); orange blends; height 1.2m (4ft); long-stemmed, useful for exhibition and cut flower; raised by Gareth Rowlands, UK, in 1984.

Brookfield Rachel
Miniature ball (NDS); purple exhibition, garden and cut flower variety; 1.1m (3.5ft) high; raised by Gareth Rowlands, UK. Available UK: National.

Brookside Cheri
Small straight cactus (ADS); dark pink, cut flower and exhibition variety; 15cm (6in) blooms on a 1.5m (4.5ft) high bush; originated by Hurt, USA, in 1971. Available USA: Dahlia Dandies, Dan's Dahlias, Elkhorn, Frey's, SB Gardens, Swan Island.

Brookside J. Cooley
Miniature informal decorative (ADS); yellow, garden and exhibition variety; height 1.2m (4ft); originated by Cooley, USA, in 1983. Awarded the Derrill Hart medal (ADS). Available USA: Clacks, Dan's Dahlias, Elkhorn, Mingus, Sea-Tac.

Brookside Snowball
Ball (ADS); white exhibition variety, excellent depth and form; 10cm (4in) blooms on strong stems, bush height 1.5m (5ft); originated by Hurt, USA, in 1976. Available USA: Alpen, Arrowhead, Capistrano, Clacks, Connell's, Dahlia Dandies, Elkhorn, Frey's, Mingus, SB Gardens, Sea-Tac, Swan Island; Canada: Candahlia, Ferncliff.

BRIAN R

BRIAN'S DREAM

BROOKSIDE CHERI

Brownie
Lilliput single (NDS); orange
garden variety, 75cm (2ft) high;
introduced by dahlia Maarse,
Holland. Available UK:
Aylett's, Butterfield, National.

Brush Strokes
Waterlily (ADS); lavender
exhibition and cut flower
variety; 13cm (5in) blooms on
a 1.4m (4.5ft) high, strong
bush; originated by N. Gitts,
USA, in 1996. Available USA:
Alpen, Connell's, Creekside,
Dan's Dahlias, Elkhorn, SB
Gardens, Swan Island; Canada:
Ferncliff.

Buffalo Nan
Single (ADS); dark blends
purple and lavender, garden
and exhibition variety; height
1.2m (4ft); originated by J.
Hart, USA, in 1998. Available
USA: Dahlia Dandies.

Bull's Pride
Giant decorative (NDS); white
exhibition variety; introduced
by B. Bull, New Zealand, in
1982. Available UK: National;
USA: Dahlia Dandies, Elkhorn.

Bumble Rumble
A collarette (ADS); light blends
dark pink and white;
exhibition and garden variety;
7.6cm (3in) blooms on a 1.1m
(3.5ft) in height; originated by
N. Gitts, USA, in 2001.
Available USA: Swan Island.

Butterball
Dwarf bedder (NDS); yellow
garden variety, 50cm (18in)
high; introduced by Lister, UK,
in 1960. Award Garden Merit,
Wisley (NDS). Available UK:
National.

C

C J's Diana
Small, straight cactus (ADS);
lavender; variety originated by
Haus, USA, in 2002.

C J's Moppet
Purple peony (ADS); originated
by Haus, USA, in 2002.

Cadet
Small, formal decorative (ADS);
white exhibition variety, height
1.5m (5ft); originated by R. &
J. Miller, USA, in 1999.
Available USA: Clacks, Elkhorn.

Camano Ariel
Medium cactus (ADS); light
blends yellow and pink;
exhibition, garden and cut
flower variety; prolific bloomer;
height 1.4m (4.5ft); originated
by R. & S. Ambrose, USA, in
1990. Available USA: Clacks,
Connell's, Creekside, Elkhorn;
elsewhere: Konishi.

Camano Choice
Small decorative (NDS), small
informal decorative (ADS);
lavender blends, excellent for
exhibition, garden and cut
flower; bush grows 1.2m (4ft)
high; long-stemmed; originated
by R. & S. Ambrose, USA, in
1979. Awarded the Derrill Hart
medal (ADS). Available UK:
National; USA: Capistrano.

Camano Classic
Medium incurving cactus
(ADS); orange exhibition
variety; originated by R. & S.
Ambrose, USA, in 1981.
Awarded the Lynn B. Dudley
medal, 1980 (ADS).

Camano Cloud
Small semi-cactus (ADS); pink,
variety excellent for exhibition
and garden; height 1.1m
(3.5ft); originated by R. & S.

Ambrose, USA, in 1978.
Awarded the Derrill Hart
medal (ADS). Available USA:
Clacks, SB Gardens.

Camano Dot
Miniature formal decorative
(ADS); yellow garden variety;
originated by R. & S.
Ambrose, USA, in 2002.
Available USA: Arrowhead,
Clacks, Creekside.

Camano Fire Storm
Medium semi-cactus (ADS);
red variety originated by R. &
S. Ambrose, USA, in 1991.
Available USA: Dan's Dahlias.

Camano Grace
Medium cactus (ADS); light
blends white and lavender,
garden variety; 1.1m (4ft) in
height; originated by R. & S.
Ambrose, USA, in 2000.
Available USA: Arrowhead.

Camano Ivory
Medium incurving cactus
(ADS); white; originated by R.
& S. Ambrose, USA, in 1989.
Awarded the Lynn B. Dudley
medal, 1988 (ADS). Available
USA: Clacks, Dahlia Dandies,
SB Gardens.

Camano Messenger
Large, incurving cactus (ADS);
light blends pink and yellow,
garden and exhibition variety,
1.2m (4ft) high plant;
originated by R. & S.
Ambrose, USA, in 1991.
Awarded the Derrill Hart
medal (ADS). Available USA:
Alpen, Clacks, Creekside,
Dahlia Dandies, Dan's Dahlias,
Elkhorn, SB Gardens.

Camano Passion
Medium semi-cactus
(unclassified); exhibition variety
1.2m (4ft) in height; originated
by R. & S. Ambrose, USA.
Available USA: Clacks.

CAMANO CLOUD

CAMANO FIRESTORM   CAMANO PASSION

Camano Pet
Star (ADS); light blends orange
and yellow exhibition variety;
height 1.5m (5ft); originated by
R. & S. Ambrose, USA, in
1997. Available USA: Alpen,
Arrowhead, Clacks, Creekside,
SB Gardens.

Camano Shadows
Medium incurving cactus
(ADS); dark blends purple and
white exhibition variety;
height 1.2m (4ft); originated
by R. & S. Ambrose, USA, in
1990. Awarded the Lynn B.
Dudley medal, 1989 (ADS).
Available USA: Clacks,
Creekside, Sea-Tac.

Camano Sitka
Large cactus (ADS); dark
blends, orange and yellow
exhibition, garden and cut
flower variety; height 1.5m
(5ft); originated by R. & S.
Ambrose, USA, in 2000.
Available USA: Arrowhead,
Clacks, Creekside.

Camano Thunder
Small, incurved cactus (ADS);
dark pink exhibition and cut
flower variety; a tall grower,
1.6m (6ft) in height; originated
by R. & S. Ambrose, USA, in
1997. Available USA: Alpen,
Clacks, Connell's, Dahlia
Dandies, Sea-Tac.

Camano Titan
Giant informal decorative
(unclassified); pink exhibition
variety; height 1.2m (4ft);
originated by R. & S. Ambrose,
USA. Available USA: Clacks.

Cameo
Small waterlily (NDS),
waterlily (ADS); yellow;
introduced by W. Tapley,
Australia, in 1986. Excellent
for exhibition, garden or cut
flower; long stems on 1.1m
(3.5ft) high plants. Available
UK: Butterfield, National,
P. & L., Scott, Station House,
Taylor; USA: Alpen, Clacks,
Dan's Dahlias, SB Gardens.

Cameo Peach
Medium formal decorative
(ADS); light blends yellow and
pink blooms on a 1.2m (4ft)
high plant; introduced by Gust,
New Zealand, in 1974.

Camilla Marie
Small informal decorative (ADS);
yellow blooms; originated by
Franklin, USA, in 2001.

Campos Gibby
Medium semi-cactus (ADS);
dark purple, blends purple
and white; originated by
D. F. Campello, USA, in 1999.
Awarded the Lynn B. Dudley
medal (ADS).

Campos Gigi
Miniature formal decorative
(ADS); light blends bronze and
yellow originated by
D. F. Campello, USA, in 1998.
Awarded the Lynn B. Dudley
medal, 1997 (ADS).

Campos Hush
Large semi-cactus (ADS);
yellow garden; variety height
1.2m (4ft); originated by
D. F. Campello, USA, in 1992.
Available USA: Arrowhead,
Clacks, Elkhorn, Mingus.

Campos Philip M
Giant decorative (unclassified);
bronze exhibition variety, 1.2m
(4ft) in height; originated by
D. F. Campello, USA.

Canby Centennial
Medium formal decorative
(ADS); dark pink exhibition
and cut flower variety; good,
18cm (7in) blooms on 1.2m
(4ft) high plants; dark foliage;
originated by Swan Island,
USA, in 1994 (centenary of
Canby Town, USA). Available
USA: Swan Island.

Candle in the Wind
Medium decorative (NDS);
white exhibition variety, growing
to a height of 1.4m (4.5ft), on
long strong stems; raised by M.
White, UK, in 1999. Named
after song adapted by Elton John
for Princess Diana's funeral
service. Available UK: Porter,
Spencer.

Candy Cupid
Miniature ball (NDS); pink
blooms, good for exhibition,
garden and cut flower; height
1.1m (3.5ft); raised by B.
Cooper, UK, in 1990. Available
UK: Abacus, Butterfield, Clark,
Cruikshank, Halls, Jones,
National, Oscroft, P. & L.,
Tivey; USA: Elkhorn.

Candy Hamilton Lilian
Small decorative (NDS); pink
exhibition, garden and cut
flower variety, height 1.1m
(3.5ft); raised by Allan Buller,
UK, in 1990. Available UK:
National.

Candy Keene
Large semi-cactus (NDS); pink
and white blended, exhibition
and garden variety; height
1.2m (4ft); raised by Terry
Clarke, UK, in 1976. Available
UK: Clark, Cruikshank, Halls,
National, Porter, Station
House; elsewhere: Jacks.

CAMANO SHADOWS

CAMANO TITAN

CAMPOS GIBBY

CAMPOS HUSH

CAMPOS PHILIP M

CANDLE IN THE WIND

CANDY CUPID

CANDY KEENE

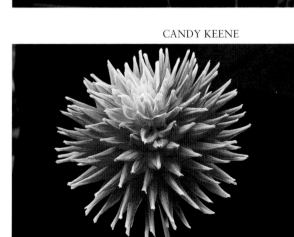

Caproz Jerry Garcia
Medium formal decorative
(ADS); red garden variety;
originated by Probizanski,
USA, in 1997. Available USA:
Arrowhead, Clacks, Creekside,
Elkhorn, Sea-Tac.

Caproz John Lennon
Medium lacinated yellow
variety (ADS); originated by
Probizanski, USA, in 2000.
Available USA: Clacks, SB
Gardens.

Capsicum
Small semi-cactus (ADS); flame-
coloured exhibition and garden
blooms; originated by Larkin &
Zydner, USA, in 1998. Awarded
the Derrill Hart medal (ADS).
Available USA: Dahlia Dandies,
Elkhorn, Mingus.

Captain Kirk
Giant decorative (unclassified);
red exhibition variety, 1.2m
(4ft) in height; raised by Peter
Cleaver, UK, in 1990.

Carol T
Small informal decorative
(ADS); yellow cut flower
variety; originated by Gene
Toote, USA, in 2000.
Available USA: Arrowhead.

Carolina Moon
Small waterlily (NDS); white
lilac blends good for
exhibition, garden and cut
flower; height 0.9m (3ft);
raised by Welch, UK, in 1990.
Available UK: Aylett's,
Cruikshank, Halls, National,
P. & L.; USA, Elkhorn.

Carstone Cobblers
Small ball (NDS); yellow
exhibition variety, 1.1m (3.5ft)

in height; raised by Joe Kidd,
UK, in 1982. Available UK:
Abacus, Jones, National.

Carstone Ruby
Small decorative (NDS and
ADS); red exhibition, garden
and cut flower variety; 1.2m
(4ft) high; raised by Joe Kidd,
UK, in 1996. Awarded the
Harry Haworth medal, 1996
(NDS). Available UK: Halls,
Oscroft, P. & L., Porter, Pratt,
Spencer; elsewhere: Jacks.

Carstone Sunbeam
Small decorative (NDS); yellow
exhibition variety, 1.2m (4ft)
high; raised by Joe Kidd, UK,
in 1991. Available UK:
National, P. & L.

Carstone Suntan
Medium semi-cactus (ADS);
bronze exhibition variety;
raised by Joe Kidd, UK, in
1996. Available UK:
Cruikshank, Halls, National,
P. & L., Spencer, Tivey.

Castle Drive
Medium decorative (NDS);
pink blends exhibition dahlia;
raised by Roger Turrell, UK, in
1991. Available UK: National,
Oscroft, P. & L., Station
House, Tivey.

Catherine Ireland
Miniature decorative (NDS);
white and lavender blended
exhibition, garden and cut
flower variety, 1.1m (3.5ft)
high; raised by H. Ireland, UK,
in 1983. Available UK:
National; USA: Dan's Dahlias.

Cecil's Star
Purple orchid (ADS); 0.9m
(3ft) high; garden and cut

flower variety; originated by
Clack, USA, in 2000. Available
USA: Clacks.

Cefn Glow
Small straight cactus (ADS);
orange exhibition and garden
variety, 1.1m (3.5ft) high; raised
by H. Hammett, UK, 1981.

Celebrity
Medium cactus (unclassified);
red garden and exhibition,
1.2m (4ft) in height; originated
USA in 1995.

Center Court
Medium formal decorative
(ADS); pristine white, garden
and cut flower variety; 8in
blooms on 1.5m (5ft) tall
plants, excellent for floral
arrangements; originated by N.
Gitts, USA, in 1994. Available
USA: Swan Island.

Cha Cha
Small straight cactus (ADS);
dark blends red and yellow,
centred 5in blooms; for cutting
or exhibition variety, on a
1.1m (4ft) high plant;
originated by Rossak,
Australia, in 1965. Available
USA: Frey's, Swan Island.

Charles H
Medium informal decorative
(ADS); bicolour orange and
white garden variety; originated
by Haugh, USA, in 1990.
Available USA: Arrowhead.

Charles McLellen
Small decorative (unclassified);
light bronze garden variety;
raised by I. Lewis, UK, in
1980.

CAPTAIN KIRK

CARSTONE COBBLERS

CARSTONE RUBY

CARSTONE SUNBEAM

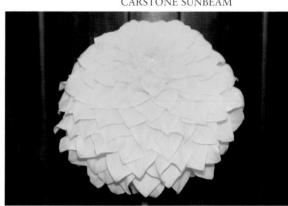

CARSTONE SUNTAN

CASTLE DRIVE

CELEBRITY

CHARLES McLELLEN

Charlie Kenwood
Miniature decorative (NDS); pink blended blooms, good for exhibition, garden and cut flower use; 0.9m (3ft) high plants; raised by C. Kenwood, UK, in 1991. Available UK: National, Station House.

Charlie Two (synonymous with **Mascot Maya** but with dissimilar foliage, NDS) Yellow-flowered, medium decorative (NDS), formal decorative (ADS); strong plant growing to 1.2m (4ft), making a full bush of exhibition and garden variety blooms; raised by E. A. Fuller, UK, in 1986. Available UK: Abacus, Aylett's, Butterfield, Clark, Cruikshank, Halls, National, Oscroft, P. & L., Porter, Pratt, Roberts, Scotts, Spencer, Station House, Tivey; USA: Clacks, Connell's, Mingus; elsewhere: Geerlings.

Cheerio
Small semi-cactus (NDS), or small incurved cactus (ADS); purple and white bicolour, excellent for garden or cut flower use, growing to 1.1m (3.5ft) in height; raised by Joe Barwise, UK, in 1953. Available UK: National, Tivey; USA: Elkhorn; elsewhere: Geerlings, Wirth.

Cheer Leader
Giant semi-cactus (ADS); lavender blooms on a 1.2m (4ft) high bush; garden and exhibition use; originated by Caldwell, USA, in 1984.

Cherokee Gold
Large informal decorative (ADS); orange garden variety, 1.1m (3.5ft) high; originated by Ricks, USA, in 1982.

Cherry Wine
Small decorative (NDS); a red variety good for garden or cut flower; 1.1m (3.5ft) in height; raised by John Crutchfield, UK, in 1970. Available UK: National, Station House; USA: Sea-Tac.

Cherwell Goldcrest
Small semi-cactus (NDS), small straight cactus (ADS); yellow blends (NDS), bronze (ADS); excellent for exhibition or garden use; 1.1m (3.5ft) high; raised by June Davis, UK, in 1996. Available UK: Abacus, Aylett's, Cruikshank, Halls, National, P. & L., Porter, Pratt, Scotts, Spencer, Taylor; USA: Arrowhead, Clacks, Mingus; Canada: Candahlia; elsewhere: Jacks.

Cherwell Lapwing
Small semi-cactus (unclassified); pink exhibition variety, 1.2m (4ft) high; raised by June Davis, UK, 2001.

Cherwell Siskin
Medium decorative (NDS), informal decorative (ADS); yellow exhibition variety, 1.2m (4ft) in height; raised by June Davis, UK, in 1999. Available UK: Cruikshank, Porter.

Cherwell Skylark
Small semi-cactus (unclassified); pink and yellow blends, exhibition variety, 1.2m (4ft) in height; raised by June Davis, UK, in 2000.

Cheryle C.
Small formal decorative (ADS); white exhibition and garden variety, 1.2m (4ft) high bush; originated by Canning, USA, in 2000.

Chessy
Single Lilliput (NDS); yellow garden variety, introduced in 1955. Available UK: Abacus, Aylett's, Butterfield, Cruikshank, National; USA: Frey's.

Cheyenne
Small lacinated variety (ADS); flame-coloured, 15cm (6in) blooms for exhibition use, on 1.4m (4.5ft) high strong bush; originated by Buddin, USA, in 1975. Available USA: Connell's, Dan's Dahlias, Mingus, SB Gardens, Swan Island.

Cheyenne Chief
Small, lacinated (ADS); variegated yellow and orange garden and exhibition variety, sport of Cheyenne; height 1.2m (4ft); originated USA in 2000. Available USA: Clacks, Connell's, Dan's Dahlias, Elkhorn.

Chilson's Pride
Small informal decorative (ADS); white/pink blends, excellent for exhibition, garden, cut flower or floral art; 10cm (4in) blooms, grows to 1.5m (5ft) high; originated by C. Chilson, USA, in 1954. Available USA: Alpen, Arrowhead, Capistrano, Clacks, Connell's, Creekside, Dahlia Dandies, Dan's Dahlias, Elkhorn, Mingus, Sea-Tac, Swan Island; Canada: Ferncliff.

Chiltern Herald
Medium semi-cactus (NDS); yellow and exhibition blooms on a 1.4m (4.5ft) high plant; raised by Keith Fleckney, UK, in 1988. Available UK: National, Oscroft, P. & L.; USA: Elkhorn.

Chiltern Impact
Small semi-cactus (unclassified); yellow exhibition variety, 1.2m (4ft) high; sport of Golden Impact; raised by Keith Fleckney, UK, in 1991.

Chimacum Julia
Medium incurving cactus (ADS); yellow exhibition variety, 1.2m (4ft) in height; originated by D. & L. Smith, USA, in 2000.

Chimacum Sunrise
Small incurved cactus (ADS); yellow exhibition and garden variety; 1.2m (4ft) high bush; originated by D. & L. Smith, USA, in 1995.

CHARLIE KENWOOD

CHARLIE TWO

CHERWELL LAPWING

CHERWELL GOLDCREST

CHERWELL SKYLARK

CHEYENNE CHIEF

CHILTERN HERALD

CHILTERN IMPACT

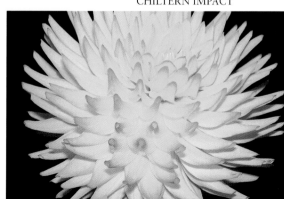

Chimacum Topaz
Medium straight cactus (ADS); light blends yellow and bronze blooms for exhibition and garden use, on a 1.2m (4ft) high plant; originated by D. & L. Smith, USA, in 1996. Awarded Lynn B. Dudley medal (ADS) 1995. Available USA: Clacks, Connell's, Dan's Dahlias, Elkhorn, Mingus, SB Gardens.

Chimborazo
Collerette dahlia (NDS); red with a collar tipped in pale yellow, growing to 90cm (3ft); excellent for exhibition and garden use; raised by John Crutchfield, UK, in 1959. Available UK,: Aylett's, National.

China Doll
Small waterlily (ADS); light pink and yellow blended 13cm (5in) blooms; prolific bloomer on a 0.7m (2ft) high plant; excellent for garden border and cut flower use; originated by Swan Island, USA in 1994. Available USA: Swan Island.

Chinese Lantern
Small decorative (NDS); flame-yellow blended blooms, garden variety, 0.9m (3ft) high plants; introduced by dahlia Maarse, Holland, in 1957. Award Merit Wisley 1964 (NDS). Available UK: National.

Chloe's Keene
Large semi-cactus (NDS); white exhibition variety, 1.2m (4ft) high; raised by Les Jones, UK, in 1995. Available UK: National.

Christine Hammett
Medium formal decorative (unclassified); bronze exhibition variety; introduced Keith Hammett, New Zealand. Available USA: Clacks.

Christmas Carol
Collerette (NDS and ADS); red, red and yellow blends for exhibition and garden use, growing to 1.1m (3.5ft) high; originated by L. Connell, USA, in 1988. Available UK: Cruikshank, Halls, National, Scotts, Station House; USA: Dan's Dahlias.

Christmas Star
Collarette (ADS); red with white collar, garden variety; 1.1m (3.5ft) high plants; originated by L. Connell, USA, in 1986.

Christopher Nickerson
Medium semi-cactus (NDS); yellow blended exhibition variety, 1.2m (4ft) tall; raised by J. Nickerson, UK, in 1991. Award Garden Merit Wisley (NDS). Available UK: National, P. & L., Scotts.

Christopher Taylor
Small waterlily (NDS); red garden and cut flower, 1.2m (4ft) high; raised by C. Taylor, UK, in 1980. Available UK: Abacus, Cruikshank, Halls, Jones, National, P. & L., Station House.

Cindy
Small or miniature decorative (NDS); yellow exhibition or garden variety, 1.1m (3.5ft) high; introduced by Cor Geerlings, Holland, in 1997. Available UK: Abacus, Cruikshank, Jones, P. & L., Scotts; USA: Mingus; elsewhere: Geerlings.

Cindy Lou
Small cactus (ADS); red exhibition variety; 1.2m (4ft) high bush; originated by Simmons, USA, in 1980.

Citron du Cap
Medium lacinated (ADS); yellow exhibition variety; height 1.2m (4ft); raised by C. Higgo, South Africa, in 2001. Available USA: Connell's.

Clair de Lune (synonymous with **Moonlight**)
Collerette (NDS); yellow with the outer petals a darker yellow than the collar; a strong-growing bush at 90cm (3ft) high, providing abundant blooms for cut flower and garden use; raised by dahlia Bruidegom, Holland, in 1946. Available UK: Cruikshank, Halls, JRG, National, Oscroft, Station House; elsewhere: Geerlings.

Clara Huston
Giant incurved cactus (ADS); orange exhibition variety, 25cm (10in) blooms with strong stems on a 1.2m (4ft) high bush; originated by Earl Huston, Canada, in 1995. Available USA: Alpen, Clacks, Creekside, Dahlia Dandies; Canada: Ferncliff; elsewhere: Konishi.

Clara Marie
Small formal decorative (ADS); dark blends, white and purple, good cut flower variety; originated by W. Almand, USA, in 1981. Available USA: Arrowhead, Clacks, Frey's.

Classic A1
Medium cactus (NDS and ADS); orange (NDS), bronze (ADS) blooms on a 1.2m (4ft) plant; useful for exhibition and garden with prolific blooms; originated by L. Connell, USA, in 1994. Available UK: Aylett's, National, Oscroft, P. & L.; USA: Dahlia Dandies, Dan's Dahlias, Elkhorn.

Classic Classic
Large semi-cactus (ADS); light blends bronze, pink and yellow exhibition variety; originated by Bishop, USA, in 2001. Available USA: Arrowhead, Clacks.

Claudette
Small lacinated (ADS); dark pink exhibition variety, 1.6m (5.5ft) in height; originated by Willoughby, Canada, in 1999. Available USA: Clacks; elsewhere: Geerlings, Wirth.

CHIMBORAZO

CHINESE LANTERN

CHLOE'S KEENE

CHRISTOPHER NICKERSON

CHRISTOPHER TAYLOR

CINDY

CLAIR DE LUNE

CLASSIC A1

Cliff Rushton
Giant decorative (unclassified); yellow-tipped exhibition variety, very tall, in excess of 1.6m (6ft); introduced by Cliff Rushton and Keith Hammett, New Zealand, in 1990.

Clint's Climax
Large decorative (NDS), or large formal decorative (ADS); lavender exhibition variety; introduced by J. Beard, South Africa, in 1987. Available UK: Abacus, National; USA: Clacks, Dan's Dahlias, Frey's, SB Gardens.

Cloverdale
Small decorative (NDS); yellow exhibition variety, growing to 1.1m (3.5ft); raised by David Boyd, UK, in 1988. Available UK: National.

Clyde's Choice
Giant formal decorative (ADS); huge, orange exhibition; 30cm (12in) blooms on a 1.3m (4.5ft) high plant of heavy growth; originated by Simon, USA, in 1989. Available USA: Clacks, Mingus, Sea-Tac, Swan Island; Canada: Candahlia, Ferncliff.

Coconut Puff
Small lacinated (ADS); white exhibition and garden variety; height 1.1m (3.5ft); originated by Surber, USA, in 1995.

Colleen Audrey
Ball (ADS); dark-red exhibition variety; 1.2m (4ft) high bush; originated by M. Hall, USA, in 2000.

Colorado Classic
Small, informal decorative (ADS); light blends pink and white exhibition and garden variety; height 1.2m (4ft); originated by C. Cook, USA, in 2001. Available USA: Arrowhead.

Colorado Moonshine
Small incurved cactus (ADS); yellow exhibition variety; originated by C. Cook, USA, in 2002. Available USA: Arrowhead.

Color Magic
Large semi-cactus (ADS); variegated yellow and dark red, exhibition and cut flower variety; height 1.5m (5ft); originated by by W. Almand, USA, in 1994. Available USA: Clacks; Dahlia Dandies.

Coltness Gem
A dwarf bedder (NDS), single red variety, 0.5m (18in) high, for garden usage; raised by Purdie in 1922; can be grown from seed. Plants available UK: National.

Comet
Anemone (NDS and ADS); dark red garden variety, growing to 0.9m (3ft) high; introduced by N. J. van Oosten, Holland, in 1952: prolific bush. Award Merit Wisley 1956 (NDS). Available UK: Blooms, National; USA: Clacks.

Como Poly
Large decorative (NDS), or large formal decorative (ADS); a lavender exhibition variety growing to 1.2m (4ft); introduced by Ray, Australia, in 1974. Available UK: National; elsewhere: Jacks.

Connecticut Dancer
Small formal decorative (ADS); variegated white and dark red variety, raised by C. Jones, USA, in 1970. Available USA: Arrowhead, Clacks, Dahlia Dandies, Dan's Dahlias, Sea-Tac.

Connie Bartlam
Medium decorative (NDS); pink blended exhibition and garden variety, 1.2m (4ft) high; raised by Tom Mantle, UK, in 1987. Available UK: Halls, National.

Conway
Small semi-cactus (NDS and ADS); pink-blended exhibition variety, growing 0.9m (3ft) high; raised by Neville Weekes, UK, in 1986. Award Garden Merit Wisley (NDS). Available UK: National.

Cool Luke
Large informal decorative (ADS); bronze exhibition variety, height 1.2m (4ft); originated by D. Hinz, USA, in 2001. Available USA: Clacks.

Copper Go American
Bronze sport of Go American, giant decorative (unclassified); exhibition variety 0.9m (3ft) high.

Coral Frills
Small lacinated (ADS); pink exhibition variety; 1.1m (3.5ft) high bush; originated by Swan Island, USA, in 1991.

Coral Gypsy
Medium straight cactus (ADS); deep pink 18cm (7in) blooms, cut flower variety useful for floral arrangements. Plants grow to 1.2m (4ft) high; originated by N. Gitts, USA, in 1996. Available USA: Swan Island.

Coral Jupiter
Giant semi-cactus (unclassified); pink exhibition variety, 1.4m (4.5ft) high; sport of Pink Jupiter.

CLIFF RUSHTON

CLINT'S CLIMAX

CLYDE'S CHOICE

COMO POLY

CONNECTICUT DANCER

CONNIE BARTLAM

COPPER GO AMERICAN

CORAL JUPITER

Coralie

Coralie
Small formal decorative (ADS); light blends pink and white, cut flower variety, height 1.2m (4ft); originated by T. Mantle, UK, in 1982. Available USA: Capistrano, Dahlia Dandies, Dan's Dahlias, Sea-Tac.

Corn Classic
Medium semi-cactus (unclassified) yellow exhibition variety originated in South Africa.

Corn Supreme
Large decorative (unclassified); yellow exhibition variety; originated in South Africa. Available USA: Arrowhead.

Cornel
Miniature or small ball (NDS), dark red ball (ADS); non-fading blooms useful for exhibition, cut flower or garden; growing to a height of 90cm (3ft) with uniform, fully revolving blooms; introduced by Cor Geerlings, Holland, in 1994. Awarded the Stanley Johnson medal. Available UK: Abacus, Butterfield, Cruikshank, Halls, National, Oscroft, P. & L., Porter, Roberts, Scotts, Spencer, Station House, Tivey; USA: Alpen, Arrowhead, Clacks, Connell's, Creekside, Dahlia Dandies, Dan's Dahlias, Elkhorn, Mingus, SB Gardens, Sea-Tac; Canada: Candahlia; elsewhere: Dgid, Engelhardt, Geerlings.

Corona
Dwarf bedder, small semi-cactus (NDS); 0.75m (2ft) in height; red garden variety; raised by Westwell. Available UK: National.

Cortez Silver
Medium decorative (NDS); 1.2m (4.0ft) high, white exhibition variety; raised by Norman Lewis, UK, in 1977. Available UK: National, Oscroft, P. & L.

Cortez Sovereign
Small semi-cactus (NDS); yellow garden variety, 1.1m (3.5ft) high; raised by Norman Lewis, UK, in 1976. Available UK: National.

Corton Olympic
Giant decorative (unclassified); bronze exhibition variety; 1.2m (4ft) high; raised by J. Harboard, UK.

Cottontail
Collerette (ADS); dark red, purple and white-collar; exhibition variety; originated by Topsvert, Holland, in 1954.

Country Boy
Medium semi-cactus (NDS); red garden variety; 1.1m (3.5ft) high; raised by A. T. Hayes, UK, in 1994. Available UK: Cruikshank, National.

Country Charm
Medium formal decorative (ADS); light blends pink and yellow exhibition variety; 1.2m (4ft) high plant; originated by Warden, USA, in 2001.

Country Gold
Medium semi-cactus (ADS); bronze exhibition variety; 1.2m (4ft) high plant; originated by Warden, USA, in 2000.

Country Sunshine
Medium informal decorative (ADS); yellow exhibition and garden variety; 1.2m (4ft) high bush; originated by Warden, USA, in 2002.

Craig Nathan
Miniature formal decorative (ADS); pink exhibition variety; 1.1m (3.5ft) high bush; originated by C. Craig, USA, in 2001.

Crazy Legs
Stellar (ADS); orange cut flower and floral art variety, with 8.5cm (3.5in) blooms, growing to a height of 1.2m (4ft) bush, with outstanding foliage; originated by N. Gitts, USA, in 1990. Available USA: Frey's, Swan Island.

Cream Alvas
Giant decorative (NDS); yellow exhibition variety, 1.2m (4ft) high, raised by E. Machin, UK, in 1990. Available UK: Cruikshank, National, P. & L.

Cream Beauty
Small waterlily (NDS), or waterlily (ADS); yellow exhibition, garden and cut flower variety, growing to a height of 1.1m (3.5ft); introduced by Cor Geerlings, Holland, in 1992. Available UK: National, Oscroft, P. & L., Tivey; elsewhere: Geerlings.

CORN CLASSIC

CORN SUPREME

CORTON OLYMPIC

COUNTRY BOY

CORNEL

CORTEZ SILVER

CREAM BEAUTY

Cream Capella
Giant decorative (unclassified); white exhibition variety, 1.2m (4ft) in height, raised by Hardy, UK, in 2000.

Cream Delight
Small semi-cactus (unclassified); yellow exhibition variety, 1.2m (4ft) in height, raised by R. F. Howes, UK, in 1994.

Cream Elegans
Small semi-cactus (NDS); pale yellow sport of Yellow Elegans, for exhibition and garden use; 1.1m (3.5ft) high; raised by B. Smith, UK, in 1998. Available UK: National, P. & L.

Cream Klankstad
Small cactus (NDS); pale yellow sport of Klankstad Kerkrade, growing to a height of 1.1m (3.5ft); raised by Frank Taylor, UK, in 1987. Available UK: National; elsewhere: Jacks.

Cream Linda
Small decorative (NDS); a yellow sport of White Linda for garden or cut flower use, growing to a height of 1.1m (3.5ft); introduced by Morton Hall, UK, in 1988. Available UK: National, Oscroft, P. & L., Scotts.

Creamy
Miniature ball (ADS); white exhibition variety; 1.2m (4ft) high; originated by P. Traff, USA, in 1993.

Creekside Betty
Small formal decorative (ADS); red exhibition variety; 1.2m (4ft) bush; originated by B. Killingsworth, USA, in 2001.

Creekside Gilly
Medium informal decorative (ADS); yellow garden variety, 1.2m (4ft) in height; originated by Brian Killingsworth, USA, in 2001. Available USA: Arrowhead, Creekside.

Creekside Marge
Orange waterlily (ADS); originated by Brian Killingsworth, USA, in 2001. Available USA: Arrowhead, Creekside.

Creekside Ruth
Small informal decorative (ADS); white exhibition variety; 1.2m (4ft) high bush; originated by B. Killingsworth, USA, in 2001.

Creekside Volcano
Small lacinated (ADS); flame; outstanding garden variety; height 1.5m (5ft); originated by Brian Killingsworth, USA, in 1997. Available USA: Alpen, Clacks, Mingus.

Creve Coeur
Giant semi-cactus (ADS); red exhibition variety on a 1.1m (3.5ft) high bush; originated by Simon, USA, in 1992. Awarded the Derrill Hart medal (ADS). Available USA: Alpen, Arrowhead, Clacks, Dahlia Dandies, Dan's Dahlias, Frey's, Mingus, SB Gardens, Sea-Tac; elsewhere: Engelhardt, Jacks, Wirth.

Crichton Honey
Small ball (NDS), or ball (ADS); orange blends (NDS) or bronze blends (ADS); exhibition or cut flower variety; 10cm (4in) blooms on a 1.1m (3.5ft) high plant; raised by Arthur Lashlie, UK, in 1976. Available UK: National; USA: Clacks, Dan's Dahlias, Elkhorn, Frey's, Mingus, SB Gardens, Sea-Tac, Swan Island.

Crossfield Ebony
Pompon (ADS); dark red exhibition or cut flower variety, 1.1m (3.5ft) high; raised by Summerscales, UK, in 1955. Available USA: Clacks, Connell's, Dan's Dahlias, Elkhorn, Sea-Tac, Swan Island.

Croydon Masterpiece
Giant informal decorative (ADS); bronze exhibition blooms, strong stems, on a 1.2m (4ft) high plant; introduced by H. Brand, Australia, in 1948. Award Merit Wisley 1952 (NDS). Available USA: Clacks, Swan Island.

Croydon Superior
Giant decorative (NDS); pink and yellow blended, exhibition variety, 1.2m (4ft) high plants; raised by H. Brand, Australia, in 1968. Available UK: National, Tivey; USA: Elkhorn.

Cryfield Bryn
Small semi-cactus (NDS); yellow exhibition and garden variety, 1.1m (3.5ft) high grower; raised by F. Wilson, UK, in 1973. Award Merit 1977 Wisley (NDS). Available UK: Halls, National.

Cryfield Keene
Large semi-cactus (NDS); pink exhibition variety, 1.4m (4.5ft) high on long stems; raised by F. Wilson, UK, in 1991. Available UK: Clark, Cruikshank, National, P. & L.

Cryfield Max
Small cactus (NDS); yellow exhibition and garden variety, growing to 1.1m (3.5ft) high; raised by F. Wilson, UK, in 1973. Award Merit 1974 Wisley (NDS). Available UK: National; USA: Dan's Dahlias.

CREAM CAPELLA

CREAM DELIGHT

CREAM ELEGANS & LEMON ELEGANS

CREAM KLANKSTAD

CREVE COEUR

CRYFIELD BRYN

CRYFIELD KEENE

Cryfield Rosie
Small ball (NDS); yellow and red blended exhibition, garden and cut flower variety; raised by F. Wilson, UK, in 1986. Available UK: National.

Crystal Anne
Medium semi-cactus (NDS); flame and white blended garden and cut flower variety; 1.1m (3.5ft) high plant; originated by L. Connell, USA, in 1992. Available UK: National; USA: Connell's, Elkhorn.

Curiosity
Collerette (NDS); bronze and red blended exhibition variety; 1.1m (3.5ft) high; introduced by dahlia Bruidegom, Holland, in 1954. Available UK: Aylett's, Cruikshank, Halls, JRG, National, Oscroft.

Cynthia Huston
Large semi-cactus (ADS); red exhibition and garden variety, blooms 25cm (10in) on a 1.1m (3.5ft) high, compact bush; originated by Earl Huston, Canada, in 1994. Available USA: Arrowhead, Dahlia Dandies, Hamilton; Canada: Ferncliff; elsewhere: Konishi.

Cynthia Louise
Large informal decorative (ADS); yellow and white exhibition sport of Kidds Climax; 25cm (10in) blooms of a 1.4m (4.5ft) high variety; originated by Swan Island, USA, in 1991. Available USA: Hamilton, Swan Island; elsewhere: Engelhardt.

Czar Willo
Pompon (ADS), purple exhibition and cut flower variety; long-stemmed, growing on a 1.2m (4ft) bush; originated in 1961. Available

USA: Arrowhead, Clacks, Dan's Dahlias, Frey's, SB Gardens.

Czeanne
Gallery dahlia (unclassified); yellow garden and pot flower; 0.6m (2ft) high; originated Belgium, 1999.

D

Daddy's Choice
Small semi-cactus (NDS); yellow garden variety; 1.2m (4ft) in height; raised by E. Richards, UK, in 1978.

Daddy's Girlie
Miniature formal decorative (ADS); purple exhibition variety; originated by Shantz, USA, in 1981. Awarded the Derrill Hart medal and Lynn B. Dudley medals in 1980 (ADS). Available USA: Clacks; elsewhere: Jacks.

Daisy's Child
Miniature single (ADS); dark blended garden variety; originated by Harold Miller, USA, in 1991.

Daleko Adonis
Large semi-cactus (unclassified); yellow exhibition variety with 25cm (10in) blooms on a plant 1.4m (4.5ft) in height; raised by George Kryzwicki, UK, in 1977. Available USA: Arrowhead, Dan's Dahlias, Elkhorn, Swan Island.

Daleko Gold
Medium decorative (NDS); orange exhibition, garden and cut flower variety on a 1.2m (3.5ft) high bush; raised by George Kryzwicki, UK, in 1976. Available UK: National, P. & L., Tivey.

Daleko Jupiter
Giant semi-cactus (NDS), large semi-cactus (ADS); red and yellow (NDS), yellow and dark pink (ADS); blended exhibition variety, 1.4m (4.5ft) high; raised by George Kryzwicki, UK, in 1979; sported Pink Jupiter (K. Hardham) 1981 and Rose Jupiter in 1986. Available UK: Abacus, Clark, Cruikshank, Halls, P. & L., Porter, Roberts, Station House, Tivey; USA: Arrowhead, Connell's, Elkhorn; elsewhere: Geerlings, Graines, Jacks.

Daleko Olympic
Large decorative (NDS); white and purple bicolour; 1.2m (4ft) high, garden and cut flower variety. Raised by George Kryzwicki, UK, in 1977.

Daleko Venus
Medium semi-cactus (NDS); lavender and white blended exhibition, garden and cut flower; 1.1m (3.5ft) in height; long-stemmed; raised by George Kryzwicki, UK, in 1975. Available UK: National.

Dana
Medium straight cactus (ADS); dark blends, yellow and red blooms, on a 1.2m (4ft) high bush; excellent garden variety; originated by W. Almand, USA, in 1979. Available USA: Connell's, Dan's Dahlias.

Dana Alice
Pompon (NDS); yellow exhibition variety, 0.9m (3ft) in height; raised by Ralph Cook, UK, in 1996.

Dana Frank
Pompon (NDS); red exhibition variety; strong plant, 1.2m (4ft) high; raised by Ralph Cook, UK, in 1996. Available UK: National, P. & L., Porter.

CRYFIELD ROSIE

DALEKO JUPITER

DALEKO VENUS

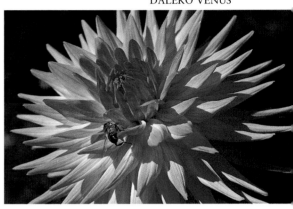

CYNTHIA LOUISE

DANA ALICE

CZEANNE

DANA FRANK

Dana Iris
Small cactus (NDS and ADS); red exhibition, garden and cut flower variety; 1.2m (4ft) high; raised by Ralph Cook, UK, in 1977. Award Garden Merit and Award Merit, 1998 Wisley (NDS). Available UK: National; USA, Sea-Tac.

Dancing Queen
Small semi-cactus (NDS); pink garden and cut variety; 1.1m (3.5ft) in height; introduced by Cor Geerlings, Holland, in 1981. Available UK: National.

Dandie de-Lite
Medium formal decorative (ADS); dark red exhibition and good cut flower variety; 1.5m (5ft) high bush; originated by Mike and Trish Valler, USA, in 2000. Available USA: Dahlia Dandies.

Dandie Lilac
Small formal decorative (ADS); purple exhibition and cut flower variety; 1.2m (4ft) high bush; originated by Mike and Trish Valler, USA, in 2000. Available USA: Dahlia Dandies.

Dandie Sparkler
Collarette (ADS); dark blends, dark red and white exhibition and cut flower; height 1.1m (3.5ft); originated by Mike and Trish Valler, USA, in 2001. Available USA: Dahlia Dandies.

Dandy
Lilliput single (NDS); purple garden variety; raised in 1959. Available UK: National.

Daniel Edward
Miniature semi-cactus (unclassified); garden and cut flower variety; abundant pink and purple blooms 9cm (3.5in) on long stems on a 1.2m (4ft) high bush; originated USA in 1989. Available USA: Swan Island.

Danjo Doc
Small, formal decorative (ADS); dark red cut flower blooms on a vigorous 1.2m (4ft) high bush; originated by Docherty, UK, in 1996. Available USA: Connell's, SB Gardens; elsewhere: Jacks.

Danum Cream
Medium semi-cactus (NDS), medium straight cactus (ADS); yellow garden and cut flower variety growing 1.1m (3.5ft) high; prolific blooming bush throughout season; raised by Fred Oscroft, UK, in 1999. Available UK: National; USA, Creekside, Mingus; Canada: Candahlia, Ferncliff.

Danum Jack
Small semi-cactus (ADS); dark-pink garden, exhibition and cut flower variety; 1.2m (4ft) high plant; originated by Fred Oscroft, UK, in 2000.

Danum Meteor
Giant semi-cactus (ADS); red exhibition variety; height 1.1m (3.5ft); raised by Fred Oscroft, UK, in 1996. Available USA: Alpen, Arrowhead, Clacks, Creekside, Mingus; Canada: Candahlia, Ferncliff; elsewhere: Jacks.

Danum Pinky
Medium semi-cactus (NDS); pink garden and cut flower variety; 1.2m (4ft) high plant; raised by Fred Oscroft, UK. Available UK: National, Oscroft, P. & L.

Danum Salmon
Medium semi-cactus (NDS); orange and pink exhibition, garden and cut flower blooms on a 1.2m (4ft) high plant; raised by Fred Oscroft, UK, in 1991. Available UK: National.

Darci Lynn
Miniature formal decorative (ADS); white exhibition and garden variety blooms on a 1.2m (4ft) high bush; originated by Anderson, USA, in 2001. Awarded the Derrill Hart medal (ADS). Available USA: Clacks.

Dare Devil
Small semi-cactus (unclassified); bright red garden and cut flower variety; prolific 15cm (6in) bloomer on a 1.2m (4ft) high bush; originated USA, 1999. Available USA: Swan Island.

Dark Delight
Small, incurving cactus (unclassified); dark red garden variety on a 1.2m (4ft) high bush. Available USA: Connell's, Frey's.

Dark Destiny
Medium lacinated (ADS); purple exhibition and garden variety; 1.2m (4ft) high bush; originated by L. Connell, USA, in 1999.

Dark Magic
Small, informal decorative (ADS); dark blended white and purple exhibition and cut flower variety; 15cm (6in) blooms on a 1.2m (4ft) high bush; introduced by Pollard, New Zealand, in 1986. Available USA: Clacks, Dahlia Dandies, Dan's Dahlias, Elkhorn, Frey's, Sea-Tac, Swan Island.

Dark Prince
Small, formal decorative (unclassified); purple garden and cut flower variety on a 1.2m (4ft) high bush; originated USA in 1995. Available USA: Connell's.

Dark Splendour
Medium cactus (NDS); red exhibition variety on 1.2m (4ft) high plant, raised by dahlia Bruidegom, Holland. Available UK: National.

DANA IRIS

DANCING QUEEN

DANUM SALMON

Darlene Vloet
Small semi-cactus (ADS); yellow garden and exhibition variety; height 1.2m (4ft); originated by Vloet, USA, in 2000. Available USA: Alpen.

Dauntless
Giant semi-cactus (NDS and ADS); red and yellow (NDS), red (ADS); exhibition blooms growing on a 1.2m (4ft) high bush; originated by B. Simon, USA, in 1985. Available UK: Cruikshank, P. & L.; USA: Connell's, SB Gardens; elsewhere: Engelhardt, Jacks.

Davenport Anita
Miniature decorative (NDS), and miniature formal decorative (ADS); orange exhibition and garden blooms on a 1.1m (3.5ft) high plant; raised by Alan Dunlop, UK, in 1988. Available UK: National; USA: Dan's Dahlias.

Davenport Honey
Miniature decorative (NDS); orange exhibition, garden and cut flower blooms on 1.2m (4ft) high bush; raised by Alan Dunlop, UK, in 1988. Available UK: Abacus, Cruikshank, National; USA: Dan's Dahlias.

Davenport Lesley
Miniature decorative (unclassified); red exhibition garden and cut flower on a bush 1.1m (3.5ft) high; introduced by Alan Dunlop, UK, in 1989.

Davenport Sunlight
Medium semi-cactus (NDS); yellow exhibition, garden and cut flower blooms on 0.9m (3ft) high plant; raised by Alan Dunlop, UK, in 1980. Available UK: Halls, National, P. & L.

Dave's Kiss
Miniature ball (NDS); purple and white bicolour, exhibition and garden blooms on a 1.1m (3.5ft) high plant; introduced by David Spencer, UK, in 1999. Available UK: Halls, P. & L., Spencer.

David Digweed
Small, formal decorative (ADS); orange garden and exhibition variety; raised by Barry Davies, UK, in 1995. Available USA: Alpen.

David Howard
Miniature decorative (NDS); orange bronze-blended blooms and dark coppery coloured foliage that sets off the blooms to great advantage; greatly used in the garden and for cut flower; grows to a height of 75cm (2.5ft); raised by D. Howard, UK, in 1965. Award Merit Wisley 1967 (NDS), Garden Merit Wisley 1995 (NDS). Available UK: Abacus, Aylett's, Halls, JRG, National, Oscroft, P. & L., Tivey; USA: Clacks, Dan's Dahlias, Sea-Tac; elsewhere: Dgid, Graines.

David Huston
Giant semi-cactus (unclassified); yellow exhibition variety on a 1.5m (4.5ft) high bush; last origination of Earl Huston in 1999. Available Canada: Ferncliff.

David Lam
Collarette (ADS); dark red exhibition and cut flower variety on a 1.2m (4ft) high bush; originated by K. & S. Williams, Canada, in 1994. Available Canada: Ferncliff.

David's Choice
Small, formal decorative (unclassified); bright red 10cm (4in) blooms; garden variety; 1.2m (4ft) high, dark foliage bush. Available Canada: Ferncliff.

DD Erica Lee
Medium straight cactus (ADS); red bloom exhibition variety; originated by Ken and Terry Diede, USA, in 2001. Awarded the Lyn B. Dudley medal (ADS).

DD Moonlight Sonata
Small, formal yellow exhibition decorative (ADS); originated by Ken and Terry Diede, USA, in 2001. Awarded the Lynn B. Dudley medal (ADS).

Debbie Boone
Small, straight cactus (ADS); white exhibition variety; originated by Lamour, Canada, in 1999. Awarded the Lynn B. Dudley medal, 1998 (ADS). Available USA: Clacks.

Deborah Ann Craven
Giant semi-cactus (NDS); red exhibition variety 1.4m (4.5ft) high; raised by A. Craven, UK, in 1988. Available UK: Cruikshank, Halls, National.

Deborah's Kiwi
Small cactus (NDS and ADS); white/pink blends (NDS), light blends (ADS); exhibition variety; grows 1.1m (3.5ft) high; raised by A. Hick, UK, in 1996 as a sport of Kiwi Gloria. Available UK: Abacus, Clark, Cruikshank, Halls, National, Oscroft, P. & L., Porter, Pratt, Scotts, Spencer, Station House, Taylor; elsewhere: Geerlings, Jacks.

Deception
Miniature formal decorative (unclassified); light pink and pink blends, garden and cut flower variety on a 1.2m (4ft) high bush; originated by L. Connell, USA, in 2000. Available USA: Connell's.

Deerwood Bo Peep
Medium informal decorative (ADS); white exhibition variety; originated by Ron Schofield, USA, in 2001.

DAUNTLESS

DAVENPORT LESLEY

DAVE'S KISS

DAVID DIGWEED

DEBORAH ANN CRAVEN

Deerwood Dandy
Small, formal decorative
(ADS); dark blends, red and
yellow exhibition blooms on a
0.9m (3ft) high bush;
originated by Ron Schofield,
USA, in 2000. Available USA:
Arrowhead, Clacks.

Deidre K
Medium lacinated (unclassified);
light blends, white and lavender
blooms on 1.4m (4.5ft) high
bush, exhibition variety;
originated by Louis and Patti
Eckhoff, USA, in 2000 (named
after their daughter).

Del Boy
Medium cactus (unclassified);
bronze exhibition variety; 1.2m
(4ft) high; raised by A. T.
Hayes, UK.

Deliah
Miniature semi-cactus
(unclassified); purple garden
and cut flower variety on a
1.2m (4ft) high bush; originated
by L. Connell, USA, in 1996.
Available USA: Arrowhead,
Connell's, Dan's Dahlias.

Denise Willo
Pompon (NDS and ADS); pink
(NDS) or light blends white
and lavender, garden and cut
flower variety; height 1.1m
(3.5ft); raised by Norman
Williams, Australia, in 1966.
Available UK: Abacus,
National; USA: SB Gardens.

Derek Sean
Miniature formal decorative
(unclassified); garden and cut
flower variety with 9cm (3.5in)
lavender blooms; prolific 1.5m
(4.5ft) high bush; originated
USA, 1990. Available USA:
Swan Island.

Desert Glow
Giant incurving cactus
(unclassified); orange exhibition
and garden variety on a 1.2m
(4ft) high bush; originated by K.

and S. Wynne, Canada, in 2002.
Available Canada: Ferncliff.

Desiree
Small, formal decorative
(unclassified); lavender and
white blended garden and cut
flower variety; early bloomer
on a 1.4m (4.5ft) high bush;
originated by L. Connell, USA,
in 2000. Available USA:
Connell's.

Deuil du Roi Albert
Medium decorative (NDS);
purple and white, bicolour
garden variety; 1.1m (3.5ft) in
height; introduced by
Defraigner and Troquay,
France, in 1936. Available UK:
National; elsewhere: Turc.

Devon Blaze
Miniature straight cactus (ADS);
red exhibition variety on a 1.5m
(4.5ft) high bush; originated by
Schmitt, USA, in 2001. Available
Canada: Ferncliff.

Devon Seduction
Small cactus (ADS); dark purple
and white exhibition and garden
variety on a 1.2m (4ft) high
bush; originated by Schmitt,
USA, in 2000. Available USA:
Clacks; Canada, Ferncliff.

Devon Tiarra
Small semi-cactus (ADS); pink
exhibition and garden variety;
originated by Schmitt, USA, in
2001.

Diane Gregory
Pompon (NDS); lavender
blends, exhibition, garden and
cut flower variety, growing to
0.9m (3ft) in height; raised by
J. Gregory, Australia, in 1947.
Available UK: National, Station
House, Tivey.

Diane Stranzek
Medium formal decorative
(ADS); yellow exhibition
variety; blooms on 1.2m (4ft)
high plant; originated by Bud

Moore, USA, in 2000. Named
after the wife of the Mayor of
Crestwood, Illinois.

Dick Westfall
Large informal decorative
(ADS); light blends, pink and
yellow exhibition and garden
variety, tall bush 1.5m (5ft)
high; originated by Havens,
USA, in 2000.

Dizzy
Collerette (unclassified); pink
with a purple centre; garden
and cut flower variety, with
10cm (4in) blooms on a 1.5m
(4.5ft) high bush; originated
USA in 1999. Available USA:
Swan Island.

Doc van Horn
Large semi-cactus (NDS); pink
exhibition variety, growing to
1.2m (4ft) in height; introduced
by dahlia Maarse, Holland, in
1978. Available UK: National,
P. & L.

Don's Delight
Pompon (ADS); white and
purple exhibition, garden and
cut flower variety; blooms on a
1.2m (4ft) high bush; originated
by Martinson, USA, in 1988.
Available USA: Clacks,
Connell's, Dahlia Dandies, Dan's
Dahlias, Elkhorn, SB Gardens.

Doodles
Small formal decorative (ADS);
pink blooms; originated by
E. Ahl, USA, in 2001.

Doris Day
Small, red flowering cactus
(NDS); growing to 90cm (3ft);
prolific blooms for garden and
cut flower use; not now used
UK for exhibition because of
green bracts showing in the
blooms. Raised by Weijers,
Holland, in 1952. Award Merit
Wisley 1959 (NDS). Available
UK: Abacus, Butterfield, Halls,
Station House, Tivey; USA:
Clacks; elsewhere: Wirth.

DEL BOY

DORIS DAY

Doris Duke
Miniature decorative (NDS); pink garden variety, growing to 1.1m (3.5ft) in height; introduced by Hackenden Nursery, UK, in 1955. Available elsewhere: Dgid.

Doris G
Medium lacinated (ADS); light blends, yellow and pink; grows to a height of 1.1m (3.5ft); garden and exhibition variety; originated by Rodewald, USA, in 1995. Available USA: Dan's Dahlias.

Doris Knight
Small cactus (NDS); purple garden and cut flower variety; 1.1m (3.5) high; raised by B. Knight, UK, in 1963. Award Merit Wisley, 1967 (NDS). Available UK: Butterfield.

Dorothy Comstock
Medium, informal decorative (ADS); deep pink variety, 1.2m (4ft) in height; originated by E. Comstock, USA, in 1972.

Double Trouble
Collarette (ADS); dark-pink and purple exhibition and cut flower variety; grows to a height of 1.2m (4ft); originated by N. Gitts, USA, in 1996.

Downham Royal
Miniature ball (NDS and ADS); purple exhibition and garden variety; 0.9m (3ft) in height; raised by John Sharp, UK, in 1972. Available UK: National; USA: Arrowhead, Clacks, Connell's, Dan's Dahlias, Mingus, SB Gardens; Canada: Candahlia, Ferncliff; elsewhere: Dgid, Graines.

Dr Caroline Rabbett
Small decorative (NDS); bronze garden and cut flower variety; introduced by P. Tivey, UK, in 1985. Available UK: National, Tivey.

Dr John Grainger
Miniature decorative (NDS); orange exhibition and garden variety, 0.9m (3ft) high; introduced by A. Lister, UK, in 1950. Available UK: National.

Dr Les
Giant semi-cactus (ADS); dark red exhibition blooms on strong stems on a 1.1m (3.5ft) high bush; originated by W. Almand, USA, in 1975. Awarded the Derrill Hart medal (ADS). Available USA: Creekside, Frey's, Swan Island.

Drummer Boy
Large formal decorative (unclassified); bright red 23cm (9in) blooms; garden variety on a 0.9m (3ft) bush; originated by Baynes, Australia, in 1960. Available USA: Hamilton, Sea-Tac, Swan Island.

Duet
Medium decorative (NDS); red and white bicolour exhibition blooms with strong stems on a 1.2m (4ft) high bush; originated by Scott, USA, in 1955. Available UK: Jager, National, Suttons; USA: Clacks, Connell's, Creekside, Dan's Dahlias, Elkhorn, Frey's, Hamilton, Mingus, SB Gardens, Sea-Tac, Swan Island; elsewhere: Dgid, Engelhardt, Turc.

Duke of Earl
Medium informal decorative (unclassified); bright red blooms on strong stems on a tall 1.6m (5ft) high bush; originated USA in 1991. Available USA: Connell's.

Dusky Lilac
Dwarf bedder (unclassified); lavender, garden variety; introduced by M. Hall, UK, in 1988.

Dustin Williams
Small, formal decorative (unclassified); yellow and purple blended, garden and cut flower variety, 10cm (4in) blooms; bush grows to a height of 1.2m (4ft); originated USA in 1997. Available USA: Swan Island.

Dusty Daydream
Medium formal decorative (ADS); light lavender, exhibition and garden variety, height 1.2m (4ft); originated by W. and C. Wynne, Canada, in 2000. Available Canada: Ferncliff.

Dutch Baby
Pompon (NDS and ADS); light pink, perfect exhibition, garden and cut flower blooms on a 1.2m (4ft) high bush. Introduced by Cor Geerlings, Holland, in 1988. Available UK: Abacus, National, Oscroft, Tivey; USA: Arrowhead, Clacks, Connell's, SB Gardens, Sea-Tac; elsewhere: Graines.

E

E. L. Judith M.
Medium semi-cactus (ADS); light blends lavender and white, originated by Norman, USA, in 2001. Awarded the Derrill Hart medal (ADS).

Earl Marc
Small cactus (NDS); white lavender blends, garden and cut flower variety, 1.1m (3.5ft) in height; raised by E. Earl, UK, in 1978. Available UK: Butterfield, National.

Easter Bonnet
Collerette (unclassified); pink with white and pink collar; garden and cut flower variety, prolific 9cm (3.5in) blooms on a 1.1m (3ft) high bush; originated USA in 2002. Available USA: Swan Island.

Easter Sunday
Collerette (NDS); white on white; excellent for garden and cut flower; grows to 0.9m (3ft); introduced by dahlia Bruidegom, Holland, in 1956. Available UK: Oscroft, Station House.

DUSKY LILAC

EARL MARC

DOROTHY COMSTOCK

DOWNHAM ROYAL

EASTER SUNDAY

Eastwood Star
Medium semi-cactus (NDS); yellow exhibition and garden variety, 1.2m (4ft) in height; raised by John Sharp, UK, in 1975. Available UK: Abacus, National, Oscroft, P. & L.

Eastwood Moonlight
Yellow medium semi-cactus (NDS); height 1.1m (3.5ft); superb blooms on long stems, widely used in the UK for exhibition and garden purposes. Raised by John Sharp, UK, in 1975, since when a number of sports have occurred (White, Lauren's, Pims). Available UK: Abacus, Clark, Cruikshank, Halls, Jones, National, Oscroft, P. & L., Porter, Pratt, Spencer, Station House, Tivey; elsewhere: Jacks.

Ed Black
Novelty star (ADS); purple and black variety with dark green foliage; originated by Donna Black, USA, in 2000. Available USA: Alpen.

Ed Johnson
Small, informal decorative (ADS); light blends, yellow and orange blends; originated by Masurat, USA, in 1997.

Edge of Gold
Large formal decorative (ADS); dark blends, dark pink and bronze garden variety on a 1.2m (4ft) high bush; originated by Rossack, Australia, in 1967. Available USA: Clacks; elsewhere: Jacks.

Edinburgh
Classified small decorative (NDS), or small formal decorative (ADS); bicolour purple and white (NDS), dark and white (ADS); garden variety, grows to 0.9m (3ft); introduced by Dobbies, UK, in 1950. Award of Merit Wisley, 1951 (NDS). Available UK: Abacus, Cruikshank, National; USA: Connell's, Elkhorn; elsewhere: Dgid.

Edith Mueller
Pompon (ADS); flame-coloured exhibition and cut flower variety; height 1.2m (4ft); introduced by Mueller, USA, in 1933. Available USA: Frey's, Swan Island.

Edna C
Medium decorative (NDS), or formal medium decorative (ADS); excellent yellow exhibition variety, grows to a height of 1.2m (4ft); originated by E. Comstock in 1968. Awarded the Lynn B. Dudley medal in 1967, and the Derrill Hart and Stanley Johnson medals (ADS). Available UK: National; USA: Alpen, Arrowhead, Clacks, Connell's, Dahlia Dandies, Dan's Dahlias, Ferncliff, SB Gardens, Sea-Tac, Swan Island; elsewhere: Dgid.

Edron Judy
Large cactus (unclassified); pink and lavender blends on a 1.5m (4.5ft) high bush; early flowering; originated by Morcilla, Canada, in 2000. Available Canada: Ferncliff.

Edron Katrina
Lacinated cactus (unclassified); 15cm (6in) exhibition variety on a 1.2m (4ft) high bush; originated by Morcilla, Canada. Available Canada: Ferncliff.

Eileen Denny (synonymous to Scottish Rhapsody)
Medium semi-cactus (NDS); white exhibition variety; grows 1.1m (3.5ft); raised by C. Kerr, UK, in 1981. Available UK: Cruikshank, National, Oscroft.

El Triunfo
Medium informal decorative (ADS); bronze exhibition variety, height 1.4m (5ft); originated by Louis and Patti Eckhoff, USA, in 2001. Available USA: Sea-Tac.

Eldon Wilson
Stellar (ADS); yellow cut flower variety, height 1.2m (4ft); originated by L. Connell, USA,

in 1992. Awarded the Derrill Hart medal (ADS).

Eleanor
Large formal decorative (unclassified); pink garden variety, 23cm (9in) blooms on a 1.5m (5ft) high bush. Available USA: Elkhorn, Swan Island.

Elgico Alan
Large semi-cactus (ADS); light blends; originated by G. Johnson, USA, in 1998. Available USA: Alpen.

Elissa
Medium incurving cactus (ADS); red variety; originated by Ed Redd, USA, in 2001.

Elizabeth Hammett
Miniature decorative (NDS), miniature formal decorative (ADS); lavender (NDS), lavender and white blends (ADS); exhibition, garden and cut flower variety, growing to 0.9m (3ft) high; raised by Keith Hammett, New Zealand, 1980. Awarded the Lynn B. Dudley medal, 1985 (ADS). Available UK: Abacus, Cruikshank, National, Scotts, Station House; USA: Clacks, Connell's, Creekside, Dahlia Dandies, Elkhorn, Mingus, Sea-Tac, Canada: Candahlia; elsewhere: Geerlings, Graines, Jacks.

Elizabeth Snowden
Collerette (NDS and ADS); white and white (NDS), lavender (ADS); exhibition and garden variety; originated by W. McClaren, USA, in 1986. Available UK: Abacus, Cruikshank, JRG, National, Oscroft, Station House; USA: Alpen, Clacks.

Ella B
Small lacinated (ADS); red exhibition and garden variety; 1.2m (4ft) high bush; originated by D. Barnes, USA, in 2001.

EASTWOOD MOONLIGHT

EASTER STAR

EDNA C

EILEEN DENNY

ELIZABETH HAMMETT

ELIZABETH SNOWDEN

Ellen Henry
Medium incurving cactus
(unclassified); white and
lavender blended, garden and
cut flower variety on a 1.2m
(4ft) high bush; originated by
L. Connell, USA, in 1991.
Available USA: Connell's.

Ellen Huston
A miscellaneous dwarf bedding
dahlia (NDS); red blooms, dark
foliage growing to a height of
45cm (18in); a useful garden
variety; originated by Earl
Huston, Canada, in 1975.
Available UK: Blooms,
Cruikshank, Halls, National,
Oscroft, Station House, Tivey;
Canada: Ferncliff; elsewhere:
Dgid, Engelhardt, Graines.

Elma Elizabeth
(synonym **Elma E**)
Large decorative (NDS), large
formal decorative (ADS); red
exhibition variety, growing to
0.9m (3ft) in height; originated
by Ed Redd, USA, in 1993.
Available UK: Abacus, Clark,
Cruikshank, Halls, National,
Oscroft, P. & L., Porter,
Roberts, Station House, Tivey;
USA: Alpen, Arrowhead,
Clacks, Connell's, Creekside,
Dahlia Dandies, Dan's Dahlias,
Elkhorn, Mingus; Canada:
Ferncliff; elsewhere: Dgid,
Geerlings, Jacks.

Elmbrook Rebel
Giant semi-cactus (NDS); red
exhibition variety growing to
1.1m (3.5ft) in height; raised
by W. Hawkins, UK, in 1982.
Available UK: National; USA:
Connell's; elsewhere: Jacks.

Elsie Huston
Large informal decorative
ADS); pink exhibition variety,
height 1.6m (5.5ft); originated
by Earl Huston, Canada, in
1989. Available USA:
Arrowhead, Clacks, Creekside,
Dan's Dahlias, Elkhorn,
Mingus, Sea-Tac; Canada:
Ferncliff.

Elvira
Peony (ADS); dark pink;
originated by Eckhoff, USA, in
1994. Available USA: Clacks,
Dan's Dahlias, Sea-Tac.

Emily C
Miniature formal decorative
(ADS); lavender; variety
originated by Canning, USA, in
1994. Awarded the Lynn B.
Dudley medal, 1993 (ADS);
awarded Derrill Hart Medal
(ADS) 1995.

Emma's Coronet
Miniature decorative (NDS),
small formal decorative (ADS);
pink and white blends (NDS),
light blends (ADS); exhibition
variety, 1.1m (3.5ft) high;
raised by J. Digweed, UK, in
1989. Available UK:
Cruikshank, JRG, National,
Porter, Station House; USA:
Connell's: Dan's Dahlias.

Emmenthal
Small decorative (NDS); orange
garden variety; raised by Cor
Geerlings, Holland, in 1988.
Available UK: Station House;
USA: Clacks.

Emory Paul
Giant informal decorative
(ADS); purple exhibition
variety, huge blooms;
introduced by Baynes,
Australia, in 1962. Available
USA: Connell's, Dan's Dahlias,
Elkhorn, Frey's, SB Gardens,
Sea-Tac, Swan Island;
elsewhere: Graines, Turc.

Encore
Large lacinated cactus
(unclassified); yellow exhibition
variety, sport of Show 'n' Tell;
28cm (11in) blooms on a 1.2m
(4ft) high bush; originated USA
in 2002. Available USA: Swan
Island.

Enfield Salmon
Large decorative (NDS); pink
bronze blends; exhibition
variety, growing to 0.9m (3ft)
high; introduced by Baynes,
Australia, in 1954. Available
UK: National; USA: Elkhorn.

England's Glory
Giant decorative (ADS);
bicolour purple and white,
exhibition variety 1.2m (4ft)
high bush; originated by
George Brookes, UK, in 1978.
Available USA: Clacks.

Envy
Giant informal decorative
(ADS); dark red exhibition and
garden variety; grows 1.1m
(3.5ft) high; originated by
Castro, USA, in 1965.
Available USA: Arrowhead,
Dan's Dahlias, Elkhorn, Frey's,
Hamilton, Swan Island.

Erik the Red
Collarette (ADS); red exhibition
and garden variety; 1.1m (3.5ft)
high bush. Awarded Lynn B.
Dudley medal (ADS); originated
by Juul, USA, in 1984.

Erika's Angel
Miniature informal decorative
(unclassified); light blends
white and purple, exhibition
and garden variety; 1.2m (4ft)
high; originated by Clack,
USA, in 2000.

Ernie Pitt
Small, decorative (NDS); pink
and yellow blends; exhibition
and garden variety, 0.9m (3ft)
high; raised by Terry Clarke,
UK, in 1978. Available UK:
National.

Eugenia Huston
Giant, informal decorative
(ADS); flame exhibition and
garden variety; originated by
Earl Huston, Canada, in 1994.
Available USA: Clacks, Elkhorn.

Eunice O
Peony (ADS); pink garden
variety; height 1.1m (3.5ft);
originated by Warden, USA, in
1986.

Evan Matthew
Collarette (ADS); dark red with
dark red collar; exhibition
variety; height 1.2m (4ft);
originated by L. Connell, USA,
in 2001. Available USA:
Connell's.

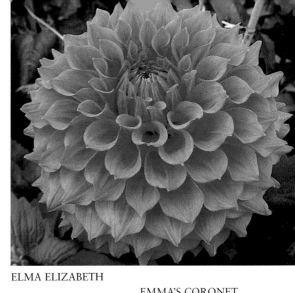

ELLEN HUSTON

ELMA ELIZABETH

ELMBROOK REBEL

EMMA'S CORONET

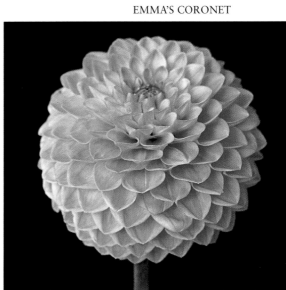

ENGLAND'S GLORY

ENVY

Evelyn Foster
Medium decorative (NDS), or medium formal decorative (ADS); white exhibition variety, growing to 1.2m (4ft) high; raised by C. Foster, UK, in 1971. Available UK: Cruikshank, Halls, National, P. & L.; USA: Elkhorn, Mingus.

Evelyn Rumbold
Giant decorative (NDS); purple exhibition variety, height 1.2m (4ft); introduced by Baynes, Australia, in 1961. Available UK: National.

Evelyn Vloet
Small, lacinated (ADS); lavender cut flower and basket variety; blooms on 1.4m (5ft) tall plants; long stems; originated by Vloet, USA, in 2000.

Evening Lady
Small, formal decorative (ADS); dark red, exhibition variety; tall grower, height 1.5m (5ft); originated by John Thiermann, USA, in 1991. Awarded the Derrill Hart medal (ADS). Available USA: Dahlia Dandies, Dan's Dahlias, SB Gardens.

Evening Mail
Giant semi-cactus (NDS); yellow exhibition variety, height 1.2m (4ft); raised by George Brookes in 1981. Award of Merit 1990 Wisley (NDS). Available UK: Cruikshank, Oscroft.

Excentric
Small, informal decorative (ADS); pink cut flower variety, height 1.1m (3.5ft); originated by N. Gitts, USA, in 1999. Available USA: Swan Island.

Exotic Dwarf
Lilliput single (NDS), mignon single (ADS); pink (NDS), dark pink blends (ADS); 30cm (1ft) high, garden variety excellent for patio pots; introduced by Nuyens, Holland, in 1965. Available UK: Halls, National; USA: Clacks.

Explosion
Small semi-cactus (NDS); white and purple bicolour; raised by Cor Geerlings, Holland, in 1965. Available UK: National; USA: Elkhorn; elsewhere: Engelhardt, Geerlings, Graines.

F

Fairway Pilot
Giant decorative (NDS); pink, blended exhibition variety, 1.2m (4ft) high; raised by Peter Cleaver, UK, in 1979. Available UK: National; USA: Mingus.

Fairway Spur
Giant decorative (NDS), giant formal decorative (ADS); bronze, pink-blended (NDS), bronze (ADS); exhibition variety, 1.2m (4ft) high, raised by Peter Cleaver, UK, in 1996. Available UK: Cruikshank, Halls, National, Oscroft, P. & L., Porter, Spencer; USA: Clacks, Mingus; elsewhere: Jacks.

Fairy Tale
Small, semi-cactus (unclassified); light pink garden variety on a 0.9m (3ft) bush; originated USA in 1999. Available USA: Swan Island.

Falcon's Future
Medium semi-cactus (ADS); light blends red and yellow; garden variety on a 1.5m (4.5ft) high bush; originated by Peck, USA, in 1995. Available USA: Dahlia Dandies, Elkhorn, Mingus; Canada: Ferncliff.

Fantasia
Large cactus (ADS); light blended yellow, exhibition variety; height 1.2m (4ft); originated USA, in 1992. Available USA: Connell's; elsewhere: Turc, Wirth.

Fascination
A miscellaneous dwarf purple bedding dahlia (NDS), with dark bronze foliage; grows to a height of 60cm (2ft): a useful garden variety; raised by Elsdon, UK, 1964. Award Merit Wisley, 1965 (NDS) and John Brown medal, Wisley (NDS) 1996. Available UK: Aylett's, Halls, National, Station House, Tivey; USA: Connell's, Dan's Dahlias, Swan Island; elsewhere: Dgid, Engelhardt, Geerlings, Graines, Wirth.

Fascination II
Peony (unclassified); bright lavender garden variety with purple foliage; 0.6m (2ft) high bush; originated USA, in 1968. Available USA: Connell's.

Fashion Monger
Collerette (NDS); pink and white exhibition and garden variety; grows 0.9m (3ft) tall; introduced by dahlia Bruidegom, Holland, in 1955. Available UK: Halls, JRG, National, Scotts; elsewhere: Wirth.

Fatima
Miniature decorative (unclassified); dark pink cut flower blooms on 1.2m (4ft) high strong plant; originated by Swan Island, USA, in 1961. Available USA: Dan's Dahlias, Mingus, Swan Island; elsewhere: Turc.

Felida Stars and Stripes
Medium formal decorative (ADS); bicolour red and white exhibition and garden variety; originated by Ted and Margaret Kennedy, USA, in 2001. Available USA: Mingus.

EVELYN FOSTER

EVELYN RUMBOLD

FAIRWAY PILOT

FAIRWAY SPUR

FASCINATION

FASHION MONGER

Fermain
Miniature decorative (NDS), miniature formal decorative (ADS); light blends, lavender and white; 0.9m (3ft) high; exhibition and garden variety, raised by Norman Flint, UK, in 1991. Available UK: Abacus, Cruikshank, National, Spencer, Station House; Canada: Candahlia.

Fern Irene
Miniature waterlily (NDS), waterlily (ADS); a yellow exhibition variety, 0.9m (3ft) in height; introduced by W. Tapley, Australia, 1985. Available UK: National, Oscroft; USA: Clacks, Dan's Dahlias, Elkhorn.

Ferncliff Ballerina
Small cactus (unclassified); salmon pink with light yellow blended; garden variety on a prolific 1.6m (5.5ft) high bush; originated by D. Jack, Canada. Available Canada: Ferncliff.

Ferncliff Copper
Small, formal decorative (ADS); orange exhibition variety, height 1.5m (5ft); originated by D. Jack, Canada, in 1990. Available USA: Alpen, Creekside, Dan's Dahlias; Canada: Ferncliff.

Ferncliff Daybreak
Small, informal decorative (unclassified); orange and white-blended garden and cut flower early variety; prolific blooms on a 1.5m (5ft) high bush; originated by D. Jack, Canada. Available Canada: Ferncliff.

Ferncliff Frenzy
Small, informal decorative (unclassified); lavender, garden and cut flower variety on a 1.5m (5ft) high, prolific bush; originated by D. Jack, Canada, in 1999. Available Canada: Ferncliff.

Ferncliff Fuego
Medium semi-cactus (ADS); flame exhibition and garden variety, 1.5m (4.5ft) high strong stems; originated by D. Jack, Canada, 1995. Available Canada: Ferncliff.

Ferncliff Illusion
Large informal decorative (ADS); white blooms with lavender tips, 20cm (8in), garden variety on a 1.5m (5ft) high bush; introduced by D. Jack, Canada, in 1994. Available USA: Creekside, Dan's Dahlias; Canada: Ferncliff.

Ferncliff Inspiration
Large, informal decorative (unclassified); 20cm (8in) lavender blooms, garden variety, 1.5m (4.5ft) high bush; introduced D. Jack, Canada, in 2000. Available Canada: Ferncliff.

Ferncliff Sunburst
Miniature cactus (ADS); yellow exhibition and garden variety, prolific 1.2m (4ft) high bush, originated by D. Jack, Canada, in 1997. Available Canada: Ferncliff.

Fernhill Champion
Medium decorative (NDS); yellow exhibition and garden variety, 1.1m (3.5ft) high; raised by E. Fuller, UK, in 1989. Available UK: National, Oscroft; elsewhere: Jacks.

Fernridge Fancy
Large semi-cactus (ADS); lavender; originated by R. Wilson, USA, in 1999.

Fidalgo Beauty
Small, lacinated (ADS) bronze variety; originated by Matthies, USA, in 1993. Awarded the Derrill Hart medal (ADS). Available USA: Connell's, Elkhorn.

Fidalgo Blacky
Miniature formal decorative (ADS); dark red, almost black, garden and cut flower variety on a 1.2m (4ft) high bush; originated by Matthies, USA, in 1993. Available USA: Connell's.

Fidalgo Climax
Fimbriated large cactus (NDS), or large lacinated cactus (ADS); yellow exhibition variety, growing to a height of 1.1m (3.5ft); originated by Matthies, USA, in 1991. A top lacinated USA bloom. Available UK: National; USA: Connell's, Dahlia Dandies.

Fidalgo Clown
Small, informal decorative (unclassified); red and white garden variety on a 1.5m (4.5ft) high bush, each bloom different; originated by Matthies, USA, in 1994. Available USA: Connell's.

Fidalgo Knight
Small, formal decorative (unclassified); good, dark red garden variety on a 1.2m (4ft) high bush; originated by Matthies, USA. Available USA: Connell's.

Fidalgo Lisa
Medium semi-cactus (ADS); dark pink, cut flower, early blooms on a 1.2m (4ft) high bush; originated by Matthies, USA, in 1993. Available USA: Connell's, Dan's Dahlias, Elkhorn.

Fidalgo Nugget
Miniature informal decorative (ADS); purple cut flower variety, early blooms on a 1.2m (4ft) high bush; originated by Matthies, USA, in 1993. Available USA: Dan's Dahlias.

FERMAIN

FERNHILL CHAMPION

FIDALGO CLIMAX

Fidalgo Snowman
Large semi-cactus (ADS); white exhibition variety on a 1.2m (4ft) high bush; originated by Matthies, USA, in 1989. Available USA: Connell's; elsewhere: Jacks.

Fidalgo Sunrise
Medium lacinated (ADS); light blends pink and yellow variety; originated by Matthies, USA, in 2001.

Fidalgo Supreme
Large decorative (NDS), medium formal decorative (ADS); yellow exhibition variety, 1.2m (4ft) high bush; originated by Matthies, USA, in 1995; awarded the Lynn B. Dudley medal in 1994 (ADS). Available UK: Aylett's, National; elsewhere: Jacks.

Fidalgo White Mafolie
Large lacinated semi-cactus (unclassified); white exhibition and garden variety; sport of Mafolie; originated by Matthies, USA, in 1995; height 1.2m (4ft). Awarded the Derrill Hart medal (ADS). Available USA: Connell's, Elkhorn.

Figurine
A small waterlily dahlia (NDS), waterlily (ADS) of pink blends; grows to a height of 1.2m (4ft) with masses of long-stemmed blooms; useful for cut flowers or the garden; raised by W. Tapley, Australia, in 1982. Award Garden Merit (NDS). Available UK: Abacus, Halls, JRG, National, P. & L., Roberts, Station House; USA: Clacks, Creekside, Dan's Dahlias, Elkhorn, Mingus, Sea-Tac.

Fiona Stewart
Small ball (NDS), miniature ball (ADS); white, pink-blended exhibition garden and cut flower variety; raised by Arthur Dashwood, UK, in 1982. Available UK: Cruikshank, National, P. & L., Scotts; USA: SB Gardens, Sea-Tac.

Fire Magic
Medium semi-cactus (ADS); flame, cut flower variety; height 1.4m (4.5ft); originated by Swan Island, USA, in 1991. Available USA: Dan's Dahlias, Elkhorn, Frey's, Swan Island; Canada: Ferncliff.

Fire Mountain
A miniature red decorative (NDS), a small decorative (ADS); height 1.1m (3.5ft); almost black foliage, much in demand for garden use; originated by Keith Hammett, New Zealand, in 1999. Available UK: Halls; USA: Clacks; elsewhere: Geerlings, Jacks.

Fire 'n' Ice
Miniature decorative (unclassified); red, with white-tipped exhibition, garden and cut flower variety on a 1.1m (3.5ft) high bush; originated Australia. Available USA: Creekside; elsewhere: Jacks.

Fire Pot
Waterlily (ADS); flame, garden variety; 0.7m (2ft) high; originated by H. Plumb, USA, in 1988. Available USA: Dan's Dahlias, Mingus, SB Gardens, Swan Island.

First Kiss
Small semi-cactus (unclassified); outstanding pink cut flower variety, much used in floral arrangement; growing

on a sturdy 1.2m (4ft) high bush; originated by Gitts, USA, in 1995. Available USA: Swan Island.

First Lady
Medium decorative (ADS); yellow exhibition and garden variety; height 0.9m (3ft); originated by E. Comstock, USA, in 1956. Available UK: National; elsewhere: Engelhardt.

Fool's Gold
Medium decorative (unclassified); yellow and bronze blended garden variety; 1.1m (3.5ft) high bush; originated USA, in 1974. Available USA: Swan Island.

Formby Alpine
Small, formal decorative (ADS); white exhibition variety, introduced by Harding, Australia, in 2000. Available USA: Clacks.

Formby Crown
Medium decorative (unclassified); lavender exhibition variety; introduced Harding, Australia, in 2000. Available UK: Spencer.

Formby Goliath
Giant informal decorative (unclassified); red garden and exhibition variety on a 1.1m (3.5ft) high bush; introduced by Harding, Australia. Available Canada: Ferncliff.

Formby Perfection
Medium decorative (NDS), medium formal decorative (ADS); lavender exhibition variety 1.1m (3.5ft) high; introduced by G. Harding, Australia, in 1975. Available UK: Cruikshank, National; USA: Arrowhead, Clacks, Creekside, Mingus.

FIDALGO SUPREME

FIGURINE

FORMBY CROWN

FIONA STEWART

FORMBY PERFECTION

Formby Supreme
Medium decorative (NDS);
yellow exhibition variety, 1.2m
(4ft) high; introduced by G.
Harding, Australia, in 1986.

Foxy Lady
Miniature decorative
(unclassified); rose and white,
cut flower variety on a 1.1m
(3.5ft) high bush, 1994 (Swan
Island). Available USA: Frey's,
Swan Island.

Frank First Kiss
Small semi-cactus
(unclassified); pink and white
cut flower and floral art variety
on a 1.2m (4ft) high bush;
originated USA, in 1995.

Frank Holmes
Pompon (NDS and ADS); white
lavender blends (NDS), pink
(ADS); exhibition, garden and
cut flower variety; 0.9m (3ft)
high; raised by E. Fuller, UK, in
1972. Available UK: Abacus,
Cruikshank, National, Oscroft,
P. & L., Station House; USA:
Arrowhead, Clacks, Frey's, SB
Gardens, Swan Island.

Frank Hornsey
Small decorative (NDS); orange
yellow blends, exhibition and
garden variety, growing to
1.2m (4ft); raised by G. J.
Chester, UK, in 1971. Available
UK: National; USA: Sea-Tac.

Frank Lovell
Giant semi-cactus (NDS);
yellow exhibition variety, 1.2m
(4ft) high; raised by Frank
Lovell, New Zealand, in 1973.
Available UK: Abacus,
National, Oscroft.

Freestyle
Small cactus (ADS); purple
exhibition variety; 0.9m (3ft)
high; raised by Eddie Durrant,
UK, in 1970. Award Merit
1973 Wisley (NDS). Available
UK: Cruikshank, National.

French Doll
Unclassified miniature
decorative; salmon pink cut

flower variety, on a 1.2m (4ft)
high plant; originated in 1994.
Available USA: Swan Island;
elsewhere: Jacks.

Frigoulet
Small cactus (ADS); dark
blends red and white bicolour,
garden variety on a 1.4m
(4.5ft) bush; originated by
Chevalier, France, in 1975.
Available USA: Connell's,
Hamilton; elsewhere: Graines.

Frilly Tilly
Small, informal decorative
(ADS); lavender variety;
originated by Hacek, USA,
in 1997.

Frits
Pompon (NDS); red and white
blends, garden and cut flower
variety; 0.9m (3ft) high;
introduced by Bos in 1943.
Available UK: National, Tivey.

Frizzy Lizzy
Small informal decorative
(ADS); exhibition variety,
height 1.6m (5.5ft); originated
by Hacek, USA, in 1997.
Available USA: Clacks.

Frodo
Small, informal decorative
(unclassified); lavender and
white, garden and cut flower
variety on a 1.2m (4ft) high
bush. Available USA: Connell's.

Frontispiece
Fimbriated giant semi-cactus or
lacinated white dahlia
(unclassified); exhibition
variety, growing to a height of
90cm (3ft); released by dahlia
Bruidegom, Holland, in 1962.
Award Merit Wisley 1965
(NDS).

Funfair
Medium formal decorative
(unclassified); yellow, red
blends; exhibition blooms on
1.4m (4.5ft) high bush;
originated in the USA in 1975.
Available USA: Connell's, Dan's
Dahlias.

Funny Face
Miniature decorative
(unclassified); light salmon and
yellow blends; cut flower
variety on a 1.2m (4ft) high
bush; originated USA, in 1985.
Available USA: Frey's, Swan
Island.

Fuzzy Wuzzy
Miniature lacinated decorative
(unclassified); pink and white
bicolour; cut flower variety,
growing to a height of 1.2m
(4ft); originated USA, in 2000.
Available USA: Swan Island.

G

G. W. Cody
Medium informal decorative
(ADS); white exhibition variety,
1.5m (5ft) in height; originated
USA, in 2001. Available USA:
Alpen, Arrowhead.

G. W.'s Babe
Miniature semi-cactus (ADS);
light blends yellow and dark
pink; exhibition variety;
originated by Wolfe, USA, in
2001.

G. W.'s Ray
Medium semi-cactus (ADS);
white exhibition variety;
originated by Wolfe, USA, in
2000. Awarded the Derrill Hart
medal (ADS).

G. W.'s Rusty
Small formal decorative (ADS);
bronze exhibition variety;
originated by Wolfe, USA, in
2000.

Gaiety
Dwarf bedder, miscellaneous
(unclassified) form; height 45cm
(18in); introduced by Roger
Aylett, UK; Award Garden
Merit Wisley (NDS) in 1997.

Gala Parade
Small, formal decorative (ADS);
lavender exhibition and garden
variety; height 1.1m (3.5ft);
raised by Terry Morgan, New
Zealand, in 1996. Available
USA: Mingus.

FORMBY SUPREME

FRANK LOVELL

FRONTISPIECE

GALA PARADE

Galator
Medium cactus (unclassified); orange-red blooms; garden variety; introduced in 1956; height 1.2m (4ft). Sported Golden Galator and Yellow Galator.

Gale Lane
Pompon (NDS); yellow-orange blends; exhibition variety, 1.2m (4ft); raised by Norman Williams, Australia, in 1967. Available UK: Cruikshank, National, P. & L.

Garden Festival
Small waterlily (NDS); orange and red bicolour, garden and cut flower variety; 1.2m (4ft) in height; raised by D. Reid, UK, in 1992. Available UK: Aylett's, Cruikshank, National, P. & L., Scotts, Tivey; USA: Mingus; elsewhere: Dgid, Geerlings, Graines, Wirth.

Garden Party
Dwarf bedder, small cactus (ADS); orange-yellow blends; garden variety; grows to a height of 60cm (2ft); introduced by van Veelen, Holland, in 1961. Award Garden Merit Wisley (NDS), 1993. Available UK: Aylett's, National; elsewhere: Dgid, Geerlings.

Gargantuan
Giant semi-cactus (ADS); light blends, pink and yellow variety; bush 1.5m (5ft) in height; originated by L. Connell, USA, in 1994. Available USA: Connell's, Creekside, Elkhorn.

Garvin
Ball (ADS); red exhibition and garden variety; 1.1m (3.5ft) high bush; originated by Simmons, USA, in 1999.

Gary
Medium semi-cactus (ADS); orange exhibition and garden variety; height 1.2m (4ft).

Awarded Lynn. B. Dudley medal (ADS); originated by Goff, USA, in 1983.

Gateshead Festival
Small, decorative (NDS); orange-pink blends; exhibition, garden and cut flower variety; raised by R. F. Howes, UK, in 1990 (named for one of a series of UK government horticultural events). Available UK: Cruikshank, Halls, National, Oscroft, Porter, Pratt, Scotts, Spencer, Station House, Taylor; USA: Elkhorn.

Gay Mini
Miniature decorative (NDS); red garden variety; raised by Terry Clarke, UK, in 1977. Available UK: Butterfield, National.

Gay Princess
Small waterlily (NDS), small informal decorative (ADS); lavender (NDS), light blends white and pink (ADS); 1.5m (5ft) in height; excellent garden and cut flower variety; raised by E. Richards, UK, in 1965. Award Merit 1972 Wisley (NDS). Available UK: Aylett's, National; USA: Capistrano, Clacks, Connell's, Dan's Dahlias, Elkhorn, SB Gardens, Swan Island.

Gay Triumph
Giant semi-cactus (NDS and ADS); bronze (NDS), orange-pink blends (ADS); exhibition and garden variety; 1.4m (4.5ft) high; originated by G. Parker, USA, in 1984. Available UK: National; USA: Creekside, Dan's Dahlias; elsewhere: Jacks, Konishi.

Geerling's Cupido
Small waterlily (NDS); orange garden variety; 1.2m (4ft) high; introduced by Cor Geerlings, Holland, in 1992. Available UK: Blooms, National; elsewhere: Dgid, Geerlings.

Geerling's Indian Summer
(synonymous **Indian Summer**)
Small cactus (NDS); red garden and cut flower; 0.9m (3ft) in height; introduced by Cor Geerlings, Holland, in 1979. Award Garden Merit, Wisley (NDS), 1993. Available elsewhere: Geerlings.

Geerling's Yellow
Small cactus (ADS); yellow cut flower variety; 1.2m (4ft) bush; introduced by Cor Geerlings, Holland, in 1993. Available USA: Connell's; elsewhere: Geerlings.

Gemma Darling
Giant decorative (NDS), giant informal decorative (ADS); white exhibition variety; 1.4m (4.5ft) high; raised by Ernie Dilley, UK, in 1994. Available UK: Cruikshank, National, Oscroft, P. & L.; Canada: Ferncliff; elsewhere: Jacks, Konishi.

Geoffrey Kent
Miniature decorative (NDS), miniature formal decorative (ADS); red exhibition and garden variety; 1.2m (4ft) in height; raised by David Kent, UK, in 1998. Available UK: Porter, Spencer, Taylor.

Gerda Juul
Small semi-cactus (ADS); light blends yellow and orange; garden and exhibition variety; 1.2m (4ft) high bush; originated by Juul, USA, in 1980.

Gerrie Hoek
Small waterlily (NDS), waterlily (ADS); pink exhibition, garden and cut flower variety; 1.1m (3.5ft) high bush; introduced by Hoek, Holland, in 1945. Available UK: Blooms, Butterfield, Jager, Jones, National, Oscroft, P. & L., Station House, Tivey; USA: Swan Island; Canada: Ferncliff; elsewhere: Dgid.

GARDEN FESTIVAL

GATESHEAD FESTIVAL

GAY TRIUMPH

GEERLING'S INDIAN SUMMER

GEMMA DARLING

GEOFFREY KENT

Giggles
Orchid (ADS); orange and purple; exhibition variety; 1.1m (3.5ft); originated by N. Gitts, USA, in 1998. Available USA: Swan Island.

Gillian
Medium cactus (ADS); yellow variety; originated by Hindry, South Africa, in 1967. Available USA: Elkhorn.

Gill's Pastelle
Medium semi-cactus (NDS); white, pink blended exhibition and cut flower variety; blooms on a 1.2m (4ft) high plant; sport of 'Pink Pastelle' family; raised by J. Newman, UK, in 1996. Available UK: Abacus, Cruikshank, National; USA: Connell's, Elkhorn.

Gilt Edge
Medium decorative (NDS); pink exhibition variety, 1.2m (4ft) high plant; raised by George Brookes, UK, in 1975. Available UK: National.

Gina Lombaert
Medium semi-cactus (NDS); pink and yellow blends; exhibition variety; 1.2m (4ft) high plant; introduced by Lombaert, Belgium, in 1959. Award Merit Wisley, 1964 (NDS). Available UK: Abacus, Blooms, National; elsewhere: Dgid.

Ginger Willo
Pompon (ADS); dark blends, yellow and bronze exhibition variety; 1.2m (4ft) in height; introduced by N. Williams, Australia, in 1988. Available USA: Clacks, Connell's, Dan's Dahlias, Frey's, SB Gardens; Canada: Ferncliff.

Gingeroo
Miniature formal decorative (unclassified); bronze exhibition and cut flower

blooms on a 1.2m (4ft) bush; originated in the USA in 1994. Available USA: Swan Island.

Gipsy Boy
Large decorative (NDS); red exhibition and garden variety; 0.9m (3ft) high plant; raised by A. T. Hayes, UK, in 1991. Available UK: Aylett's, National, P. & L., Tivey.

Giraffe
Double orchid (NDS), novelty double centre (ADS); yellow and bronze (NDS), bronze (ADS); cut flower variety, growing to 0.9m (3ft) high; introduced by Hoek, Holland, in 1948. Available UK: National; USA: Clacks; elsewhere: Dgid.

Gitts Attention
Small informal decorative (ADS); white cut flower variety on a 1.2m (4ft) high bush; fimbriated, tipped petals; originated by N. Gitts, USA, in 2000. Awarded the Derrill Hart medal (ADS). Available USA: Arrowhead, Clacks, Swan Island.

Gitts Perfection
Large decorative (NDS), large informal decorative (ADS); lavender and white blended exhibition variety, on a 1.1m (3.5ft) high bush; originated by N. Gitts, USA, in 1997. Available UK: National; USA: Clacks, Creekside, Elkhorn, Mingus, Swan Island; elsewhere: Dgid, Geerlings, Jacks.

Glass Cock
Miniature formal decorative (unclassified); bicolour purple and white, garden and cut flower variety; 1.2m (4ft) high bush; originated USA, in 1996. Available USA: Connell's.

Glen Echo
Miniature formal decorative (ADS); purple garden and cut flower variety; 1.2m (4ft) tall bush; originated by Curnow, New Zealand, 1993. Available USA: Connell's.

Glenafton
Pompon (NDS); purple and red blends, exhibition variety; 1.2m (4ft) high plant; raised by W. Cann, UK, in 1965. Available UK: National, P. & L.

Glenbank Honeycomb
Pompon (NDS); yellow blends, exhibition, garden and cut flower variety; 1.1m (3.5ft) in height; introduced by G. Davidson, Australia, in 1985. Available UK: National, Oscroft, Station House.

Glenbank Twinkle
Miniature cactus, white and purple blends (NDS and ADS); excellent as a garden variety (NDS); 0.9m (3ft) in height; profuse blooms. Originated by Garfield Davidson in 1982, currently ranking sixth (ADS) in top fifty all-time winning varieties. Awarded the Stanley Johnson medal 2001. Available UK: JRG, National; USA: Clacks, Dahlia Dandies, Dan's Dahlias, Swan Island; elsewhere: Jacks.

Glenn Ruth
Miniature formal decorative (ADS); flame-coloured variety; 1.2m (4ft) bush; originated by Morin, USA, in 1995. Awarded the Derrill Hart medal.

Glenplace
Pompon (unclassified); dark purple, cut flower variety; 1.2m (4ft) high bush; raised in the UK in 1982. Available USA: Alpen, Arrowhead, Clacks, Connell's, Dan's Dahlias, Elkhorn, Frey's, SB Gardens.

GILLS' PASTELLE

GLENBANK HONEYCOMB

GILLIAN

GITTS PERFECTION

GLENBANK TWINKLE

Glenvalley Kathy
Small semi-cactus (unclassified); yellow and red bicolour; height 0.9m (3ft); originated USA in 1969. Available USA: Alpen, Capistrano, Clacks, Dahlia Dandies, Elkhorn, Mingus, SB Gardens.

Gloria Romaine
Small, decorative (NDS); purple blended, garden and cut flower variety; 1.1m (3.5ft) high plant; raised by G. Titchard, UK, in 1977. Available UK: National, P. & L., Tivey.

Glorie van Heemstede
Waterlily (NDS); yellow garden and cut flower variety, growing to a height of 0.9m (3ft); has stood the test of time. Raised by Bakker, Holland, in 1947. Award Merit 1986 Wisley (NDS). Available UK: Aylett's, Blooms, Butterfield, Halls, JRG, National, Oscroft, P. & L., Roberts, Station House, Tivey; USA: Sea-Tac; elsewhere: Dgid, Geerlings.

Go American
Giant decorative (NDS); bronze-blended exhibition variety; 0.9m (3ft) tall bush; originated by Stanley Johnson, USA, in 1959. Available UK: Halls, National, P. & L., Station House, Tivey.

Golden Egg
Miniature waterlily (unclassified); yellow, prolific blooms on a 1.2m (4ft) high bush; USA introduction in 1980. Available USA: Frey's, SB Gardens, Swan Island.

Golden Fizz
Miniature ball (NDS); yellow garden variety, 1.1m (3.5ft) high; raised by Staite, UK, in 1960. Available UK: National.

Golden Heart
Medium semi-cactus (NDS and ADS); flame and orange blends (NDS), or flame (ADS); garden variety; introduced by dahlia Bruidegom, Holland, in 1955. Available UK: National; USA: Connell's.

Golden Impact
Medium semi-cactus (NDS and ADS); yellow (NDS) light blends, yellow and orange exhibition, garden and cut flower variety; 1.2m (4ft) high bush; raised by Gordon Littlejohn, UK, in 1989. Available UK: Clark, Cruikshank, Halls, National, P. & L., Spencer, Station House; elsewhere: Jacks.

Golden Leader
Small decorative (NDS); orange garden variety; 1.1m (3.5ft) high; introduced by dahlia Bruidegom, Holland, in 1945. Available UK: National.

Golden Symbol
Medium semi-cactus (NDS); yellow exhibition and garden variety; 1.2m (4ft) high; last sport of the Symbol family; raised by Eric Payne, UK, in 1993. Available UK: Abacus, Cruikshank, Jones, National, Station House; USA: Mingus.

Golden Willo
Pompon (NDS and ADS); orange and yellow blends (NDS), or bronze (ADS); exhibition variety; 0.9m (3ft) high; introduced by N. Williams in 1961. Available UK: National, Tivey.

Golden Years
Large semi-cactus (ADS); bronze exhibition blooms on a 1.4m (4.5ft) high bush; originated by W. Almand, USA, in 1987. Available USA: Connell's.

Goldie Gull
Anemone (ADS); light blends, yellow and pink exhibition variety; height 1.5m (5ft); originated by Gullikson, USA, in 1998. Available USA: Alpen, Capistrano, Clacks, Dahlia Dandies, Dan's Dahlias.

Gollum
Peony (unclassified); red garden variety with dark foliage similar to Bishop of Llandaff on strong stems; height 1.2m (4ft). Available USA: Connell's.

Gonzo Grape
Miniature formal decorative (unclassified); deep purple blooms, excellent cut flower variety; prolific bloomer on a 1.2m (4ft) high bush; originated USA in 2000. Available USA: Swan Island.

Good Earth
Medium cactus (NDS); pink and white blends; garden variety; 1.2m (4ft) high; introduced by Ballego, Holland, in 1952. Award Merit Wisley 1956 (NDS). Available UK: National; elsewhere: Dgid.

Goodwill
Small, informal decorative (ADS); light blends, pink and yellow cut flower variety; height 1.2m (4ft); vigorous grower; originated by L. Connell, USA, in 1991. Available USA: Dan's Dahlias.

Gordon Lockwood
Pompon (ADS); purple exhibition variety; 1.1m (3.5ft) tall; raised by Lockwood, UK, in 1983.

Goya's Venus
Small semi-cactus (NDS); bronze, purple blends, garden and cut flower variety; 1.1m (3.5ft) high; raised by Piper, UK, in 1962. Available UK: National.

Grace Rushton
Small waterlily (unclassified); red garden and cut flower variety; 1.1m (3.5ft) in height; raised by Cliff Rushton, New Zealand, in 1994.

GLORIE VAN HEEMSTEDE

GO AMERICAN

GOLDEN IMPACT

GRACE RUSHTON

Grand Duc
Collarette (NDS); red and yellow bicolour; height 0.9m (3ft); exhibition and garden variety; introduced by Cor Geerlings, Holland, in 1956. Available UK: National, Oscroft, Station House; elsewhere: Geerlings.

Grandma Juul
Medium incurved cactus (ADS); purple garden and exhibition variety; height 1.2m (4ft) plant; originated by Juul, USA, in 1989.

Grand Willo
Pompon (ADS); lavender exhibition variety; height 1.5m (4.5ft); introduced by N. Williams, Australia, in 1961. Available USA: Alpen, Clacks, Connell's, Dan's Dahlias, SB Gardens.

Grants Gold
Star (ADS); yellow exhibition and garden variety 1.1m (3.5ft) high plant; originated by Clack, USA, in 2001.

Grenidor Pastelle
Medium semi-cactus (NDS and ADS); pink and yellow blends (NDS), or light blends orange and yellow (ADS); exhibition, garden and cut flower; 1.2m (4ft) high; raised by John Carrington, UK, in 1988. Many sports including Pink (1981) and Gil's (1996). Available UK: Abacus, Butterfield, Clark, Cruikshank, Halls, JRG, National, Oscroft, P. & L., Porter, Pratt, Roberts, Spencer, Station House, Tivey; USA: Dahlia Dandies, Dan's Dahlias, Sea-Tac; elsewhere: Engelhardt, Geerlings, Graines, Jacks, Wirth.

Gurtla Twilight
Pompon (NDS and ADS); white and pink blends (NDS), or light blends white and/or purple (ADS); excellent exhibition variety, growing to 0.9m (3ft) in height; raised by Bill Wilkinson, UK, in 1996. Available UK: Halls, National, Oscroft, P. & L., Porter, Station House.

Gypsy Girl
Small formal decorative (ADS); variegated lavender and purple garden variety; originated by Parrella, in 1948.

H

H G Chad E
Large cactus (ADS); red exhibition variety; height 1.4m (4.5ft); originated by R. Jones, USA, in 2000. Available USA: Arrowhead.

H G Sunrise
Medium incurving cactus (ADS); yellow exhibition and garden variety; 1.2m (4ft) high bush; originated by R. Jones, USA, in 2000. Available USA: Dahlia Dandies.

Hallmark
Pompon (NDS and ADS); pink and lavender blends (NDS), dark pink (ADS); released in the UK by N. Williams, Australia, in 1960; excellent exhibition variety. Available UK: Cruikshank, P. & L., Spencer, Station House; USA: Capistrano, Clacks, SB Gardens.

Hallwood Coppernob
Miniature decorative (NDS); bronze garden and cut flower variety; 1.1m (3.5ft) high; raised by D. Passey, UK, in 1996. Available UK: National; USA: Elkhorn.

Hamari Accord
Large semi-cactus (NDS), or medium semi-cactus (ADS); pure yellow growing to a height of 1.2m (4ft); excellent for exhibition, garden and cut flower. Wisley RHS award Merit (1991), Wisley RHS award Garden Merit (1994), RHS award Merit Exhibition Purposes (1993), Stredwick Medal (NDS) 1998. Winner of the American Dahlia Society Stanley Johnson medal in 1992; a top winner raised by W. (Pi) Ensum in 1986. Available UK: Abacus, Aylett's, Cruikshank, Halls, National, Oscroft, P. & L., Spencer, Station House, Tivey; USA: Alpen, Arrowhead, Capistrano, Clacks, Connell's, Creekside, Dahlia Dandies, Dan's Dahlias, Elkhorn, SB Gardens, Sea-Tac; Canada: Candahlia, Ferncliff; elsewhere: Jacks.

Hamari Bride
Medium semi-cactus (NDS); white exhibition variety on a 1.2m (4ft) high plant; raised by W. (Pi) Ensum, UK, in 1963. Award Merit Wisley 1965; award Garden Merit (NDS). Most Ensum varieties have the prefix 'Hamari', Hindustani for 'our house'. Available UK: Aylett's, National, Oscroft, P. & L.

GRENIDOR PASTELLE

GURTLA TWILIGHT

HALLMARK

HALLWOOD COPPERNOB

HAMARI ACCORD

HAMARI BRIDE

Hamari Girl
Giant decorative (NDS), large decorative (ADS); pink (NDS), dark pink (ADS); exhibition variety; height 0.9m (3ft); raised by W. (Pi) Ensum, UK, in 1960. Award Merit Wisley 1966 (NDS). Available UK: Cruikshank, Halls, National, Oscroft, P. & L., Tivey; USA: Dan's Dahlias, Elkhorn; elsewhere: Dgid, Turc.

Hamari Gold
A giant flowered decorative (NDS), large informal decorative (ADS); with bronze exhibition blooms on strong stems if restricted to three blooms per plant; a garden variety if unrestricted grows to a height of 90cm (3ft); raised by W. (Pi) Ensum in 1984. Award Merit 1984 Wisley; award of Garden Merit 1993. Available UK: Cruikshank, Halls, National, Oscroft, P. & L., Roberts, Spencer, Station House, Taylor; USA: Clacks, Creekside, Elkhorn; Canada: Candahlia; elsewhere: Geerlings, Graines, Jacks.

Hamari Katrina
Large semi-cactus (NDS), medium semi-cactus (ADS); yellow exhibition, garden and cut flower; strong grower to a height of 1.2m (4ft); raised by W. (Pi) Ensum, UK, in 1972. Award Merit 1976 Wisley (NDS). Available UK: Abacus, Jones, National, Oscroft, P. & L., Roberts, Tivey; USA: Clacks; elsewhere: Wirth.

Hamari Rose
Small ball or miniature ball (NDS), or ball (ADS); pink exhibition and excellent garden variety, growing to 0.9m (3ft) tall; raised by W. Ensum, UK, in 1993. Award of Garden Merit 1996, award Merit 1997 Wisley, award Garden Merit (NDS). Available UK: Aylett's, Cruikshank, Halls, JRG, National, Oscroft, P. & L., Scotts, Tivey; USA: Elkhorn; elsewhere: Dgid, Geerlings.

Hamari Sunshine
Large decorative (NDS), medium informal decorative (ADS); yellow garden variety; height 0.9m (3ft); with pointed petals; raised by W. Ensum, UK, in 1996. Award Garden Merit Wisley 1997. Available UK: Halls, National, P. & L., Porter; USA: Mingus; elsewhere: Jacks.

Hamilton Amanda
Small decorative (NDS), small formal (ADS); yellow exhibition and garden variety; 1.4m (4.5ft) high bush; introduced by Hamilton, Canada, in 1994. Award Merit Wisley 1994 (NDS). Available UK: National; USA: Dahlia Dandies; Canada: Candahlia.

Hamilton Midnight
Miniature informal decorative (ADS); purple exhibition and garden variety; 1.4m (4.5ft) high plant; introduced by Hamilton, Canada, in 1999.

Hana Hitosuji
Giant cactus (ADS); light blends pink and yellow exhibition variety; 1.2m (4ft) high plant; introduced by Kinoshi, Japan, in 1998.

HAMARI GIRL

HAMARI GOLD

HAMARI KATRINA

HAMARI ROSE

HAMARI SUNSHINE

HAMILTON AMANDA

Hamilton Lillian
Small decorative (NDS), small formal decorative (ADS); bronze pink blends (NDS), light blends orange and yellow (ADS); 1.2m (4ft) bush; exhibition, garden and cut flower variety introduced by Hamilton, Canada, in 1986. Award Garden Merit (NDS), the Lynn B. Dudley 1985, Derrill Hart and Stanley Johnson medals (ADS). Available UK: Abacus, National, P. & L.; USA: Arrowhead, Capistrano, Clacks, Connell's, Creekside, Dahlia Dandies, Mingus, SB Gardens, Sea-Tac; Canada: Candahlia, Ferncliff.

Hannah Baker
Medium lacinated cactus (ADS); light blends pink and yellow, exhibition variety; originated by Nowotarski, USA, in 2001. Awarded the Derrill Hart medal (ADS). Available USA: Arrowhead, Clacks.

Hans Ricken
Small waterlily (NDS); yellow garden and cut flower variety; 1.1m (3.5ft) bush; raised by Cor Geerlings, Holland, in 1977. Available UK: National.

Happy Hanny
Small waterlily (NDS); pink exhibition, garden and cut flower variety; introduced by Cor Geerlings, Holland, in 1977. Available elsewhere: Geerlings.

Harlequin
Small formal decorative (ADS); red and white bicolour garden and exhibition blooms on a 1.2m (4ft) high bush; originated by Kutschara, USA, in 1980.

Harriet Collins
Large, incurved cactus (ADS); garden variety, growing to 1.2m (4ft) tall bush; raised by H. Collins, USA, in 1989. Available USA: Connell's, Hamilton.

Harvest
Large fimbriated semi-cactus (NDS), large lacinated (ADS); 1.2m (4ft) bush; orange exhibition and garden variety; introduced by Phil Traff, USA, in 1992. Available UK: National; USA: Clacks, Dahlia Dandies.

Harvest Amanda
Lilliput (unclassified); tiny single orange blooms; garden and patio pot variety; 0.6m (2ft) high; introduced by Ian Butterfield, UK, in 1995. Award Garden Merit Wisley 1997 (NDS).

Harvest Samantha
Lilliput (unclassified); single pink blooms; excellent for garden and patio pot use; grows to a height of 0.9m (3ft); introduced by Ian Butterfield, UK, in 1995. Award of Garden Merit, 1996.

Hawaii
Collarette (ADS); purple with white colour; exhibition and garden variety; height 1.1m (3.5ft); introduced by C. Geering, Holland, in 1958.

Hayley Jane
Small semi-cactus (NDS and ADS); white with purple blends, growing to a height of 1.2m (4ft); prolific cut flower and garden variety; raised by G. Titchard of the UK in 1978. Available UK: Abacus, JRG, National, Oscroft, P. & L.; USA: Clacks, Dan's Dahlias; elsewhere: Dgid, Engelhardt, Jacks, Konishi.

Heather Marie
Miniature semi-cactus (ADS); pink garden variety; strong stems on a 1.2m (4ft) bush; originated by Swan Island, USA, in 1983. Available USA: Swan Island.

Hee Haugh
Small semi-cactus (ADS); orange exhibition and cut flower on a 1.4m (4.5ft) bush; originated by Haugh, USA, in 1989. Available USA: Frey's, Swan Island.

Helen's Dallas
Medium semi-cactus (ADS); dark red variety; originated by H. Bair, USA, in 1999. Available USA: Clacks, Dan's Dahlias, Elkhorn.

Helen's Norma Jean
Miniature formal decorative (ADS); dark red variety; originated by H. Bair, USA, in 2001.

Helen's White
Waterlily (ADS); white garden and exhibition variety; originated by H. Bair, USA, in 2001. Available USA: Clacks.

Herbert Smith
Small semi-cactus (ADS); dark pink, outstanding cut flower and good exhibition variety on a 1.2m (4ft) bush; originated by H. Smith, USA, in 1967. Available USA: Mingus, Swan Island.

High Flyer
Medium formal decorative (ADS); white flushed, exhibition variety; 1.5m (5ft) high bush; originated USA in 2001. Available elsewhere: Jacks.

HAMILTON LILLIAN

HARVEST

HARVEST AMANDA

HAYLEY JANE

HELEN'S DALLAS

HIGH FLYER

Hi Lite
Small semi-cactus (unclassified); red cut flower variety; 1.4m (4.5ft) tall bush; originated by Swan Island in 1991. Available USA: Swan Island.

Higherfield Champion
Small semi-cactus (NDS); yellow exhibition and garden variety; 1.1m (3.5ft) high plant; raised by D. Pickles, UK. Available UK: National.

Highgate Lustre
Medium semi-cactus (NDS); bronze blends, garden and cut flower variety; 1.2m (4ft) high; raised by W. Robinson, UK, in 1980. Available UK: National.

Highgate Robbie
Small ball (unclassified); excellent dark red garden variety; height 1.1m (3.5ft); raised by W. Robinson, UK, in 1967.

Highgate Torch
Medium semi-cactus (NDS); flame, garden variety; height 1.1m (3.5ft); raised by W. Robinson, UK, in 1968. Award Merit 1980 Wisley (NDS). Available UK: National.

Highlighter
Large formal decorative (ADS); yellow exhibition and garden variety; height 1.2m (4ft); originated by Wynn, USA, in 2000.

High Noon
Small semi-cactus (ADS); bronze exhibition variety; 1.2m (4ft) high bush; originated by K. Larkin, USA, in 1997.

Hillary Dawn
Medium cactus (ADS); dark pink, early blooming cut flower and garden variety; 1.2m (4ft) high bush; originated USA in 1995. Available USA: Clacks, Dan's Dahlias, Elkhorn.

Hillcrest Albino
Medium semi-cactus (NDS); white; good exhibition, garden and cut flower variety; height 1.2m (4ft); raised by Les Jackson, UK, in 1991. Award Garden Merit Wisley 1993. Available UK: Cruikshank, National, P. & L.; USA: Dan's Dahlias.

Hillcrest Amour
Small decorative (NDS), formal small decorative (ADS); white and lavender blended exhibition variety; 1.2m (4ft) high bush; raised by Les Jackson, UK, in 1992. Available UK: Cruikshank, National, P. & L.; USA: Sea-Tac.

Hillcrest Blaze
Small cactus (NDS); yellow-red bicolour garden variety, 1.1m (3.5ft) high; raised by Les Jackson, UK, in 1992. Available UK: National.

Hillcrest Bobbin
Small ball (NDS), or ball (ADS); purple (NDS) or lavender (ADS); exhibition and garden variety; 1.2m (4ft) high; raised by Les Jackson, UK, in 1992. Available UK: National, P. & L.; USA: Arrowhead, Mingus, SB Gardens.

Hillcrest Carmen
Small, formal decorative (ADS); lavender exhibition and garden variety; 0.9m (3ft) high plant; raised by Les Jackson, UK, in 1998. Available USA: Clacks, Elkhorn, Mingus.

Hillcrest Chelsey
Small, formal decorative (ADS); orange variety; raised by Les Jackson, UK, in 2001. Available USA: Clacks.

HILLCREST ALBINO

HILLCREST AMOUR

HILLCREST BLAZE

HILLCREST BOBBIN

HILLCREST CARMEN

HILLCREST CHELSEY

Hillcrest Delight
Medium decorative (NDS), or
informal decorative (ADS);
orange exhibition variety; 1.2m
(4ft) high; raised by Les
Jackson, UK, in 1996.
Available UK: Cruikshank,
Halls, P. & L., Spencer; USA:
Connell's.

Hillcrest Desire
Small cactus (NDS); pink,
bronze-blended exhibition,
garden and cut flower variety;
1.2m (4ft) high plant; raised by
Les Jackson, UK, in 1991.
Available UK: Abacus, Aylett's,
Clark, Cruikshank, Halls,
National, P. & L., Spencer.

Hillcrest Divine
Small or miniature decorative
(NDS), or small formal
decorative (ADS); pink
exhibition and garden variety;
raised by Les Jackson, UK, in
1998. Available UK: Abacus,
Clark, Cruikshank, Halls; USA:
Dahlia Dandies; elsewhere:
Jacks.

Hillcrest Fiesta
Medium semi-cactus (ADS);
light blended red and yellow;
raised by Les Jackson, UK,
1995. Available USA:
Connell's, Elkhorn.

Hillcrest Hannah
Miniature decorative (NDS), or
miniature formal decorative
(ADS); yellow exhibition
variety; 1.2m (4ft) high; raised

by Les Jackson, UK, 1999.
Available UK: Cruikshank,
Spencer, Taylor; USA:
Connell's.

Hillcrest Heights
Large semi-cactus (NDS); white
exhibition variety; 1.2m (4ft)
high plant; raised by Les
Jackson, UK, in 1993.
Available UK: Abacus,
National, P. & L.; elsewhere:
Jacks.

Hillcrest Hilton
Large semi-cactus (NDS);
yellow exhibition variety; 1.2m
(4ft) high; raised by Les
Jackson, UK, in 1992.
Available UK: Cruikshank,
National, Oscroft, P. & L.;
USA: Connell's.

HILLCREST DELIGHT

HILLCREST DESIRE

HILLCREST DIVINE

HILLCREST FIESTA

HILLCREST HANNAH

HILLCREST HILTON

Hillcrest Kismet
Medium decorative (NDS), or small formal decorative (ADS); pink exhibition variety; 1.1m (3.5ft) high; raised by Les Jackson, UK, 2000. Available UK: Clark, Cruikshank, Halls, National, Oscroft, P. & L., Pratt, Spencer, Station House; USA: Arrowhead, Mingus.

Hillcrest Margaret
Miniature formal decorative (ADS); light blends yellow and pink; raised by Les Jackson, UK, in 2001.

Hillcrest Pearl
Medium decorative (NDS), white exhibition variety; 1.2m (4ft) high; raised by Les Jackson, UK, in 1992. Available UK: National, P. & L.

Hillcrest Regal
Collerette (NDS and ADS); red on red (NDS), purple (ADS); grows to a height of 1.1m (3.5ft); excellent for exhibition, cut flower or garden use; introduced by Les Jackson, UK, in 1996. Available UK: Abacus, National, Oscroft.

Hillcrest Royal
Medium cactus (NDS), or medium incurved cactus (ADS); purple exhibition, garden and cut flower variety; raised by Les Jackson, UK, in 1991. Award Garden Merit Wisley (NDS). Available UK: Halls, National, Oscroft, P. & L.; USA: Clacks, Dan's Dahlias, Mingus; elsewhere: Engelhardt, Wirth.

Hillcrest Suffusion
Small decorative (NDS), or small formal decorative (ADS); orange blends (NDS), or light blends, pink and yellow; height 0.9m (3ft); raised by Les Jackson, UK, in 1991. Available UK: Clark, Cruikshank, JRG, National, Oscroft, Spencer, Station House; USA: Creekside; elsewhere: Geerlings, Jacks.

Hillcrest Trueform
Medium decorative (NDS); orange exhibition variety; 1.2m (4ft) high plant; raised by Les Jackson, UK, in 1994.

Hillcrest Ultra
Small decorative (NDS); yellow, pink-blended exhibition and garden variety; 1.1m (3.5ft) tall. Raised by Les Jackson, UK, in 1993. Available UK: National; USA: Mingus; elsewhere: Jacks.

Hissy Fitz
Small lacinated semi-cactus (ADS); yellow exhibition and long-stemmed cut flower variety, on a 1.2m (4ft) bush; originated by N. Gitts, USA, in 1999. Available USA: Swan Island.

Hit Parade
Medium semi-cactus (NDS); red garden variety; 0.9m (3ft) high; introduced by dahlia Bruidegom, Holland, in 1963. Available UK: National.

HILLCREST KISMET

HILLCREST MARGARET

HILLCREST REGAL

HILLCREST ROYAL

HILLCREST TRUEFORM

HILLCREST ULTRA

Holland Festival
Giant decorative (NDS), or giant informal decorative (ADS); orange white bicolour exhibition variety, 1.2m (4ft) high; introduced by dahlia Bruidegom, Holland, in 1960 Award Merit Wisley 1962 (NDS). Available UK: Cruikshank, National, Tivey; USA: Elkhorn; elsewhere: Dgid, Engelhardt, Turc.

Holland Herald
Large semi-cactus (unclassified); red cut flower and garden variety; 1.2m (4ft) tall; long-stemmed one-time exhibition variety; raised by dahlia Bruidegom, Holland, 1967. Award Merit Wisley, 1969 (NDS).

Hollyhill High Time
Small formal decorative (ADS); purple exhibition variety; originated by T. & M. Kennedy, USA, in 2001. Available USA: Mingus.

Homer T
Large semi-cactus (ADS); red exhibition and garden variety; 1.2m (4ft) in height; originated by W. Almand, USA, in 1990.

Honey
Dwarf bedder anemone (NDS), anemone (ADS); bronze, pink blends (NDS), or light blended pink and yellow (ADS); garden and patio pot variety; 0.3m (12in) high; raised by Ballego, Holland, in 1956. Available UK: Abacus, National; elsewhere: Turc.

Honeymoon Dress
Small decorative (NDS), or small formal decorative (ADS); pink blends (NDS), or pink

(ADS); 0.9m (3ft) high exhibition, garden and cut flower variety; raised by Les Jones, UK, in 1981. Available UK: Halls, National, Oscroft, P. & L.; elsewhere: Jacks.

Honka
Miscellaneous star (NDS), or orchid (ADS); yellow garden and cut flower variety, good for basketwork; raised by Kieffer, USA, in 1990. Available UK: JRG, Oscroft, Station House; USA: Capistrano, Clacks, Connell's, Creekside, Dahlia Dandies, Dan's Dahlias, Frey's, SB Gardens; Canada: Ferncliff.

Horn of Plenty
Miniature decorative (unclassified); red, free-flowering garden variety; height 1.2m (4ft); introduced by dahlia Bruidegom, Holland, in 1959. Award Merit Wisley, 1962 (NDS).

Horse Feathers
Novelty double centre (ADS); white garden variety; 0.9m (3ft) high bush; introduced by Geerlings, Holland, in 1995. Available USA: Alpen, Clacks, Elkhorn.

Horst Athalie
Small cactus (NDS); yellow blended exhibition variety, 1.5m (5ft) tall; raised by J. Wheatley, UK, in 1998. Available UK: Porter, Spencer.

Hugh Mather
Miniature waterlily (NDS); orange garden and cut flower variety, 0.9m (3ft) high; raised by Bertie Barnes, UK, in 1965. Available UK: Cruikshank, National, Station House.

Hulin's Carnival
Miniature formal decorative (ADS); variegated white and red cut flower and exhibition variety; some blooms white splashed purple, some white, some purple; height 1m (3.5ft); originated by Hulin, USA, in 1954. Available USA: Creekside, Dan's Dahlias, Frey's, SB Gardens, Swan Island; Canada: Ferncliff; elsewhere: Graines.

Hy Abalone
Large cactus (ADS); white exhibition variety; height 1.1m (3.5ft); originated by Wayne Holland, Canada, in 2002.

Hy Bill D.
Medium informal decorative (ADS); lights blends yellow and lavender; exhibition variety; 1.1m (3.5ft) in height; originated by Wayne Holland, Canada, in 2000.

Hy Clown
Small formal decorative (ADS); light blends yellow and bronze; exhibition variety; 1.1m (3.5ft in height; originated by Wayne Holland, Canada, in 1995.

Hy Fashion
Ball (ADS); lavender, exhibition variety; free flowering on a 1.1m (3.5ft) high bush; originated by Wayne Holland, Canada, in 1999. Available UK: Porter, Spencer; Canada: Ferncliff.

Hy Fire
Miniature ball red (ADS); exhibition variety, 0.9m (3ft) high bush; originated by Wayne Holland, Canada, in 1996. Available UK: Arrowhead, Elkhorn; Canada: Ferncliff.

HOLLAND FESTIVAL

HORST ATHALIE

HUGH MATHER

HY FASHION

Hy Lustre
Ball (ADS); dark blends, orange and bronze, exhibition variety; tall grower 1.5m (5ft) high bush; originated by Wayne. Holland, Canada, in 1999. Available UK: Porter; USA: Clacks, Mingus; Canada: Candahlia.

Hy Maize
Ball (ADS); light blends yellow and orange, exhibition and garden variety; height of bush 1.5m (5ft); originated by Wayne Holland, Canada, in 2000. Available USA: Arrowhead; Canada: Ferncliff.

Hy Mallow
Ball (ADS); purple garden and exhibition variety, 1.6m (5.5ft) tall bush; originated by Wayne Holland, Canada. In 2000 awarded the Derrill Hart medal (ADS). Available USA: Arrowhead, Clacks, Creekside; Canada: Ferncliff.

Hy Mom
Giant incurved cactus (ADS); white variety, 1.2m (4ft) in height; originated by Wayne Holland, Canada, in 2001. Available USA: Arrowhead, Clacks; Canada: Ferncliff.

Hy Sockeye
Small formal decorative (ADS); red exhibition variety, height 1.5m (4.5ft); originated by Wayne Holland, Canada, in 2001; early to medium flowering (USA).

Hy Suntan
Miniature ball (ADS); bronze exhibition and garden variety,

1.4m (5ft) tall bush; originated by Wayne Holland, Canada, in 2000. Available USA: Arrowhead; Canada: Candahlia, Ferncliff.

I

I Lyke It
Small semi-cactus (NDS); red exhibition variety; 1.2m (4ft) in height; raised by Bill Mark, UK, in 1996. Available UK: National, P. & L., Porter.

Ice Carnival
Miniature formal decorative (ADS); variegated white and lavender exhibition and garden variety; 1.2m (4ft) in height; originated by D. Jack, Canada, in 1996.

Ice Cream Beauty
Small waterlily (unclassified); pale yellow, excellent garden and cut flower variety; introduced by Ballego, Holland, in 1988. Award Garden Merit 1994 Wisley (NDS).

Idaho Red
Small, formal decorative (unclassified); red-tipped white, early blooming, cut flower variety on a 1.2m (4ft) high bush; originated USA in 1980. Available USA: Connell's.

Illini Faith
Small informal decorative (ADS); yellow exhibition and garden variety; 1.2m (4ft) in height; originated by A. White, USA, in 2001.

Imp
Lilliput (NDS); orange red blended garden variety; 0.6m (2ft) in height; originated by Dahliadel, USA, in 1941. Available UK: Aylett's, Butterfield, National.

Imperial Wine
Small informal decorative (ADS); exhibition and cut flower variety; height 1.2m (4ft); originated by N. Gitt, USA, in 2000.

Ina Spurs
Miniature decorative (NDS); red garden variety, 0.9m (3ft) high; raised by Neville Weekes, UK, in 1970.

Inca Dambuster
Giant semi-cactus (NDS and ADS); yellow exhibition and garden variety; tall at 1.5m (5ft); raised by George Brookes, UK, in 1975. Award Merit 1984 Wisley (NDS). Available UK: Halls, National, Station House, Tivey; Canada: Ferncliff; elsewhere: Jacks.

Inca Matchless
Medium decorative (NDS); yellow blended exhibition variety; 1.2m (4ft) in height; raised by G. Brookes, UK, in 1972. Award Merit 1978 Wisley (NDS). Available UK: Abacus, National, Tivey.

Inca Metropolitan
Large decorative (unclassified); yellow exhibition and garden variety; 1.2m (4ft) in height; raised by G. Brookes, UK, in 1978. Award Garden Merit 1993 Wisley (NDS).

HY LUSTRE

HY SUNTAN

ICE CREAM BEAUTY

I LYKE IT

INCA DAMBUSTER

Inca Royale
Large decorative (NDS); lavender exhibition variety, 1.2m (4ft) high plant; raised by G. Brookes, UK, in 1986. Award of Merit 1990 Wisley (NDS). Available UK: National.

Indian Summer (synonym Geerlings Indian Summer)
Small cactus (unclassified); red garden and cut flower; 0.9m (3ft); raised by Holm, UK, in 1979. Available UK: Abacus, Halls, National, Oscroft, P. & L., Station House, Tivey; elsewhere: Geerlings.

Inflammation
Lilliput (single) (NDS), mignon single (ADS); bronze garden and patio pot variety; height 0.45m (18in); introduced by Ballego, Holland, in 1961. Award Garden Merit Wisley (NDS). Available UK: Butterfield; USA: Dahlia Dandies, Dan's Dahlias, Frey's, Swan Island.

Informal Fires
Small, informal decorative (ADS); flame exhibition blooms on 1.2m (4ft) high bush; originated by Dan and Kathy Franklin, USA, in 2000. Available Canada: Ferncliff.

Inglebrook Jill
Collerette (NDS); red and red exhibition garden and cut flower variety; height 1.1m (3.5ft); unknown New Zealand raising in 1996. Available UK: Aylett's, JRG, National.

Inland Dynasty
Giant semi-cactus (NDS and ADS); yellow exhibition variety; 1.2m (4ft) high bush; originated by Anselmo, USA, in 1992. Award of Derrill Hart and Stanley Johnson medals (ADS). Available UK: Cruikshank, National, Oscroft, P. & L.; USA: Alpen, Clacks, Connell's, Dahlia Dandies, Dan's Dahlias, Mingus, SB Gardens; Canada: Ferncliff; elsewhere: Jacks, Konishi.

Innocence
Large waterlily (ADS); light blended white and lavender; long-stemmed, cut flower and exhibition variety; tall grower at 1.5m (5ft); raised in Australia in 1986. Available USA: Dan's Dahlias, Swan Island.

Intrigue
Small, formal decorative (unclassified); salmon pink, cut flower variety; 1.2m (4ft) high bush; originated by Swan Island, USA, in 2002. Available USA: Swan Island.

Iola
Large formal decorative (ADS); deep red, exhibition variety; height 1.5m (4.5ft); originated by Ed Redd, USA, in 1989. Available USA: Arrowhead, Clacks, Connell's, Elkhorn; Canada: Candahlia, Ferncliff.

Ira
Medium, incurving cactus (ADS); flame, long-stemmed exhibition variety; originated by Bishop, USA, in 2000. Available USA: Clacks.

Irene Florence
Medium semi-cactus (unclassified); dark red exhibition variety; 1.2m (4ft) high bush; originated by L. Connell, USA, in 1992. Available USA: Connell's.

Irene's Pride
Giant semi-cactus (NDS and ADS); orange (NDS), bronze (ADS); exhibition variety; 1.3m (4.5ft) high bush; originated by Szalkowski, USA, in 1990. Awarded the Derrill Hart medal (ADS). Available UK: Cruikshank; USA: Alpen, Clacks, Connell's, Elkhorn, Mingus, SB Gardens; Canada: Candahlia, Ferncliff.

Iris
Pompon (NDS and ADS); purple (NDS), dark red (ADS); exhibition variety; height 0.9m (3ft); raised by Mann, Germany, in 1974. Available UK: Abacus, Cruikshank, National.

Irisel
Medium lacinated (ADS); light blended pink and yellow variety 1.2m (4ft) in height; introduced by Cyril Higgo, South Africa, in 1995. Available USA: Arrowhead, Clacks, Dan's Dahlias.

Island Blaze
Medium cactus (unclassified); yellow and orange exhibition and cut flower variety; 1.2m (4ft) in height; originated by R. & S. Ambrose, USA, in 1987. Available USA: Clacks, Dan's Dahlias, Mingus.

Island Survivor
Medium semi-cactus (ADS); orange exhibition variety; originated by R. & S. Ambrose, USA, in 1993.

Island View Twister
Medium informal decorative (ADS); bronze exhibition variety; originated by Willoughby, USA, in 2000.

INCA ROYALE

INFLAMMATION

INLAND DYNASTY

IOLA

IRENE'S PRIDE

IRISEL

Islander

Large informal decorative
(ADS); dark pink garden and
exhibition variety; 1.2m (4ft) in
height; originated by Wicks,
USA, in 1983.

Isle of Fire

Small semi-cactus (ADS); flame
exhibition variety; originated
by R. & S. Ambrose, USA, in
1984.

Ivanetti

Ball or miniature ball (NDS),
or ball (ADS); purple (NDS) or
dark red (ADS); exhibition,
garden and cut flower; 1.1m
(3.5ft) in height; introduced by
Cor Geerlings in 1999.
Available UK: Halls, Oscroft, P.
& L., Scotts, Spencer;
elsewhere: Dgid, Geerlings.

Ivor's Rhonda

Pompon (NDS); lavender
exhibition and garden variety;
height 1.1m (3.5ft); raised by
I. Jones, UK, in 2000. Available
UK: Abacus, Station House.

Ivory Palaces

Giant informal decorative
(ADS); yellow exhibition
variety; tall at 1.5m (5ft) high;
originated by Simmon, USA, in
1992. Available USA: Alpen,
Arrowhead, Clacks, Connell's,
Dahlia Dandies, Dan's Dahlias,
Elkhorn, Mingus, SB Gardens;
Canada: Ferncliff.

Ixtapa

Small incurving cactus
(unclassified); pink and yellow

blended; garden variety, tall at
1.5m (5ft) high. Available USA:
Connell's.

J

Jabberbox

Miniature formal decorative
(unclassified); peach pink,
garden and cut flower variety;
prolific bloomer on a 1.2m
(4ft) bush; originated USA in
1995. Available USA: Dan's
Dahlias, Frey's, Swan Island.

Jackie Magson

Medium semi-cactus or small
semi-cactus (NDS), or medium
semi-cactus (ADS); orange
exhibition variety; height 1.2m
(4ft); sport from Andrew
Magson, raised by Bill Mark,
UK, in 1996. Available UK:
Abacus, National, P. & L.,
Spencer.

Jackie S.

Miniature ball (ADS); bronze
exhibition and garden variety;
1.2m (4ft) in height; originated
by Rodewald, USA, in 1993.

Jacqueline Tivey

Small decorative (NDS); pink
blended garden and cut flower
variety; raised by P. Tivey, UK.
Available UK: National, Tivey.

Jacy

Miniature informal decorative
(ADS); dark blends white and
deep pink; garden and

exhibition variety; 1.1m (3.5ft)
in height; originated by
McClaren, USA, in 1984.

Jaldec Jerry

Giant semi-cactus (NDS); pink
blended exhibition variety;
1.2m (4ft) high; raised by
Derek Hewlett, UK, in 1987.
Available UK: National; USA:
Elkhorn.

Jaldec Joker

Small semi-cactus (unclassified);
red and white bicolours, garden
variety; 1.2m (4ft) high; raised
by Derek Hewlett, UK, in 1991.
Award Garden Merit Wisley
1995 (NDS).

Jaldec Jolly

Small cactus (unclassified); red
and white bicoloured, garden
variety; height 1.2m (4ft);
raised by Derek Hewlett, UK,
in 1990. Award of Garden
Merit Wisley 1995 (NDS).

Jamboree

Medium decorative
(unclassified); orange red,
garden variety; a compact bush
1.1m (3.5ft) high; originated by
Swan Island, USA, in 1993.
Available USA: Swan Island.

Jamie

Small straight cactus (ADS);
lavender exhibition variety;
1.2m (4ft) high bush;
originated by Ed Redd, USA, in
1994. Awarded the Lynn B.
Dudley medal, 1993 (ADS).
Available USA: Arrowhead,
Creekside.

ISLE OF FIRE

IVANETTI

IVOR'S RHONDA

IVORY PALACES

JACKIE MAGSON

JALDEC JERRY

Jan Lennon
Large semi-cactus (ADS); light blends, lavender and white exhibition variety; introduced by Sibley, Australia, in 1978. Available USA: Clacks, SB Gardens; elsewhere: Jacks.

Janal Amy
Giant semi-cactus (NDS), large semi-cactus (ADS); yellow exhibition variety; height 1.4m (4.5ft); raised by A. Jones, UK, in 1999. Available UK: Cruikshank, Halls, Oscroft, P. & L., Pratt, Spencer; USA: Arrowhead, Clacks, Mingus.

Janal Cameron
Giant informal decorative (ADS); pink exhibition variety; raised by A. Jones, UK, in 2000. Available USA: Clacks, Mingus.

Jane
Small incurved cactus (ADS); purple exhibition and garden variety; originated USA in 1993.

Jane Horton
Collerette (NDS); pink and pink exhibition and garden variety; introduced in 1991. Available UK: National.

Janet Goddard
Small decorative (NDS); red and bronze blended garden and cut flower variety; height 1.1m (3.5ft); raised by A. Shaw, UK, in 1979. Available UK: National.

Japanese Bishop
Peony (ADS); red blooms on almost black foliage; exhibition and cut flower variety; height 0.9m (3ft); introduced in 1960. Available USA: Connell's, Dahlia Dandies, Dan's Dahlias, Frey's, Sea-Tac, Swan Island.

Jax Tinker
Small semi-cactus (ADS); white exhibition variety, 1.2m (4ft) in height; originated by Crawford, USA, in 1997.

Jazzy
Collarette (ADS); pink, pink and white collar exhibition and cut flower, heavy blooming variety; height 1.1m (3.5ft); originated by Swan Island, USA, in 1996. Available USA: Clacks, Swan Island.

Jean Fairs
Miniature waterlily (NDS); orange bronze blends, cut flower variety; 1.1m (3.5ft); raised by John Crutchfield, UK, in 1955. Available UK: Butterfield, National, Station House.

Jean Marie
Medium formal decorative (unclassified); lavender-tipped, white garden variety sport of Duet; height, 1.1m (3.5ft); introduced in Holland. Available USA: Swan Island.

Jean McMillan
Small semi-cactus (NDS); pink blended exhibition, garden and cut flower variety; 1.2m (4ft) high; raised by Neville Weekes, UK, in 1995. Available UK: Halls, P. & L.; elsewhere: Geerlings.

Jeanette Carter
Miniature decorative (NDS); yellow pink blends exhibition, garden and cut flower variety; 1.1m (3.5ft) in height; raised by Eric Carter, UK, in 1988. Award Garden Merit (NDS). Available UK: National.

Jeanne Gervis
Medium semi-cactus (ADS); dark-red garden and exhibition variety; 1.2m (4ft) in height; originated by E. Redd, USA, in 1991.

Jeannie LeRoux
Small lacinated (ADS); light blends white and lavender; garden and exhibition variety; 1.2m (4ft) in height; originated by Steenfoot, USA, in 1992.

Jeanne W
Small, lacinated (ADS); white exhibition variety, originated by Nowotarski, USA, in 2001.

Jeff Miner
Medium cactus (ADS); yellow exhibition variety; 1.2m (4ft) in height; originated by Miner, USA, in 1996.

Jenna
Small, informal decorative (unclassified); lavender and pink cut flower and garden variety on a 1.4m (4.5ft) lush bush; originated by Swan Island, USA, in 1995. Available USA: Swan Island.

JAN LENNON

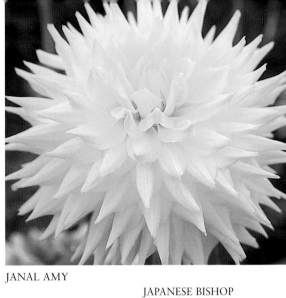

JANAL AMY

JANAL CAMERON

JAPANESE BISHOP

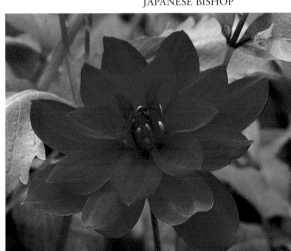

JEAN McMILLAN

JEANETTE CARTER

Jennie
Fimbriated, classified as a medium semi-cactus (NDS), or medium lacinated (ADS); yellow and pink blends, or light blends white and lavender; an exhibition and garden variety growing to a height of 1.1m (3.5ft). Awarded the Lynn B. Dudley medal 1992 (ADS); originated by Phil Traff, USA, in 1993. Available UK: Cruikshank, National; USA: Alpen, Arrowhead, Clacks, Dahlia Dandies, Dan's Dahlias, SB Gardens; elsewhere: Geerlings, Graines, Wirth.

Jennie Too
Medium lacinated (ADS); pink exhibition and garden variety, originated by Phil Traff, USA, in 1993. Available USA: Creekside.

Jennifer Lynn
Medium semi-cactus (ADS); light blended yellow and pink cut flower variety on a 1.2m (4ft) high bush; originated by Swan Island, USA, in 1981. Available USA: Swan Island.

Jennifer's Wedding
Informal, medium decorative fimbriated (unclassified); deep purple blooms, garden and cut flower variety; height 1.2m (4.5ft); originated by Swan Island, USA, in 2001. Available USA: Swan Island.

Jeremy Boldt
Giant formal decorative (ADS); variegated lavender and white exhibition variety; originated by Cunningham, USA, in 1999.

Jerita
Medium semi-cactus (unclassified); bright pink garden variety, strong grower on a 1.4m (4.5ft) high bush; originated by L. Connell, USA, in 1993. Available USA: Connell's, Dan's Dahlias.

Jescot Jim
Small decorative (NDS); yellow exhibition, garden and cut flower variety; 1.1m (3.5ft) in height; raised by E. Cooper, UK, in 1948. Award of Merit Wisley (NDS), 1950. Available UK: National; elsewhere: Dgid.

Jescot Julie
Classified as a miscellaneous double orchid (NDS), or a stellar dahlia (ADS); dark blends of orange and purple: an eye-catching dahlia for garden and cut flower use, particularly for floral art; height of 90cm (3ft); introduced by E. Cooper, UK, in 1974. Award Merit 1976 Wisley (NDS). Available UK: Aylett's, Butterfield, National, Station House; USA: Sea-Tac; elsewhere: Dgid.

Jessica
Small semi-cactus (NDS), small cactus (ADS); yellow and red bicolour, exhibition, garden and cut flower variety; 0.9m (3ft) in height; originated by Hale, USA, in 1988. Awarded the Stanley Johnson medal (ADS). Available UK: National; USA: Alpen, Arrowhead, Clacks; elsewhere: Engelhardt, Geerlings, Graines.

Jessica Crutchfield
Small waterlily (unclassified); yellow cut flower and garden variety, growing to 1.2m (4ft) high; introduced by John Crutchfield in 1968. Award Garden Merit Wisley, 1995 (NDS).

Jessie G
Small ball or miniature ball (NDS), ball (ADS); purple exhibition and garden variety; 1.4m (4.5ft) high bush; originated by L. Connell, USA, in 1994. Awarded the Derrill Hart and Stanley Johnson medals (ADS). Available UK: Cruikshank, JRG, National, Oscroft, P. & L., Scotts, Station House; USA: Alpen, Arrowhead, Clacks, Connell's, Creekside, Dahlia Dandies, Dan's Dahlias, Mingus, SB Gardens, Sea-Tac; Canada: Candahlia, Ferncliff.

Jessie Ross
Dwarf bedder (miniature decorative) (NDS); pink garden variety; 35cm (14in) in height; raised by A. Lister, UK, in 1950. Available UK: National.

Jess-Kelly
Ball (ADS); yellow exhibition variety; originated by Suttell, Canada, in 1999.

Jess-Louis
Small semi-cactus (ADS); yellow variety originated by Suttell, Canada, 2000.

Jess-Lynn
Miniature formal decorative (ADS); orange exhibition variety, 1.2m (4ft) high bush; originated by Suttell, Canada, in 1993. Awarded the Derrill Hart medal. Available USA: Dahlia Dandies.

Jil
Small cactus (unclassified); deep lavender and white, slightly lacinated, cut flower (floral art) blooms on a compact 0.9m (3ft) high bush; originated by Swan Island, USA, in 1994. Available USA: Swan Island.

JENNIE

JESSICA

JESSIE G

Jill's Delight
Medium flowered decorative (unclassified); pink garden variety; height 1.4m (4.5ft) raised by Dr Lester, UK, in 1989. Award Garden Merit Wisley (NDS).

Jim
Miniature formal decorative (ADS); bicolour dark red and white variety; originated by Ieffer, USA, in 2000.

Jim Brannigan
Large semi-cactus (NDS); red exhibition variety; 1.4m (4.5ft) tall plant; raised by A. Brannigan, Ireland, in 1981. Available UK: Abacus, Halls, National, Tivey; elsewhere: Jacks.

Jitterbug
Miniature formal decorative (ADS); pink garden and cut flower variety; compact 0.9m (3ft) tall bush; originated by Swan Island, USA, in 1995. Available USA: Frey's, Swan Island.

Jo
Waterlily (unclassified); creamy yellow, cut flower variety on a 1.2m (4ft) high bush; originated by L. Connell, USA, in 1994. Available USA: Connell's.

Jo Anne
Medium semi-cactus (NDS), medium cactus (ADS); yellow exhibition and garden variety; height 1.2m (4ft); introduced by W. Trotter, Australia, in 1998. Available UK: National, Scotts; elsewhere: Jacks.

Joan Beecham
Small waterlily (NDS); orange blended garden variety; 1.1m (3.5ft) high; raised by R. Beecham, UK, in 1990. Available UK: Cruikshank, National, P. & L., Station House, Tivey.

Joanna Petite
Pompon (unclassified); salmon pink cut flower variety on a 1.1m (3.5ft) high bush; originated by Swan Island, USA, in 1992. Available USA: Swan Island.

Jocondo
Giant decorative (NDS); purple exhibition variety; 1.2m (4ft) in height; introduced by dahlia Bruidegom, Holland, in 1960. Available UK: Halls, National; USA: Clacks.

Johann
Pompon (NDS); red exhibition, garden and cut flower variety; 1.2m (4ft) tall; raised by E. Hunt, UK, in 1971. Available UK: Cruikshank, Halls, National, P. & L.; USA: Clacks, Connell's.

John Bramelett
Medium informal decorative (ADS); purple garden variety, compact bush, 1.1m (3.5ft) high; originated by Swan Island, USA, in 2000. Available USA: Elkhorn, Sea-Tac, Swan Island.

John Prior
Small waterlily (NDS); red garden and cut flower variety; 1.1m (3.5ft) in height; raised in 1988. Available UK: National.

John Street
Small waterlily (NDS); red garden variety, 1.5m (5ft) tall; raised by John Crutchfield, UK, in 1977. Award Merit 1977 Wisley (NDS); award Garden Merit Wisley (NDS). Available UK: Butterfield, National, Station House.

Jomanda
Small ball and miniature ball (NDS), small formal decorative (ADS); excellent orange exhibition and garden variety; 1.2m (4ft) high; introduced by Cor Geerlings, Holland, in 1996. Award Garden Merit Wisley (NDS). Available UK: Abacus, Butterfield, Cruikshank, Halls, JRG, National, Oscroft, P. & L., Porter, Roberts, Scotts, Spencer, Station House, Tivey; USA: Arrowhead, Connell's, Creekside, Dan's Dahlias, Elkhorn, Mingus, SB Gardens; Canada: Candahlia, Ferncliff; elsewhere: Dgid, Geerlings, Konishi.

Jorja
Medium semi-cactus (ADS); red exhibition variety; originated by Phil Traff, USA, in 1996. Available USA: Connell's.

Jo's Choice
Miniature decorative (NDS); red exhibition (in its day) and garden variety; 1.1m (3.5ft) high; raised by Joe Sharp, UK, in 1959. Award Merit 1974 Wisley (NDS). Available UK: Butterfield, National.

Joy Ride
Small semi-cactus (unclassified); hot pink and lavender garden and cut flower variety; 1.1m (3.5ft) in height; originated by Swan Island, USA, in 1995. Available USA: Swan Island.

Joyce Green
Giant semi-cactus (NDS); pink blended exhibition variety; 1.4m (4.5ft) high; raised by H. Gowar, UK. Available UK: Cruikshank, National.

Juanita
Medium cactus (ADS); dark red exhibition variety on a 1.2m (4ft) high bush; originated by Healey, South Africa, in 1951. Available USA: Creekside, Dahlia Dandies, Elkhorn, Frey's, Swan Island.

JILL'S DELIGHT

JO ANNE

JOMANDA

JORJA

Judy Albert
Miniature formal decorative
(ADS); purple exhibition
variety; 1.4m (4.5ft) high bush;
originated by Nowotarski,
USA, in 2000. Awarded the
Derrill Hart medal (ADS).
Available Canada: Ferncliff.

Julio
Miniature ball (NDS); pink
exhibition and garden variety;
1.2m (4ft) tall; introduced by
Cor Geerlings, Holland, in
1996. Available UK: National,
Scotts, Unwin; elsewhere: Dgid.

Jura
Small semi-cactus (NDS); white
and purple bicolour; garden
and cut flower variety; 1.2m
(4ft) in height; raised by Cor
Geerlings, Holland, in 1988.
Available UK: National, Scotts;
elsewhere: Turc, Wirth.

Just Peachy
Small cactus (ADS); pink garden
and cut flower variety; 1.2m
(4ft) in height; originated by
L. Connell, USA, in 1986.
Available USA: Alpen,
Arrowhead, Capistrano, Clacks,
Connell's, Dahlia Dandies,
Dan's Dahlias, Elkhorn, Sea-
Tac; Canada: Ferncliff.

Just So
Mignon (unclassified); purple
bloom garden and patio pot
variety on a 0.3m (12in) bush
(late season); originated in the
USA in 1978. Available USA:
Frey's, Swan Island.

Justin
Medium lacinated cactus
(unclassified); lavender garden
variety on a 1.2m (4ft) high
strong bush; originated USA.
Available USA: Connell's.

Juul's Allstar
Star (unclassified); pink; height
0.6m (2ft); originated by Juul,
USA, in 2000. First
commercially released scented
dahlia. Available USA: Juul;
UK: Winchester.

Juul's Lotus
Waterlily (ADS); white
exhibition variety; originated by
Juul, USA, in 1998. Awarded
the Derrill Hart medal (ADS).
Available USA: Clacks, Dan's
Dahlias, SB Gardens.

Juul's Star
Orchid (ADS); white exhibition
and garden variety; originated
by Juul, USA, in 1983.
Awarded the Lynn B. Dudley
medal, 1982 (ADS). Available
USA: Arrowhead, Clacks,
Connell's, Dan's Dahlias,
Elkhorn.

K

Kaapse Nooi
Medium lacinated (ADS); dark
blends red and orange exhibition
variety; raised by Cyril Higgo,
South Africa, in 1991.

Kaja
Miniature ball (ADS); yellow
exhibition variety; originated
USA in 2000.

K-Andy
Collarette (ADS); dark red,
dark red collar/exhibition
variety; originated by
Anderson, USA, in 1999.
Awarded the Derrill Hart
medal. Available USA:
Arrowhead, Clacks, Dahlia
Dandies, Elkhorn, SB Gardens;
Canada: Ferncliff.

Karenglen
A striking red miniature
decorative (NDS), miniature
formal decorative (ADS);
excellent for exhibition, garden
or cut flower, a prolific
bloomer; grows to a height of
1.2m (4ft); raised by Gerry
Woolcock, UK, in 1990.
Available UK: Abacus,
Butterfield, Cruikshank, Halls,
JRG, National, Oscroft, P. &
L., Porter, Scotts, Spencer,
Station House, Taylor, Tivey;
USA: Creekside; elsewhere:
Dgid, Geerlings, Jacks.

Kari Blue
Waterlily (ADS); lavender cut
flower and exhibition variety on
a 1.4m (4.5ft) bush; introduced
by D. Smythe, New Zealand, in
1996. Available USA: Clacks,
Connell's, Dan's Dahlias,
Elkhorn, Mingus, SB Gardens.

Kari Dancer
Small cactus (ADS); light blends
pink and white variety;
originated by D.
Smythe, New Zealand, in 1999.
Available USA: Connell's.

Kari Fruit Salad
Miniature straight cactus (ADS);
dark blends yellow and red;
garden, cut flower and exhibition
variety; prolific bloomer on a
1.2m (4ft) high bush; originated
by D. Smythe, New Zealand, in
1999. Available USA: Alpen,
Connell's; Canada: Ferncliff.

Kari Lemon
Waterlily (ADS); yellow garden
and exhibition variety; raised
by D. Smythe, New Zealand, in
1999. Available USA:
SB Gardens.

Kari Quill
Miniature cactus (ADS); light
blends lavender and white
garden variety; tall grower,
1.5m (5ft) in height; introduced
by D. Smythe, New Zealand, in
1994. Available USA: Clacks,
Connell's, Dan's Dahlias.

Kari Smokey
Waterlily (ADS); mauve-pink
prolific garden and cut flower
variety; 1.2m (4ft) bush;
introduced by D. Smythe, New
Zealand, in 1992. Available
USA: Connell's, Dan's Dahlias.

Karras 150
Small semi-cactus (NDS), small
straight cactus (ADS); white
exhibition and garden variety;
1.1m (3.5ft) high; raised by A.
Petters, Australia, in 1996.
Available UK: Cruikshank,
Halls, National, P. & L.; USA:
Alpen, Arrowhead, Clacks,
Connell's, Mingus; Canada:
Candahlia.

JULIO

JUSTIN

KARI FRUIT SALAD

KARRAS 150

KARENGLEN

Kasasagi
Pompon (ADS); flame cut flower and exhibition variety; 1.1m (3.5ft) high; originated in Japan in 1960. Available USA: Connell's, SB Gardens, Swan Island.

Kate's Pastelle
Medium semi-cactus (unclassified); exhibition variety; pale pink sport of Primrose Pastelle; height 1.2m (4ft); originated in the UK in 2000.

Katherine Marie
Small semi-cactus (ADS); light blends, exhibition variety; originated by Anderson, USA, in 2001. Available USA: Clacks.

Katherine Temple
Small cactus (unclassified); lavender cut flower variety; strong grower on a 1.5m (5ft) bush; originated USA in 1987. Available USA: Connell's.

Kathleen's Alliance
Small cactus (NDS and ADS); pink (NDS), or purple (ADS); exhibition, garden and cut flower height, 0.9m (3ft); originated by K. Davidson, UK, in 1989. Award Garden Merit Wisley (NDS). Available UK: Halls, National, Oscroft, Roberts.

Kathryn's Cupid
Miniature ball (NDS); pink exhibition, garden and cut flower variety; height 0.9m (3ft); raised by Gregory, USA, in 1987. Available UK: Abacus, Cruikshank, Jones, National, Oscroft, P. & L., Roberts, Scotts, Station House.

Kathy's Choice
Miniature cactus (ADS); yellow exhibition dahlia, 1.2m (4ft) bush; originated by Dick Canning, USA, in 1999. Awarded the Lynn B. Dudley medal, 1998 (ADS). Available

USA: Alpen, Clacks, Dahlia Dandies, Dan's Dahlias, SB Gardens; elsewhere: Jacks.

Katie Dahl
Miniature, formal decorative (ADS); pink garden and patio pot variety; height 0.3m (12in); raised by Keith Hammett, New Zealand, in 1996.

Katisha
Miniature decorative (NDS); orange bronze blends, garden and cut flower variety; 1.1m (3.5ft) in height; raised by John Crutchfield, UK, in 1960. Available UK: National, Tivey.

Katja
Small ball or miniature ball (NDS); yellow exhibition and garden variety; 1.1m (3.5ft) high variety, introduced in 1997. Available UK: National, Tivey; elsewhere: Dgid.

Keating Mary
Small lacinated cactus (ADS); dark blends, purple and white variety; originated by Willoughby, Canada, in 2001.

Keating Tiptoe
Medium formal decorative (ADS); bicolour red and white variety, originated by Willoughby, Canada, in 2000.

Keith H
Waterlily (ADS); light blends, yellow and red exhibition variety; originated by Miller, 1987. Available USA: Connell's, Dan's Dahlias, Elkhorn, SB Gardens, Sea-Tac; Canada: Ferncliff.

Keith's Choice
Medium decorative (NDS), medium formal decorative (ADS); red (NDS), dark red (ADS); exhibition variety, 1.2m (4ft) high bush; originated by L. Connell, USA, in 1991; named by Keith Hammett. Awarded

the Derrill Hart medal (ADS). Available UK: Abacus, Cruikshank, Halls, National, P. & L.; elsewhere: Jacks.

Kellie Ann
Giant semi-cactus (unclassified); white-tipped lavender exhibition variety on a 1.2m (4ft) high bush; originated by L. Connell, USA, in 1991. Available USA: Connell's, Elkhorn.

Kelsea Carla
Small semi-cactus (ADS); light blends of pink and yellow; grows to a height of 1.2m (3ft); good for exhibition, garden and cut flowers; raised by Tony Hindle, UK, in 1998.

Keltie Peach
Medium decorative (NDS); orange pink blends, exhibition variety; 1.2m (4ft) in height; raised by D. Payne, UK, in 1999. Available UK: Halls, P. & L.

Kelvin Floodlight
Giant decorative (NDS), giant formal decorative (ADS); yellow exhibition variety, 1.4m (4.5ft) in height; introduced by McDougall, Australia, in 1959. Available UK: National, Suttons; USA: Dahlia Dandies, Frey's, Hamilton; elsewhere: Dgid, Engelhardt, Turc.

Kenora Amethyst
Ball (ADS); purple exhibition variety, originated by Gordon Leroux, USA, in 1989. Awarded the Derrill Hart medal (ADS).

Kenora Canada
Medium semi-cactus (ADS); yellow exhibition variety, 1.2m (4ft) high bush; originated by Gordon Leroux, USA, in 1987. Awarded the Lynn B. Dudley medal in 1986 (ADS). Available USA: Creekside, Elkhorn; elsewhere: Jacks.

KATE'S PASTELLE

KELSEA CARLA

KATHRYN'S CUPID

KELTIE PEACH

KATIE DAHL

KEITH'S CHOICE

KENORA CANADA

Kenora Challenger
White, large semi-cactus (NDS), white medium semi-cactus (ADS). In the UK, possibly the contender for the best ever exhibition large semi-cactus. Originated in 1991 by Gordon Leroux, USA, this variety grows to a height of 1.2m (4ft) with blooms of massive depth on long, straight, strong stems. Awarded the Stredwick medal in 2002 (NDS), and the Lynn B. Dudley medal in 1989 (ADS). Available UK: Abacus, Clark, Cruikshank, National, Oscroft, P. & L., Pratt, Spencer, Station House, Taylor; USA: Alpen, Arrowhead, Clacks, Dahlia Dandies, Dan's Dahlias, SB Gardens, Sea-Tac; elsewhere: Geerlings, Jacks.

Kenora Christmas
Small, formal decorative (ADS); red exhibition and garden variety; height 1.4m (4.5ft); originated by Gordon Leroux, USA, in 1993. Available USA: Arrowhead, Creekside, SB Gardens, Sea-Tac; Canada: Ferncliff.

Kenora Clyde
Giant semi-cactus (NDS and ADS); white exhibition variety; 1.4m (4.5ft) high bush; originated by Gordon Leroux, USA, in 1988. Awarded the

Lynn B. Dudley medal 1987 (ADS). Available UK: National; USA: Clacks, Dahlia Dandies, Elkhorn, Hamilton, SB Gardens; Canada: Ferncliff; elsewhere: Jacks.

Kenora Dazzler
Miniature informal decorative (ADS); dark blends purple and white exhibition and garden variety; 1.2m (4ft) in height; originated by Gordon Leroux, USA, in 1994.

Kenora Fireball
Ball (ADS); red exhibition variety, 1.2m (4ft) in height; originated by Gordon Leroux, USA, in 1986. Awarded the Lynn B. Dudley 1985, and the Derrill Hart medals. Available USA: Arrowhead, Dahlia Dandies, SB Gardens.

Kenora Frills
Medium lacinated semi-cactus (ADS); dark pink, strong-stemmed garden variety on a 1.2m (4ft) high bush; originated by Gordon Leroux, USA, in 1996. Available USA: Elkhorn, Sea-Tac.

Kenora Jubilee
Large semi-cactus (ADS); white exhibition and garden variety; 1.2m (4ft) in height; originated by Gordon Leroux, USA, in 2002.

Kenora Lisa
Medium formal decorative (ADS); pink exhibition variety; height 1.2m (4ft); originated by Gordon Leroux, USA, in 1990. Available USA: Alpen, Clacks, Connell's, Creekside, Dahlia Dandies, Dan's Dahlias, Hamilton, SB Gardens, Sea-Tac.

Kenora Macop-B
Medium lacinated (ADS); dark red exhibition variety; originated by Gordon Leroux, USA, in 1992. Available USA: Alpen, Creekside; elsewhere: Engelhardt, Graines.

Kenora Majestic
Medium cactus (ADS); light blends lavender and white; excellent exhibition and garden variety; 1.2m (4ft) in height; originated by Gordon Leroux, in USA, in 2002.

Kenora Moonbeam
Small, informal decorative (ADS); yellow exhibition variety, originated by Gordon Leroux, USA, in 1992. Awarded the Lynn B. Dudley medal, 1991 (ADS). Available USA: Clacks, Creekside, Sea-Tac.

Kenora Ontario
Medium incurved cactus (ADS); light blends white and lavender garden variety 1.2m (4ft) in height; originated by Gordon Leroux, in USA, in 1983.

KENORA CHALLENGER

KENORA CHRISTMAS

KENORA CLYDE

KENORA FIREBALL

KENORA FRILLS

KENORA LISA

KENORA MACOP-B

KENORA MOONBEAM

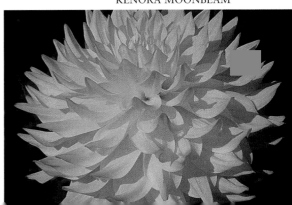

Kenora Passion
Small, informal decorative (ADS); light blends, pink and yellow variety; originated by Gordon Leroux, USA, in 1991.

Kenora Petite
Miniature semi-cactus (NDS); pink exhibition variety, 1.2m (4ft) high bush; originated by Gordon Leroux, USA, in 1993. Available UK: National.

Kenora Sunburst
Large, informal decorative (ADS); yellow exhibition variety, 1.2m (4ft) in height; raised by Gordon Leroux, USA, in 1984. Awarded the Lynn B. Dudley 1983 and the Derrill Hart medals (ADS). Available USA: Sea-Tac; Canada: Candahlia.

Kenora Sunset
Medium semi-cactus (NDS and ADS); yellow and red bicolour (NDS), flame (ADS); grows to a height of 1.2m (4ft). Excellent free-flowering exhibition and good garden variety; originated by Gordon Leroux, USA, in 1996. Available UK: Abacus, Butterfield, Halls, Oscroft, P. & L., Pratt, Scotts, Spencer, Station House, Tivey; USA: Arrowhead, Clacks, Dahlia Dandies, SB Gardens; elsewhere: Dgid; Geerlings, Jacks, Konishi, Wirth.

Kenora Superb
Large semi-cactus (ADS); light blends orange and yellow garden and exhibition blooms on strong stems; originated by Gordon Leroux, USA, in 1992. Available USA: Alpen; elsewhere: Wirth.

Kenora Tonya
Ball (ADS); lavender exhibition and garden variety; originated by G. Leroux, USA, in 1990.

Kenora Valentine
Red, large decorative (NDS), large formal decorative (ADS); growing to a height of 1.2m (4ft); in the UK blooms can be oversize for exhibition purposes. Originated Gordon Leroux, USA, in 1990. Available UK: Abacus, Aylett's, Halls, National, Oscroft, Tivey; USA: Sea-Tac; Canada: Candahlia; elsewhere: Geerlings, Graines.

Kenora Wildfire
Giant or large decorative (NDS), large informal decorative (ADS); red exhibition variety, 1.2m (4ft) high; originated by Gordon Leroux, USA, in 1989. Awarded the Lynn B. Dudley medal, 1988 (ADS). Available UK: National, P. & L.; USA: Alpen, Clacks, Creekside, Dahlia Dandies, Dan's Dahlias, Elkhorn, Mingus, SB Gardens; Canada: Ferncliff.

Ken's Coral
Waterlily (ADS); flame exhibition and cut flower variety, 1.2m (4ft) in height; introduced by Farquhar, Australia, in 1989. Available USA: Clacks, Connell's.

Ken's Flame
Waterlily (ADS); flame, cut flower variety on a 1.2m (4ft) bush; early blooms; introduced by Farquhar, Australia, in 1989. Available USA: Alpen, Clacks, SB Gardens.

Ken's Orchid
Orchid (ADS); white exhibition variety; originated by Masurat, USA, in 1995. Awarded the Derrill Hart medal (ADS).

Kidd's Climax
Giant decorative (NDS), large formal decorative (ADS); exhibition blooms of light blends of yellow and pink; this popular long-lived variety was raised by Ted Kidd, New Zealand, in 1940. Award Merit 1973 Wisley (NDS). Available UK: Abacus, Cruikshank, Halls, National, Oscroft, P. & L., Tivey; USA: Arrowhead, Clacks, Connell's, Dahlia Dandies, Dan's Dahlias, Elkhorn, Hamilton, Mingus, SB Gardens, Sea-Tac, Swan Island; elsewhere: Engelhardt, Geerlings, Jacks, Wirth.

Kikukomachi
Novelty double centre (ADS); yellow exhibition and garden variety, 0.9m (3ft) in height; originated by Konishi, Japan, in 1995.

Kimberley Robin
Miniature formal decorative (ADS); dark pink exhibition variety, 1.2m (4ft) in height; originated by W.H. Smith, New Zealand, in 1967.

Kimpuu
Medium informal decorative (ADS); bicolour yellow and white exhibition and garden variety, 1.2m (4ft) in height; introduced by Konishi, Japan, in 1989.

Kims Marc
Small cactus (NDS); yellow-blended exhibition, garden and cut flower variety; 1.1m (3.5ft) in height; raised by B. Fowler, UK, in 1980. Available UK: Butterfield, National.

Kingston
Miniature cactus (unclassified); lemon yellow tipped pink cut flower variety on a 0.9m (3ft) bush; originated USA in 1984. Available USA: Connell's, Dan's Dahlias.

Kiwi Brother
Small semi-cactus (NDS); pink bronze blended exhibition variety, 1.2m (4ft) in height; raised by Eddie Durrant, UK, in 1975. Available UK: National.

KENORA PASSION

KENORA SUPERB

KENORA SUNSET

KENORA TONYA

KENORA VALENTINE

KENORA WILDFIRE

KEN'S CORAL

KIDD'S CLIMAX

Kiwi Gloria
Small cactus (NDS and ADS); with lavender blends (NDS), light blends white and dark pink blooms on plants growing to 1.2m (4ft) in height; excellent exhibition blooms; raised by Eddie Durrant, UK, in 1988. Available UK: Abacus, Clark, Cruikshank, Halls, National, Oscroft, P. & L., Porter, Pratt, Spencer, Station House, Taylor, Tivey; USA: Clacks, Elkhorn; Canada: Candahlia; elsewhere: Geerlings, Jacks.

K-K-K Katie
Orchid (ADS); orange exhibition variety; originated by van Dyke, USA, in 1996. Available USA: Alpen, Clacks, Dan's Dahlias, Elkhorn.

Klankstad Kerkrade
Small yellow cactus (NDS and ADS); growing to a height of 90cm (3ft); excellent for exhibition, garden and cut flowers. Introduced by dahlia Bruidegom, Holland, in 1954. Award Merit Wisley 1959 (NDS); subsequently sported White Klankstad (1967), Majestic Kerkrade (1973), Pink Kerkrade (1987) and Lady Kerkrade (1987). Available UK: National, Oscroft, P. & L., Roberts, Station House, Tivey.

Klondyke
Medium semi-cactus (ADS); white cut flower and exhibition variety; height 1.2m (4ft); originated by Ed Redd, USA, in 1992. Awarded the Lynn B. Dudley medal, 1991 (ADS). Available elsewhere: Graines, Wirth.

Koko Puff
Pompon (unclassified); orange cut flower and garden variety on a 0.9m (3ft) high plant; originated in the USA in 1991. Available USA: Swan Island.

Kolchelsee
Miniature decorative (NDS); red garden variety; 1.1m (3.5ft) in height; introduced by D. McCann, New Zealand, in

1961. Available UK: National; elsewhere: Dgid.

Komet
Anemone (unclassified); red garden variety, height 1.1m (3.5ft); originated Holland.

Koppertone
Waterlily (unclassified); bronze and orange cut flower variety, height 1.4m (4.5ft); originated USA in 1982. Available USA: Swan Island.

Korb Dandy Lady
Miniature formal decorative (ADS); purple exhibition variety; originated by D. Korb, USA, in 2001.

Korb Dan's Dandy
Small, lacinated (ADS); pink exhibition variety; originated by D. Korb, USA, in 2001.

Korb Martha R
Medium lacinated (ADS); light blends, pink and white exhibition variety, height 1.2m (4ft); originated by D. Korb, USA, in 2000.

Korb Purple Persuasion
Small formal decorative (ADS); purple variety originated by D. Korb, USA, in 2000.

Korb Quill's Pride
Small, lacinated (ADS); pink variety; originated by D. Korb, USA, in 2001.

Korb Red Rebel
Giant incurving cactus (ADS); red variety, originated by D. Korb, USA, in 2001.

Korb Ruby Forte
Large semi-cactus (ADS); red exhibition variety, 0.9m (3ft) high bush; originated by D. Korb, USA, in 2000. Available USA: Clacks; Canada: Ferncliff.

Korb Splendid Lady
Miniature formal decorative (ADS); 1.5m (5.5ft) tall; variety originated by D. Korb, USA, in 2000.

Korb Summer Gala
Small, informal decorative (ADS); dark blends, purple and white, originated by D. Korb, USA, in 2001. Available USA: Clacks.

Korb White Delight
Medium lacinated (ADS); white exhibition variety, 1.2m (4ft) high bush; originated by D. Korb, USA, in 2000. Available USA: Dahlia Dandies.

Kotare Jackpot
Small semi-cactus (NDS and ADS); red garden and exhibition height, 0.9m (3ft); introduced by Peter Burrell, New Zealand, in 1994. Available UK: National, P. & L.; USA: Clacks.

Kotare Jubilee
Small semi-cactus (unclassified); yellow garden variety; height 1.2m (4ft); introduced by P. Burrell, New Zealand, in 2000.

Kotare Magic
Small decorative (NDS); red exhibition variety; 0.9m (3ft) high bush; introduced by Peter Burrell, New Zealand, in 1998.

Kracker Jac
Waterlily-type, small decorative (unclassified); orange bronze garden and cut flower variety; height 1.4m (4.5ft); originated USA in 2000. Available USA: Swan Island.

Kristin
Small semi-cactus (ADS); dark blends, dark red and yellow cut flower and garden variety on a 1.2m (4ft) high bush; prolific grower. Originated L. Connell, USA, in 2001. Available USA: Connell's.

Kung Fu
Small decorative (NDS); red exhibition variety, tall plant 1.8m (6ft); raised by Norman Lewis, UK, in 1976. Available UK: National, Tivey.

KIWI GLORIA

KOMET

KLONDYKE

KOTARE MAGIC

Kym Willo
Pompon (NDS); orange bronze
blended garden variety, 1.1m
(3.5ft) in height; raised by
Norman Williams, Australia, in
1963. Available UK: National.

Kyodi Yusaki
Small cactus (ADS); dark red,
exhibition variety, originated in
Japan in 1992.

L

L'Ancresse
Small ball or miniature ball
(NDS), ball (ADS); white
exhibition variety; height 1.4m
(4.5ft); raised by Norman Flint,
UK, in 1982. Available UK:
Abacus, Aylett's, Cruikshank,
Halls, Jones, JRG, National,
Oscroft, P. & L., Porter, Scotts,
Station House; USA: Clacks,
Dan's Dahlias, Elkhorn,
Mingus, Swan Island;
elsewhere: Engelhardt, Wirth.

L.A.T.E.
Miniature ball (NDS),
miniature formal decorative
(ADS); light blends orange pink
(NDS), or orange yellow (ADS);
exhibition and garden variety;
1.2m (4ft) high; introduced by
T. Cleghorn, UK, in 1999.
Available UK: Abacus,
Cruikshank, Halls, JRG,
National, P. & L., Porter,
Roberts, Spencer, Station House;
USA: Clacks, Elkhorn, Mingus.

La Bomba
Collarette (ADS); dark red with
dark red collar; originated by
Eckhoff, USA, in 2001.
Available USA: Sea-Tac.

La Cierva
Collerette (NDS); purple tipped
white with a white collar;
exhibition and garden variety;
introduced by Entrup,
Germany, in 1939. Available
UK: National, Scotts;
elsewhere: Wirth.

La Corbiere
Miniature ball (NDS); pink
blended exhibition, garden and
cut flower variety; 1.2m (4ft) in
height; raised by Norman Flint,
UK, in 1985. Available UK:
National, P. & L.

La Gioconda
Collerette (NDS); red and
yellow with red collar;
exhibition variety; introduced
by Mayergmelin, Germany, in
1943. Available UK: National;
elsewhere: Dgid.

Lady Darlene
Medium formal decorative
(ADS); dark blends red and
yellow exhibition variety; 1.2m
(4ft) high bush; originated by
Grimm, USA, in 1984.
Available USA: Arrowhead,
Dahlia Dandies, Mingus.

Lady Kerkrade
Small cactus (NDS and ADS);
light blends lavender and white
exhibition, garden and cut
flower variety; 1.2m (4ft) in
height; raised by D. Walker,
UK, in 1987. Available UK:
National, Roberts, Station
House, Tivey; USA:
Arrowhead, Dan's Dahlias,
Elkhorn; elsewhere: Jacks.

Lady Lael
Waterlily (unclassified); yellow
cut flower and garden variety
on a 1.2m (4ft) high bush;
originated USA in 1998.
Available USA: Clacks,
Connell's.

Lady Linda
Small decorative (NDS); yellow
exhibition, garden and cut
flower variety; height 1.1m
(3.5ft); raised by Norman
Lewis, UK, in 1980. Available
UK: Abacus, Butterfield,
Cruikshank, Halls, National,
Oscroft, P. & L., Scotts, Tivey;
USA: Frey's, Sea-Tac, Swan
Island; elsewhere: Jacks.

Lady Orpah
Small decorative (NDS); yellow
and bronze blends; exhibition,

garden and cut flower variety;
raised by R. Mahon, UK, in
1985. Available UK: National.

Lady Sunshine
Small semi-cactus (NDS);
yellow exhibition and garden
variety; strong stems on a bush
1.2m (4ft) in height; introduced
by Ballego, Holland, in 1970.
Available UK: National.

Lambada
Small formal decorative (ADS);
orange garden and exhibition
variety; originated by Ghio,
USA, in 1998.

Lara Anne
Medium semi-cactus (ADS);
red exhibition variety, 1.2m
(3.5ft) high bush; originated by
Ed Redd, USA, 2000.

Last Dance
Miniature formal decorative
(ADS); light blends lavender
and white cut flower and
exhibition variety on a 1.4m
(4.5ft) bush; originated by N.
Gitts, USA, in 1994. Available
USA: Clacks, Elkhorn, Frey's,
Swan Island.

Laura Marie
Miniature ball (NDS), ball
(ADS); red exhibition garden
and cut flower variety; 1.2m
(4ft) high; raised by Norman
Lewis, UK, in 1988. Available
UK: National, P. & L., Scotts,
Station House, Tivey.

Lauren Michele
Waterlily (ADS); lavender with
purple reverse, cut flower and
exhibition variety; prolific
bloomer on a 1.5m (5ft) bush;
originated by N. Gitts, USA, in
1990. Available USA: Clacks,
Connell's, Creekside, Frey's, SB
Gardens, Sea-Tac, Swan Island;
Canada: Ferncliff.

Laurence Fisher
Medium semi-cactus (NDS);
yellow exhibition garden and
cut flower; 1.4m (4.5ft) high;
raised by E. Fisher, UK, in
1985. Available UK: National.

L.A.T.E.

LADY KERKRADE

LAURA MARIE

Lauren's Moonlight
(synonymous **Pim's Moonlight**)
Medium semi-cactus (NDS);
yellow exhibition and garden
variety; 1.2m (4ft) in height;
raised by Wagstaff, UK, in
1988. Available UK: Abacus,
Clark, Cruikshank, Halls,
National, Oscroft, P. & L.,
Pratt, Spencer; USA: Mingus.

Lavender Athalie
Small cactus (NDS), small
semi-cactus (ADS); lavender
exhibition variety; 1.4m
(4.5ft); raised by T. Dale, UK,
in 1991. Available UK:
National, Oscroft, P. & L.,
Scotts; USA: Dan's Dahlias,
Sea-Tac.

Lavender Chiffon
Small cactus (unclassified);
white-edged pink garden
variety on a bush 1.2m (4ft)
high; originated USA in 1971.
Available USA: Frey's, Swan
Island; elsewhere: Engelhardt.

Lavender Line
Small cactus (ADS); light
blends lavender and white
exhibition variety, 1.2m (4ft)
high bush; originated by L.
Connell, USA, in 1998;
awarded the Lynn B. Dudley
medal 1997 (ADS). Available
USA: Capistrano, Connell's;
Canada: Candahlia, Ferncliff.

Lavender Nunton Harvest
Small decorative (NDS);
exhibition, garden and cut
flower variety; height 1.2m
(4ft); sport of Nunton Harvest;
raised in the UK in 1982.
Available UK: National,
Oscroft, Station House.

Lavender Perfection
Giant decorative (NDS), large
formal decorative (ADS);
lavender garden variety, 1.2m
(4ft) high; raised by H.
Johnston, New Zealand, in
1941. Available UK: National;
USA: Elkhorn; elsewhere: Dgid.

Lavender Ruffles
Giant informal decorative
(unclassified); lavender garden
variety on a 0.9m (3ft) high
bush; a sport of purple Tahejio,
originated USA in 2000. Award
Merit Wisley (NDS) 1952.
Available USA: Swan Island.

Lavender Symbol
Medium semi-cactus (NDS);
lavender and yellow blends;
exhibition variety; 1.2m (4ft) in
height. Raised in the UK in
1980 as one of the Symbol
sports. Available UK: Tivey

Lavengro
Giant decorative (NDS), large,
informal decorative (ADS);
lavender and bronze blends
(NDS); raised Bertie Barnes;
UK, in 1953. Award Merit
Wisley (NDS) 1958. Available
for 2003, UK: National, P. &
L.; elsewhere: Turc.

Le Batts Premier (synonymous
Le Batts Prime)
Small decorative (NDS), small
formal decorative (ADS);
exhibition garden and cut
flower; height 1.1m (3.5ft);
originated by Batts, USA, in
1985. Available UK: National,
Oscroft; USA: Clacks, Elkhorn.

Le Castel
Waterlily (unclassified); white
cut flower variety on a 1.4m
(4.5ft) high bush; originated
USA. Available USA: Elkhorn,
Swan Island.

Le Vonne Splinter
Giant semi-cactus (NDS and
ADS); bronze blends exhibition
variety; 1.4m (4.5ft) in height;
originated by Paul Comstock,
USA, in 1978. Awarded the
Lynn B. Dudley (ADS) 1977
and the Derrill Hart medals
(ADS). Available UK:
Cruikshank, National, P. & L.;
elsewhere: Jacks.

Lemon Candy
Small formal decorative
(unclassified); yellow tipped
white cut flower variety; 1.2m

(4ft) high bush; sport of Candy
Cane; originated USA in 1995.
Available USA: Dan's Dahlias,
Swan Island.

Lemon Cane
Small formal decorative
(unclassified); yellow white
tipped cut flower variety on a
1.2m (4ft) high bush; sport of
Candy Cane; originated USA in
1999. Available USA: Connell's;
elsewhere: Engelhardt.

Lemon Elegans
A small yellow semi-cactus
(NDS and ADS); producing
deep exhibition and cut-flower
blooms in profusion on tall
plants of 1.2m (3.5ft);
introduced by Cor Geerlings,
Holland, in 1988. Available
UK: Abacus, Butterfield,
Cruikshank, Halls, JRG,
National, Oscroft, P. & L.,
Pratt, Spencer; elsewhere:
Jacks.

Lemon Meringue
Small informal decorative
(ADS); bright yellow cut flower
variety on a 1.2m (4ft) high
bush; early bloomer; originated
by Bonneywell, USA, in 1995.
Available USA: Connell's,
Creekside, Dan's Dahlias;
Canada: Ferncliff.

Lemon Kiss
Medium formal decorative
(unclassified); yellow garden
variety on a 1.2m (4ft) bush;
originated USA in 1993.
Available USA: Swan Island.

Lemon Shiffon
Small formal decorative
(unclassified); soft yellow cut
flower and floral art variety;
1.2m (4ft) bush; originated
USA in 1998. Available USA:
Swan Island.

Lemon Swirl
Waterlily (unclassified); lemon
garden flower variety; prolific
blooms on a 1.2m (4ft) bush;
originated by L. Connell, USA,
in 1996. Available USA:
Connell's.

LAUREN'S MOONLIGHT

LAVENDER SYMBOL

LAVENGRO

LAVENDER ATHALIE

LAVENDER LINE

LE VONNE SPLINTER

LEMON ELEGANS

Lemon Tart
Small semi-cactus
(unclassified); yellow cut flower
and exhibition variety; 0.6m
(2ft) in height; prolific;
originated USA in 1992.
Available USA: Swan Island.

Lemon Zing
Miniature ball (NDS), small
formal decorative (ADS);
yellow exhibition, garden and
cut flower variety; 1.2m (4ft) in
height; raised by T. Cleghorn,
UK, in 1999. Available UK:
Abacus, Cruikshank, Halls, P.
& L., Spencer; USA: Creekside,
Dan's Dahlias.

Leonardo
Gallery miniature decorative
(unclassified); garden variety;
height 0.4 (1.45ft). Available
UK: Blooms, JRG, National,
Porter; elsewhere: Dgid.

Leopold Classic
Medium decorative
(unclassified); yellow exhibition
variety on a 1.2m (4ft) plant;
raised by Phil Watson, UK, in
2000.

Leycett
Giant decorative (NDS); orange
blends exhibition and garden
variety; 1.4m (4.5ft) in height;
raised by Tom Bebbington, UK,
in 1978. Available UK:
National, Oscroft.

Liberator
Giant decorative (NDS); red
exhibition variety; 1.2m (4ft) in
height; introduced by Harris,
Australia, in 1941. Available
UK: National, Oscroft.

Libretto
Collerette (NDS); purple and
white blends, purple collar,
garden variety 1.1m (3.5ft)
high; introduced by F.
Topsvoort, Holland, in 1955.
Available UK: National:
elsewhere: Geerlings.

Lifesize
Large decorative (NDS); yellow
exhibition variety, 1.2m (4ft);

raised by Brother Simplicius,
UK, in 1968. Available UK:
Cruikshank, National.

Light Accord
Medium semi-cactus (ADS);
yellow exhibition variety;
originated by Ed Redd, USA, in
2000. Awarded the Lynn B.
Dudley medal, 1999 (ADS).
Available USA: Arrowhead.

Light Music
Large cactus (NDS), medium
incurving cactus (ADS);
lavender exhibition variety;
1.5m (5ft) tall; introduced by
Ballego, Holland, in 1966.
Available UK: National;
elsewhere: Engelhardt.

Lil Buddy
Miniature ball (unclassified);
purple garden variety on strong
1.1m (3.5ft) bush; originated
by L. Connell, USA, in 1992.
Available USA: Connell's.

Lilac Athalie
Small cactus (NDS); lavender
exhibition, garden and cut
flower variety, on a 1.2m (4ft)
high plant; raised in the UK in
1987. Available UK: National;
elsewhere: Jacks.

Lilac Mist
Small incurving cactus
(unclassified); lavender, cut
flower variety, on a 1.4m
(4.5ft) high bush; originated in
the USA in 1985. Available
USA: Swan Island.

Lilac Willo
Pompon (NDS and ADS);
lavender exhibition, garden and
cut flower variety; 1.2m (4ft) in
height; raised by Bob Porter,
UK, in 1978. Available UK:
National, P. & L.; USA:
Clacks, SB Gardens.

Lilian Ingham
Miniature decorative (NDS),
small cactus (ADS); bronze
(NDS), deep purple (ADS);
raised by R. Ingham, UK, in
1989.

Lilian Stewart
Medium lacinated
(unclassified); dark pink garden
variety on a 1.2m (4ft) bush;
originated USA in 1998.
Available USA: Connell's.

Lilianne Ballego
Miniature decorative (NDS);
bronze garden and cut flower
variety; height 1.1m (3.5ft);
raised by Ballego, Holland, in
1954. Available UK: Halls,
National.

Linda's Chester
Small cactus (NDS); orange
and yellow blends, exhibition,
garden and cut flower variety;
sport of Paul Chester; raised by
J. Watson, UK, in 1991.
Available UK: Butterfield,
Cruikshank, National, P. & L.,
Station House; USA: Mingus.

Lindy
Small informal decorative
(unclassified); rose-pink cut
flower variety on a 1.2m (4ft)
high bush; originated USA in
1996. Available USA: Swan
Island.

Lions' International
Small formal decorative (ADS);
dark pink exhibition variety;
originated by Pfuhl, USA, in
1965. Awarded the Derrill Hart
medal (ADS).

Lipoma
Miniature ball (NDS); lavender,
garden variety; 1.1m (3.5ft) in
height; raised by Mayer
Gmelin, Germany, in 1943.
Available UK: National;
elsewhere: Dgid.

Lipstick
Medium lacinated (ADS);
bicolour, yellow and red,
exhibition and garden variety;
1.2m (4ft) high bush;
introduced by D. Kent, UK, in
1998. Available USA:
Arrowhead, Elkhorn, Mingus.

LIBRETTO

LIFESIZE

LIGHT ACCORD

LILIAN INGHAM

LINDA'S CHESTER

LILAC ATHALIE

LIPSTICK

Lisa
Waterlily (unclassified); lavender and white; early blooming; prolific; cut flower variety; tall, at 1.5m (5ft); originated USA in 1986. Available USA: Dan's Dahlias, Elkhorn; Canada: Ferncliff.

Lismore Carol
Pompon (NDS); orange blends, exhibition and garden variety; 1.1m (3.5ft) in height; raised by Bill Franklin, UK, in 2000. Available UK: Halls, National, P. & L., Porter.

Lismore Moonlight
Pompon (NDS and ADS); yellow exhibition variety; height 1.1m (3.5ft); raised by Bill Franklin, UK, in 1998. Available Aylett's, Cruikshank, Halls, National, P. & L., Pratt, Spencer; elsewhere: Geerlings.

Lismore Peggy
Pompon (NDS); pink blended exhibition and garden variety; 1.1m (3.5ft) in height; raised by Bill Franklin, UK, in 1985. Available UK: JRG, National, P. & L., Porter, Spencer, Station House.

Lismore Sunset
Pompon (NDS and ADS); orange yellow blended (NDS), flame (ADS); exhibition, garden and cut flower variety; 1.1m (3.5ft) high plant; raised by Bill Franklin, UK, in 1998. Available UK: Abacus, Cruikshank, Halls, National, P. & L., Spencer, Station House; USA: Creekside.

Lismore Willie
Small waterlily (NDS); a prolific provider of exhibition, garden and cut-flower blooms, orange blends; very tall at 1.5m (5ft); raised by Bill Franklin, UK, in 1992. Available UK: Abacus, Aylett's, Butterfield, Cruikshank, Halls, JRG, National, Oscroft, P. & L., Station House; USA: Clacks, Mingus.

Little Caesar
Miniature ball (ADS); orange exhibition variety; originated by Hacek, USA, in 1993. Awarded the Derrill Hart medal. Available USA: Arrowhead, Clacks, Creekside, Dan's Dahlias, SB Gardens.

Little Dorrit
Lilliput (single) (NDS); purple garden variety; 0.6m (2ft) in height; introduced in 1976. Award Garden Merit Wisley (NDS). Available UK: Butterfield, National, Station House.

Little Glenfern
Miniature cactus (unclassified); yellow garden and cut flower variety; prolific bloomer; height 1.1m (3.5ft); originated in Australia in 1980.

Little J
Miniature semi-cactus (ADS); light blends lavender and white; originated by L. Connell, USA, in 1998. Available USA: Clacks, Connell's.

Little Lamb
Miniature cactus (unclassified); pure white cut flower variety (weddings) on a 1.2m (4ft) bush; originated by Swan Island, USA, in 1974. Available USA: Frey's, SB Gardens.

Little Laura
Miniature ball (ADS); light blends, orange and yellow, early blooming garden variety; originated by Frank Turton, Australia, in 1991. Available USA: Connell's.

Little Royal
Miniature formal decorative (ADS); purple exhibition variety; originated by Takeuchi, USA, in 1985. Awarded the Derrill Hart medal (ADS).

Little Sally
Pompon (NDS); flame garden variety; 1.1m (3.5ft) high; introduced by J. Gregory, Australia, in 1961. Award Merit Wisley, 1963 (NDS). Available UK: Halls, National.

Little Scottie
Pompon (ADS); yellow cut-flower and garden variety; 1.2m (4ft) in height; introduced in Australia in 1989. Available USA: Connell's, Dan's Dahlias, SB Gardens; Canada: Ferncliff.

Little Show-off
Collarette (ADS); purple garden variety on a 1.2m (4ft) bush; originated by L. Connell, USA, in 1991. Awarded the Lynn B. Dudley medal, 1990 (ADS). Available USA: Clacks, Dahlia Dandies, Dan's Dahlias.

Little William
Miniature ball (unclassified); red and white tipped, dwarf bedding garden variety; height 70cm (2ft); introduced by dahlia Bruidegom, Holland, in 1954.

Little Willo
Pompon (ADS); white garden and exhibition variety; introduced by N. Williams, Australia, in 1935. Available USA: Alpen, Clacks, SB Gardens.

Lloyd Huston
Giant semi-cactus (NDS), large semi-cactus (ADS); bronze yellow blends (NDS), orange (ADS); exhibition and garden variety; 1.2m (4ft) high; originated by Earl Huston, Canada, in 1983. Available UK: National, Oscroft, P. & L.; USA: Clacks, Elkhorn.

Lois V
Medium lacinated cactus (ADS); yellow garden variety on a bush 1.2m (4ft) high; originated by Schoen, USA, in 1991.

Lollipop
Miniature formal decorative (unclassified); orange cut-flower variety on a 1.1m (3.5ft) high bush; originated by Swan Island, USA, in 1990. Available USA: Frey's, Swan Island; elsewhere: Engelhardt, Konishi.

LISMORE MOONLIGHT

LITTLE J

LITTLE LAMB

LISMORE SUNSET

LITTLE LAURA

LISMORE WILLIE

LOIS V

Longwood Dainty
Peony (ADS); orange exhibition and garden variety; 0.9m (3ft) in height; introduced by Robbie, New Zealand, in 1990. Awarded the Derrill Hart medal (ADS); prolific bloomer. Available Canada: Ferncliff.

Loretta
Miniature decorative (NDS); small formal decorative (ADS); lavender exhibition and garden variety; 1.1m (3.5ft) in height; raised by Cor Geerlings, Holland, in 1996. Available UK: Cruikshank, JRG, National, Porter, Scotts, Station House, Tivey; USA: Arrowhead.

Lorilli Dawn
Waterlily (unclassified); light pink, miniature cut-flower and excellent floral art blooms; 1.2m (4ft) high; originated USA in 1993. Available: USA, Connell's, Swan Island.

Lorona Dawn
Novelty, double centre (ADS); purple with white collar, exhibition variety; height 1.5m (4.5ft); originated by K. Williams, Canada, in 2000. Prolific blooms. Available Canada: Ferncliff.

Loud Applause
Medium semi-cactus (unclassified); yellow garden and cut flower variety, long-stemmed; height 1.2m (4ft); introduced by Lindhout, Holland, in 1993. Award Garden Merit 1993 Wisley (NDS).

Love Potion
Small semi-cactus (unclassified); hot pink; garden, exhibition and cut flower variety; 1.2m (4ft) high bush; originated USA in 1999. Available USA: Swan Island.

Lovely Lana
Large, informal decorative (ADS); lavender exhibition variety; originated by D. Hinz, USA, in 2001. Available USA: Clacks, Dahlia Dandies, Mingus.

Love's Comet
Anemone (ADS); red exhibition variety, 1.5m (5ft) high bush; originated by Shinn, Canada, in 2000.

Love's Dream
Small waterlily (NDS); red-blended garden and cut flower variety; 1.1m (3.5ft) in height; raised by Piper, UK, in 1957. Available UK: National.

Love's Sasha
Small lacinated (ADS); flame exhibition variety; originated by Shinn, Canada, in 2000.

Lula Pattie
Giant decorative (NDS), giant informal decorative (ADS); white exhibition variety; 1.1m (3.5ft) in height; originated by Clack, USA, in 1960. Awarded the Derrill Hart medal. Available UK: Cruikshank; USA: Connell's, Sea-Tac, Swan Island; Canada: Ferncliff.

Lune de Cap
Medium lacinated (ADS); bright yellow exhibition variety on a 1.2m (4ft) high bush; introduced by Cyril Higgo, South Africa, in 2000. Available USA: Connell's.

Lupin Amy
Orchid (ADS); dark blends, red and orange exhibition variety; originated by W. Morin, USA, in 2001.

Lupin Beth
Waterlily (ADS); yellow exhibition variety originated by B. Jones, USA, in 2001. Awarded the Lynn B. Dudley medal.

Lupin Cardinal
Small formal decorative (ADS); dark red exhibition and garden variety; originated by W. Morin, USA, 1992. Awarded the Derrill Hart medal (ADS). Available USA: Dan's Dahlias.

Lupin Mandi
Small semi-cactus (ADS); dark pink exhibition variety; originated by B. Jones, USA, in 2001.

Lupin Peltier
Giant lacinated cactus (ADS); light blends, exhibition variety on a 1.2m (4ft) high bush; originated by B. Jones, USA, in 1993. Available USA: Elkhorn, Sea-Tac.

Lupin Sheila
Orchid (ADS); dark pink exhibition variety, 1.2m (4ft) high bush; originated by W. Morin, USA, in 2000. Awarded Lynn B. Dudley 1999, and the Derrill Hart medals (ADS). Available USA: Clacks.

Lupin Tori
Mignon single (ADS); white garden and exhibition variety; originated by B. Jones, USA, in 1997. Awarded Derrill Hart medal 1996 (ADS). Available USA: Clacks, Dan's Dahlias.

Lydia Suckow
Medium incurving cactus (ADS); bicolour purple and white garden variety on a 1.2m (4ft) bush; originated by Russell, USA, in 1964. Available USA: Connell's, Dan's Dahlias.

LORILLI DAWN

LORETTA

LULA PATTIE

LUPIN PELTIER

M

M B B
Miniature formal decorative (ADS); variegated lavender and purple variety; originated by Bloomfield, USA, in 1993. Available USA: Clacks, SB Gardens.

Maarn
Miniature ball (unclassified); orange cut flower variety; 1.4m (4.5ft) high; raised in Holland. Available USA: Clacks, Swan Island.

MAB
Small lacinated (ADS); pink variety; originated by D. Barnes, USA, in 2001.

Mabel Ann
Giant decorative (NDS), large formal decorative (ADS); bronze yellow blends (NDS), light blends orange and yellow (ADS); exhibition variety; 1.3m (4.5ft) high bush; raised by Ray Adley, UK, in 1995. Available UK: Cruikshank, National, Oscroft, P. & L.; USA: Capistrano, Dahlia Dandies, Elkhorn, Mingus; elsewhere: Geerlings, Jacks.

Mabel Avis
Small, lacinated (ADS); pink variety; originated by Barton, USA, in 2000. Available USA: Capistrano.

Mack Medium
Informal decorative (ADS); dark blends; H. Miller, USA, in 1999.

Madison Moment
Small formal decorative (ADS); purple variety, originated by C. Craig, USA, in 2001.

Magic Moment
Medium semi-cactus (ADS); white, excellent exhibition and cut flower variety; 1.4m (4.5ft) high bush; originated by L. Connell, USA, in 1983. Awarded the Stanley Johnson medal (ADS). Available USA: Alpen, Arrowhead, Clacks, Creekside, Dahlia Dandies, Dan's Dahlias, Elkhorn, SB Gardens, Sea-Tac, Swan Island; Canada: Candahlia; elsewhere: Engelhardt.

Magically Dunn
Small formal decorative (ADS); bicolour white blooms, tipped lavender; cut and exhibition variety; introduced Swan Island, USA, in 2001. Available USA: Swan Island.

Magnificat
Miniature decorative (NDS); red garden variety; 1.1m (3.5ft) high plant; introduced by Bakker, Holland, in 1955. Available UK: JRG, National.

Maisie Mooney
Giant decorative (NDS), large informal decorative (ADS); white exhibition variety; originated by Mooney, Canada, in 1994. Available UK: National; USA: Alpen, Clacks, Connell's, SB Gardens; Canada: Candahlia; elsewhere: Jacks.

Majestic Athalie
Small cactus (NDS), small semi-cactus (ADS); light blends yellow and pink, raised garden and exhibition variety; tall at 1.5m (5ft) high; raised in UK in 1982. Available UK: National, P. & L., Scotts; USA: Sea-Tac.

Majestic Kerkrade
Small cactus (NDS), small, straight cactus (ADS); pink and yellow blends (NDS), light blends (ADS); originated by H. Hadow, USA, in 1977. Available UK: JRG, National; USA: Arrowhead, Clacks, Dan's Dahlias.

Majjas Symbol
Medium semi-cactus (NDS); yellow orange blends exhibition, garden and cut flower variety; 1.2m (4ft) high bush; raised by P. A. Dawson, UK, in 1994. Available UK: National.

Maki
Giant informal decorative (unclassified); pink-striped purple exhibition variety; height 1.2m (4ft); sport of Emory Paul; introduced in 1980. Available USA: Swan Island.

Maltby Fanfare
Collerette (NDS); purple with white collar; exhibition variety; 1.2m (4ft) high plant; introduced by Cunnard, New Zealand, in 1995. Available UK: Cruikshank, National.

Maltby Vanilla
Small formal decorative (ADS); white variety; Cunnard, New Zealand, in 1990.

Manor Gold
Ball (ADS); yellow variety; originated by Boyer, USA, in 1986.

Manor Sunset
Medium semi-cactus (ADS); flame variety, originated by Boyer, USA, in 1984. Available USA: Hamilton.

Man's Adam N
Miniature ball (ADS); lavender variety; originated by Manwell, USA, in 2001.

Man's Alley Cat
Miniature ball (ADS); deep pink variety; originated by Manwell, USA, in 2000. Available USA: Clacks.

Man's Leandra
Small formal decorative (ADS); pink variety; originated by Manwell, USA, in 2001.

Man's Nyika
Novelty double centre (ADS); pink variety; originated by Manwell, USA, in 2000.

Man's Orange Sherbet
Same (ADS); bicolour orange and white variety; originated by Manwell, USA, in 1998.

MAISIE MOONEY

MAJESTIC ATHALIE

MABEL ANN

MAGIC MOMENT

MAJESTIC KERKRADE

Marcy Lynn
Medium lacinated (ADS); dark blends red and yellow variety; originated by Vandament, Canada, 1999.

Mardi Gras
Miniature formal decorative (unclassified); orange and yellow exhibition and cut flower variety; 1.2m (4ft) high bush. Originated USA in 1999. Available USA: Connell's, Swan Island.

Maren
Miniature ball (ADS); orange variety; originated by Lorenzen, Germany, in 1993. Available USA: Dan's Dahlias; Canada: Ferncliff.

Margaret Alexander
Single (ADS); red variety; originated by Masurat, USA, in 1997.

Margaret Anne
Miniature decorative (NDS); yellow exhibition and garden variety; 0.9m (3ft) high plant; raised by Terry Clarke, UK, in 1977. Available UK: Aylett's, Butterfield, National, P. & L., Tivey; elsewhere: Geerlings, Jacks.

Margaret Duross
Giant formal decorative (unclassified); orange garden variety; tall at 1.5m (5ft) in height; originated in 1954. Available USA: Swan Island.

Margaret Ellen
Medium cactus (unclassified); pink and white cut flower and garden variety, 1.2m (4ft) high plant; originated by Swan Island, USA, in 2000; named for Margaret Gitts. Available USA: Swan Island.

Margaret Haggo
Waterlily (ADS); light blends yellow and orange variety; originated by R. Ingham, New Zealand, in 2000.

Margaret Jean
Giant formal decorative (ADS); lavender exhibition variety; 1.2m (4ft) in height; by George Brookes, UK, in 1977.

Marie Schnugg
Star (miscellaneous) (NDS), orchid (ADS); red garden variety; 1.1m (3.5ft); originated by McNulty, USA, in 1973. Awarded the Lynn B. Dudley medal 1972 (ADS). Available UK: National, Station House; USA: Arrowhead, Clacks, Connell's, Creekside, Dan's Dahlias, Frey's.

Marika
Medium lacinated (unclassified); white and lavender, garden variety; 1.2m (4ft) high bush; introduced South Africa in 1997. Available USA: Dan's Dahlias.

Marilyn Anne
Small formal decorative (ADS); bicolour purple and white; originated by Parkes, USA, in 1991.

Mariner's Light
Small semi-cactus (NDS and ADS); yellow exhibition and garden variety; 1.1m (3.5ft) high bush; raised by John Sharp, UK, in 1970. Award Garden Merit Wisley (NDS). Available UK: National.

Mariposa
Collerette (NDS); pink and pink collar, exhibition and garden variety; 0.9m (3ft) high plant; introduced by Topswoort, Holland, in 1958. Available UK: Abacus, National; elsewhere: Geerlings.

Mark Damp
Large semi-cactus (NDS); bronze orange blends; 1.2m (4ft) high; raised by Phil Damp, UK. Available UK: National.

Mark Hardwick
Giant decorative (NDS), or giant informal decorative (ADS); yellow exhibition variety; 0.9m (3ft) high plant; raised by M. Hardwick, UK, in 1985. Available UK: Cruikshank, Halls, National, Oscroft, P. & L.; USA: Elkhorn, Mingus; elsewhere: Geerlings, Graines.

Mark Lockwood
Pompon (NDS and ADS); lavender exhibition, garden and cut flower variety; 1.2m (4ft) high plant; raised by A. Lockwood, UK, in 1975. Available UK: Abacus, National, Tivey; USA: Clacks, Dahlia Dandies, Dan's Dahlias, SB Gardens.

Mark's Memory
Miniature formal decorative (ADS); red variety; originated by Riordan, USA, in 2001.

Marlene Joy
Fimbriated medium semi-cactus (NDS); small, lacinated; 1.2m (4ft) high; white and pink blends garden and cut flower variety; introduced by Steenfort, USA, in 1989. Available UK: Abacus, Cruikshank, Halls, Jones, National, P. & L., Scotts, Station House; USA: Clacks, Connell's, Dahlia Dandies, Dan's Dahlias, Elkhorn, Sea-Tac, Swan Island; elsewhere: Dgid.

Mar-Lo Aunt Margie
Small, informal decorative (ADS); light blends lavender and white variety; originated by H. Morgan, USA, in 1995.

MARGARET ANN

MARGARET JEAN

MARK HARDWICK

MARLENE JOY

MARIE SCHNUGG

Marmalade
Small, informal decorative
(ADS); orange exhibition and
cut flower variety, on a bush
1.4m (4.5ft) high; originated by
N. Gitts, USA, in 1993.
Available USA: Swan Island.

Marshmallow Sky
Collarette (unclassified); white,
splashed pink, with white
splashed pink collar garden
variety; 1.4m (4.5ft) high plant;
introduced USA in 1987.
Available USA: Clacks,
Connell's, Dan's Dahlias.

Marta
Giant, informal decorative
(ADS); red exhibition variety;
originated by Simon, USA, in
1994. Available USA:
Hamilton; Canada: Ferncliff.

Martha Lee
Small, informal decorative
(ADS); light blends lavender and
yellow; originated by Masurat,
USA, in 1995. Awarded the
Derrill Hart medal (ADS).

Martin's Neat
Small cactus (ADS); light blends
yellow and bronze variety, by T.
Martin, New Zealand, in 1998.
Available elsewhere: Jacks.

Martin's Red
Pompon (NDS); orange red
blends, 1.1m (3.5ft) high bush;
introduced by T. Martin, New
Zealand, in 2000. Available
UK: Halls, National, P. & L.

Martin's Yellow
Pompon (NDS and ADS);
yellow exhibition and garden
variety; introduced by T. Martin,
New Zealand, in 1980.
Available UK: Abacus,
Cruikshank, Halls, National, P.
& L.; USA: Clacks.

Marvellous Mans
Medium lacinated cactus
(unclassified); white and
lavender blended exhibition
variety; 1.5m (5ft) high bush;

originated by Mellinger, USA,
in 2001. Available USA:
Connell's.

Marvellous Mel
Medium lacinated (ADS); light
blends pink and white garden
variety on a 1.4m (4ft) high
bush; originated by Mellinger,
USA, in 1999. Available USA:
Connell's.

Marvellous Sal
Medium formal decorative
(unclassified); pink garden
variety on a 1.2m (4ft) high
bush; originated by Mellinger,
USA. Available elsewhere: Jacks.

Mary
Small formal decorative (ADS);
light blends lavender and white
garden and exhibition variety,
0.9m (3ft) high; introduced by
Rice, Australia, in 1984.
Available USA: Arrowhead,
Clacks, Connell's, Dan's
Dahlias, Elkhorn, SB Gardens.

Mary Eveline
Collerette (NDS and ADS);
purple red collar (NDS), or
dark red, white collar (ADS);
exhibition; garden and cut
flower variety; 1.1m (3.5ft)
high plant; introduced by W.
Chamberlain, New Zealand, in
1987. Available UK: Aylett's,
Halls; USA: Alpen, Clacks,
Swan Island.

Mary Hammett
Miniature decorative (NDS);
white exhibition, garden and
cut flower variety; introduced
by Keith Hammett, New
Zealand, in 1990. Available
UK: Abacus; USA: Alpen,
Clacks, Creekside, Elkhorn, SB
Gardens, Sea-Tac.

Mary Jennie
Miniature semi-cactus (ADS);
cut flower and floral art
variety; 0.6m (2.5ft) in height;
originated USA in 1988.
Available USA: Connell's.

Mary Jo
Miniature semi-cactus (ADS);
pink, early prolific exhibition
and cut flower variety; 0.6m
(2.5ft) in height; originated by
Ranfz, USA, in 1968. Awarded
the Stanley Johnson medal
(ADS). Available USA: Alpen,
Clacks, Dahlia Dandies, Dan's
Dahlias, SB Gardens, Sea-Tac,
Swan Island; Canada: Ferncliff.

Mary Magson
Medium semi-cactus or small
semi-cactus (NDS); yellow
exhibition variety; 1.1m (3.5ft)
high plant; raised by Bill Mark,
UK, in 1998. Available UK:
National, P. & L., Spencer.

Mary Morris
Small lacinated (unclassified);
yellow, early blooming cut
flower variety on a 1.2m (4ft)
high bush; originated in USA in
1984. Available USA:
Connell's.

Mary Munns
Pompon (unclassified);
lavender, cut flower variety;
0.9m (3ft) high bush;
originated USA in 1928.
Available USA: Dan's Dahlias,
Swan Island.

Mary Partridge
Waterlily (NDS and ADS); red
(NDS); dark red (ADS);
exhibition, garden and cut
flower variety; 0.9m (3ft) high
plant; raised by Cor Geerlings,
Holland, in 1991. Available
UK: National, Oscroft, P. & L.;
Canada: Ferncliff.

Mary Pitt
Miniature decorative (NDS),
miniature formal decorative
(ADS); white exhibition,
garden and cut flower; 1.1m
(3.5ft) high plant; raised by
Ernie Pitt, UK, 1991. Available
UK: National.

MARTIN'S YELLOW

MARY EVELINE

MARY PARTRIDGE

MARY PITT

MARY MAGSON

Mary Richards
Small decorative (unclassified); white tipped pink, garden variety, 1.2m (4ft) in height; raised by A. Drewer, UK, in 1952. Award Merit Wisley 1952 (NDS).

Mascot Maya (synonymous to **Charlie Two**)
Medium decorative (NDS); yellow exhibition variety, 1.2m (4ft) high plant; raised by S. Mellen, UK, in 1994. Available UK: JRG, P. & L., Spencer, Station House; USA: Mingus.

Master David
Miniature ball (ADS); flame exhibition variety; originated by E. Comstock, USA, in 1969. Awarded the Lynn B. Dudley medal in 1968, and the Derrill Hart medal (ADS). Available USA: Creekside, Dan's Dahlias.

Masurao
Giant formal decorative (ADS); red exhibition variety; Konishi, Japan, in 1994. Available USA: Clacks, Mingus; elsewhere: Jacks.

Match
Small semi-cactus (NDS and ADS); outstanding bicoloured white and purple, prolifically blooming garden variety, much used in the UK for floral art purposes; raised by A. Hindry, South Africa, in 1965. Available UK: National, Station House, Tivey; USA: Dan's Dahlias, Frey's, SB Gardens; elsewhere: Geerlings, Graines.

Matchmaker
Small, informal decorative (unclassified); white-edged lavender cut flower variety; 1.2m (4ft) high bush; originated USA in 1986. Available USA: Connell's, Dan's Dahlias, Elkhorn, Frey's, Sea-Tac, Swan Island.

Matilda Huston
Small semi-cactus (ADS); red exhibition and cut flower

variety; height 0.6m (2.5ft); originated by Earl Huston, Canada, in 1978. Available USA: Dan's Dahlias, Frey's, Swan Island; Canada: Ferncliff; elsewhere: Engelhardt.

Matthew Juul
Miniature single (ADS); dark blends orange and dark red variety; originated by Juul, USA, in 1996. Awarded the Lynn B. Dudley 1995 and Derrill Hart medals (ADS). Available USA: Clacks, Dan's Dahlias.

Mauve Climax
Large, formal decorative (ADS); pink exhibition variety on a 1.2m (4ft) high bush; originated by L. Connell, USA, in 1979. Awarded the Lynn B. Dudley medal 1978 (ADS). Available USA: Connell's, Dan's Dahlias, Elkhorn.

Mazama
Waterlily (unclassified); dark pink garden variety, 15cm (6in) blooms on good stems on a 1.5m (5ft) high bush. Available USA: Connell's.

Meiro
Small decorative (NDS); lavender, garden variety; 1.1m (3.5ft) high; introduced by Ogue, UK, in 1961. Available UK: National, Tivey.

Melanie Jane
Medium semi-cactus (NDS); lavender and white blends, garden and cut flower variety; 1.1m (3.5ft) high plant; introduced by W. Trotter, Australia. Available UK: National.

Melissa M
Miniature formal decorative (unclassified); pink cut flower garden variety; 1.4m (4.5ft) high bush; originated USA in 1992. Available USA: Swan Island.

Melqua Heat
Waterlily (ADS); flame; variety originated by Cruger, USA, in

1996. Available USA: Clacks, Mingus.

Meredith's Marion Smith
Small, decorative (NDS); pink and white blends; exhibition and garden variety; 1.2m (4ft) high plant; raised by J. Meredith, UK, in 1995. Available UK: Cruikshank, National.

Mi Wong
Pompon (NDS and ADS); pink and white blends (NDS), light blends lavender and white (ADS); exhibition variety; 1.2m (4ft) high; raised by E. Hunt, UK, in 1976. Available UK: Cruikshank, Halls, National, P. & L., Porter, Station House; USA: Alpen, Clacks, Creekside.

Michel K
Small semi-cactus (unclassified); lavender cut flower variety on a 1.2m (4ft) high bush; introduced USA in 1991. Available USA: Connell's.

Michele Mignot
Medium informal decorative (unclassified); pink exhibition and garden variety; height 1.5m (5ft); originated USA in 1958. Available USA: Swan Island.

Mickey
Collerette (unclassified); dark red with yellow collar, cut flower and exhibition variety on a 1.4m (4.5ft) high bush; originated USA in 1989. Available USA: Swan Island.

Mick's Peppermint
Medium semi-cactus (NDS), giant semi-cactus (ADS); white and red variegated, garden variety; 1.2m (4ft) high bush; originated by M. Senior, USA, in 1992. Available UK: Dgid, National, P. & L.; USA: Clacks; elsewhere: Geerlings, Graines, Wirth.

MASCOT MAYA

MATCH

MEREDITH'S MARION SMITH

MASURAO

MI WONG

Midnight
Pompon (ADS); purple cut
flower and floral art variety, on
a 1.1m (3.5ft) high bush;
originated by Harry Stredwick,
UK, in 1945. Available USA:
Swan Island.

Midnight Dancer
Small formal decorative (ADS);
purple exhibition variety on a
1.1m (3.5ft) high bush;
originated by N. Gitts, USA, in
1992. Available USA: Dan's
Dahlias, Swan Island.

Midnight Moon
Small formal decorative (ADS);
light blends, white and
lavender garden and exhibition
variety; 1.2m (4ft) high bush;
originated by N. Gitts, USA, in
1998. Available USA: Swan
Island; elsewhere: Jacks.

Minerva Bryan
Novelty double centre (ADS);
lavender garden variety;
originated by L. Havens, USA,
in 2000.

Minerva Eva
Single (ADS); purple garden
variety; originated by L.
Havens, USA, in 1998.

Minerva Maiden
Small cactus (ADS); light
blends, pink and yellow;
originated by L. Havens, USA,
in 2001.

Minerva Snowboy
Small semi-cactus (ADS); white
exhibition variety; originated
by L. Havens, USA, in 1997.
Awarded the Lynn B. Dudley
1996 and the Derrill Hart
medals. Available USA: Sea-
Tac.

Mingus Ashley
Ball (ADS); purple exhibition
variety; originated by Mingus,
USA, in 2001. Awarded the
Derrill Hart medal. Available
USA: Arrowhead, Mingus.

Mingus Erica
Star (ADS); orange, garden
variety; height 1.2m (4ft);

originated by Mingus, USA, in
1999. Available USA: Clacks,
Mingus.

Mingus Frank
Small straight cactus (ADS);
exhibition variety; originated
by Mingus, USA, in 2001.
Awarded the Derrill Hart
medal (ADS).

Mingus Kathrine
Medium cactus (ADS);
lavender, exhibition variety; tall
grower, 1.6m (5.5ft), early to
mid-season (USA); originated
by Mingus in 2000. Available
USA: Arrowhead, Clacks,
Dahlia Dandies, Mingus;
Canada: Ferncliff.

Mingus Nicole
Large informal decorative
(ADS); light blends pink and
yellow, exhibition variety; 1.4m
(4.5ft) in height; originated by
Mingus, USA, in 2000.
Awarded the Derrill Hart
medal. Available USA:
Arrowhead, Mingus.

Mingus Paula
Small, lacinated (ADS); light
blends, pink and yellow
exhibition variety; tall, 1.5m
(5ft) in height; originated by
Mingus, USA, in 2000. Available
USA: Dahlia Dandies, Elkhorn,
Mingus.

Mingus Steven
Large, informal decorative
(ADS); purple exhibition
variety; height 1.5m (5ft);
originated by Mingus, USA, in
1998. Awarded the Derrill Hart
medal (ADS); mid-season (USA).
Available USA: Clacks, Dahlia
Dandies, Mingus; Canada:
Ferncliff.

Mingus Tracy Lynn
Medium semi-cactus (ADS);
lavender exhibition variety on
a 1.2m (4ft) high bush;
originated by Mingus, USA, in
1997. Available USA: Mingus.

Mingus Wesley
Large, informal decorative
(ADS); light blends, lavender

and white exhibition variety;
height 1.5m (5ft); originated by
Mingus, USA, in 1997; mid-
season (USA). Available USA:
Capistrano, Clacks, Dahlia
Dandies, Dan's Dahlias,
Elkhorn, Mingus; Canada:
Ferncliff; elsewhere: Konishi.

Mingus Whitney
Giant informal decorative
(ADS); light blends, lavender
and white exhibition variety on
a 1.2m (4ft) high bush;
originated by Mingus, USA, in
1997. Available USA: Clacks,
Mingus.

Mini Red
Miniature semi-cactus (NDS),
miniature cactus (ADS); red
exhibition variety; 1.2m (4ft)
high; originated by W. Almand,
USA, in 1988. Available UK:
National; USA: Clacks.

Minley Carol
A pompon variety (NDS); good
all-rounder for exhibition,
garden and cut flower
purposes; this variety grows to
a height of 1.1m (3.5ft);
introduced by Bill Wilkins, UK,
in 1983. Sported 'Red Carol' in
1994. Available UK: National.

Minley Linda
Pompon (NDS); orange
exhibition, garden and cut
flower variety; 1.1m (3.5ft)
high bush; originated by Bill
Wilkinson, UK, in 1983.
Available UK: National,
Oscroft, Station House, Tivey;
elsewhere: Geerlings.

Minx (synonym **Willo's Violet**)
Pompon (NDS and ADS);
purple blends, exhibition
variety; height 1.1m (3.5ft);
raised by Ray Adley, UK, in
1997. Available UK: National,
Pratt; Canada: Ferncliff.

Miss America
Giant incurving cactus (ADS);
light blends, yellow and pink
variety; originated by Berzau,
USA, in 1967. Awarded the
Lynn B. Dudley medal, 1966
(ADS).

MINGUS TRACY LYNN

MINGUS WESLEY

MINGUS WHITNEY

MINLEY CAROL

Miss Delilah
Medium formal decorative (unclassified); pink exhibition and cut flower variety; prolific bush; 1.2m (4ft) high; introduced by Swan Island, USA, in 2002. Available USA: Swan Island.

Miss Ellen
Miscellaneous star (unclassified); pink exhibition variety; some scent; raised by Kit Strange, UK, in 2000.

Miss McGee
Waterlily (ADS); white variety; originated by Eckhoff, USA, in 2001. Available USA: Sea-Tac.

Miss Midwest
Medium semi-cactus (ADS); dark pink, exhibition variety; originated by Moore, USA, in 1972. Awarded the Lynn B. Dudley medal, 1971 (ADS).

Miss Rose Fletcher
Small semi-cactus (ADS); pink cut flower and floral art variety on a 1.2m (4ft) high bush; introduced Australia in 1948. Available USA: Connell's, Dan's Dahlias, Elkhorn, Frey's, Swan Island.

Miss Vary
Medium semi-cactus (ADS); variegated white and purple; originated by W. Holland, Canada, in 1999.

Misthill Beauty
Small cactus (NDS); pink and yellow blends, exhibition variety; 1.1m (3.5ft) in height; raised by F. Currie, UK, in 1983. Available UK: JRG, National, Station House.

Misthill Contessa
Small formal decorative (ADS); orange exhibition and garden variety; 0.9m (3ft) high plant; raised by F. Currie, UK, in 1996. Available USA: Creekside; elsewhere: Jacks.

Misthill Delight
Miniature decorative (NDS); white exhibition, garden and cut flower variety; 1.2m (4ft) in height; raised by F. Currie UK in 1974. Award Merit 1979 Wisley (NDS). Available UK: National, P. & L., Tivey; elsewhere: Wirth.

Mistral
Medium lacinated (ADS); dark blends, purple and white garden variety; height 1.1m (3.5ft); originated by R. Surber, USA, in 1996. Available USA: Dahlia Dandies, Dan's Dahlias.

Mme. Stappers
Dwarf bedder (unclassified); red garden variety much used at Anglesey Abbey, UK.

Mo Bay's Honey
Miniature ball (ADS); bronze variety; originated by H & B. Brown, USA, in 1995. Awarded the Derrill Hart medal (ADS).

Molly Mooney
Small semi-cactus (unclassified); yellow garden variety; raised by Mooney, Canada, in 1997.

Mom's Special
Large informal decorative (unclassified); variegated light blends and dark lavender; 1.2m (4ft) high bush; originated USA in 1991. Available USA: Connell's, Frey's.

Mona Lisa
Large semi-cactus (unclassified); lavender and white exhibition variety; tall 1.5m (5ft) high bush; originated USA in 1994. Available USA: Connell's, Dan's Dahlias, Elkhorn.

Monk Marc
Small cactus (NDS), small semi-cactus (ADS); pink exhibition, garden and cut flower variety, 1.2m high; raised by B. Fowler, UK, in 1972. Available UK: Butterfield, JRG, National.

Monkstown Diane
Small cactus (NDS); pink blends exhibition, garden and cut flower variety; 1.2m (4ft) in height; raised by B. Fowler, UK, in 1994. Available UK: National, P. & L.; USA: Elkhorn.

Moonfire
Single dwarf bedder (NDS), single (ADS); orange and bronze blends (NDS), and dark blends, bronze, yellow and red (ADS) with bronze foliage; an excellent garden variety; height 1.1m (3.5ft); introduced by Walter Jack, New Zealand, in 1998. Available UK: Abacus, Aylett's, Halls, National, Oscroft, Taylor, Tivey; Canada: Ferncliff.

Moonglow
Large semi-cactus (NDS), yellow garden variety; 1.2m (4ft) high plant; raised by Robens, USA, in 1945. Available UK: National; elsewhere: Dgid, Engelhardt.

Moonlight Sonata
Small, informal decorative (ADS); dark blends, yellow and orange; originated by Wyn, USA, in 2001. Available Canada: Ferncliff.

Moonstruck
Medium informal decorative (ADS); yellow cut flower variety on a 1.1m (3.5ft) high compact bush; originated by N. Gitts, UK, in 1996. Available USA.

Moor Place
A pompon (NDS and ADS); purple-bloomed exhibition variety, growing to a height of 1.1m (3.5ft); introduced by Alan Nennham, UK (named for a local golf course), in 1955. Available UK: Abacus, Clark, Cruikshank, Halls, JRG, National, Oscroft, P. & L., Porter, Roberts, Spencer, Station House, Taylor, Tivey; USA: Alpen, Clacks, Dan's Dahlias, Elkhorn, SB Gardens; elsewhere: Geerlings.

MISS ELLEN

MISTHILL CONTESSA

MONKSTOWN DIANE

MOOR PLACE

MISTRAL

Moray Susan
Waterlily (ADS); dark blends, dark red and yellow variety; 1.2m (4ft) bush; introduced by McLaughlin in 1995. Available USA: Alpen, Clacks, Connell's, Mingus, SB Gardens.

Morgenster
Medium, lacinated (ADS); white garden variety on a 0.9m (3ft) high bush; introduced by Cyril Higgo, South Africa, in 1996. Available USA: Connell's, Dan's Dahlias, Frey's.

Morley Lady
Small decorative (NDS); yellow exhibition, garden and cut flower variety; 1.2m (4ft) high; raised by Neville Weekes, UK, in 1983. Available UK: National.

Morley Lass
Small cactus (unclassified); yellow exhibition and garden variety; 1.2m (4ft) in height; raised by Neville Weekes, UK, in 1985.

Morning Star
Miniature, informal decorative (unclassified); white and lavender blends, early blooming, cut flower variety on a 1.2m (4ft) high bush; originated USA in 1995. Available USA: Clacks, Connell's.

Morning Sun
Medium formal decorative (ADS); bronze, garden variety; height 1.5m (4.5ft); originated by Haugh, USA, in 2000. Available Canada: Ferncliff.

Mr Brett
Medium semi-cactus (ADS); red garden variety on a 1.2m (4ft) high bush; originated by Bateman, USA, in 1976. Available USA: Connell's, Creekside.

Mr Jones
Collarette (ADS); red exhibition variety; originated by W. Morin, USA, in 1999.

Awarded the Lynn B. Dudley medal (ADS).

Mr Larry
Giant semi-cactus (ADS); flame garden variety on a 1.2m (4ft) high bush; originated by Clack, USA, in 1975.

Mr Ralph
Medium formal decorative (ADS); dark blends, bronze and orange exhibition variety; originated by Holicky, USA, in 1992. Available USA: Capistrano, Swan Island.

Mrs A. Woods
Medium formal decorative (ADS); lavender garden and exhibition variety; 1.4m (4.5ft) in height; raised by Douglas, Australia, in 1955.

Mrs Black
Pompon (unclassified); garden variety, on a 1.2m (4ft) high bush; originated USA in 1991. Available USA: Swan Island.

Mrs Bates
Medium incurving cactus (ADS); light blends, pink and yellow variety; originated by Bishop, USA, in 2001. Available USA: Arrowhead, Clacks.

Mrs McDonnell Quill
Large decorative (NDS); red and white bicolour; exhibition variety; 1.4m (4.5ft) high; introduced by Douglas, New Zealand. Available UK: Cruikshank, Halls, National; USA: Clacks; elsewhere: Konishi.

Mulloy's Moment
Small formal decorative (ADS); white exhibition variety; originated by Beekman, USA, in 1999. Awarded the Derrill Hart medal. Available USA: Arrowhead.

Mummy's Favourite
Small decorative (NDS); bronze and red blends; garden cut

flower variety; 1.1m (3.5ft) high; raised by P. Tivey, UK, in 1985. Available UK: National.

Muriel
Collerette (unclassified); orange tipped yellow, with yellow collar; garden variety, on a 1.2m (4ft) bush; introduced Australia. Available USA: Connell's.

Murray Petite
Small semi-cactus (ADS); pink cut flower variety; 1.2m (4ft) in height; introduced by Selleck, Australia, in 1990. Available USA: Arrowhead, Elkhorn; Canada: Ferncliff.

My Beverly
Small lacinated (ADS); dark pink and yellow exhibition variety; Simmons, USA, in 1999. Available USA: Arrowhead, Creekside, Elkhorn, Mingus.

My Joy
Collerette (unclassified); pink with yellow collar, cut flower variety on a 1.4m (4.5ft) high bush; originated USA in 1991. Available USA: Frey's, Swan Island.

My Lynda
Medium cactus (ADS); yellow variety; originated by Szala, USA, in 2001.

My Wife
Medium lacinated (ADS); red exhibition variety; originated by Mingus, USA, in 1996. Awarded the Derrill Hart medal (ADS). Available USA: Alpen, Arrowhead, Capistrano, Dahlia Dandies, Dan's Dahlias, Elkhorn, Mingus.

Myrtle's Lace
Medium lacinated (ADS); light blends, pink and yellow variety; originated by Bloomfield, USA, in 2001. Available USA: Clacks.

MORAY SUSAN

MORLEY LASS

MR RALPH

MORGENSTER

MY BEVERLY

Mystique
Small formal decorative (unclassified); light orange cut flower and exhibition variety; 1.5m (5ft) tall; originated USA in 1994. Available USA: Dan's Dahlias, Swan Island.

N

Nagel's Solidlite
Medium incurving cactus (ADS); light pink blends, pink and yellow exhibition variety; introduced by Nagels, Belgium, in 1951. Available USA: Clacks, Connell's.

Nancy Ann
Miniature ball (ADS); bronze variety; originated by Rumple, USA, in 1998. Available USA: Elkhorn.

Nancy M
Miniature formal decorative (ADS); bicolour lavender and white garden variety; height 1.1m (3.5ft); originated by Moore, USA, in 1998. Available Canada: Ferncliff; elsewhere: Konishi.

Nancy Margaret
Medium semi-cactus (NDS); white exhibition and garden variety; 1.2m (4ft) high; raised by Neville Weekes, UK, in 1900. Available UK: Cruikshank, JRG.

Nankyoku
Giant formal decorative (ADS); white exhibition variety; introduced by Konishi, Japan, in 1984. Available USA: Dan's Dahlias.

Nantenan
Large semi-cactus (unclassified); yellow, one-time top exhibition variety, 1.4m (4.5ft) high, strong-stemmed plant; raised by dahlia Bruidegom, Holland, in 1961. Award Merit Wisley, 1962 (NDS).

Narcoma Princess
Waterlily (ADS); light blends orange and yellow; variety introduced Australia in 1988.

Nargold
Medium fimbriated semi-cactus (NDS), medium lacinated (ADS); orange (NDS), flame (ADS); variety growing to a height of 1.2m (4ft) with strong, long stems and striking blooms; excellent for garden or exhibition purposes; this variety was introduced by Cyril Higgo, South Africa, in 1994. Winner of the Lynn B. Dudley medal 1993 (ADS). Available UK: Aylett's, National; USA: Alpen, Arrowhead, Dahlia Dandies, Dan's Dahlias, Elkhorn, SB Gardens; elsewhere: Geerlings, Graines.

Narnia
Medium formal decorative (unclassified); yellow and orange blends, very tall exhibition variety; 1.8m (6ft) tall bush; originated by L. Connell, USA, in 1992. Available USA: Dan's Dahlias, Elkhorn.

Natalie
Medium incurving cactus (ADS); purple variety, originated by R. & J. Miller, USA, in 1998. Available USA: Clacks.

Nationwide
Small, decorative (NDS); orange yellow blended garden and cut flower variety; 1.3m (4.5ft) high plant; originated by H. Stanners, UK, in 1980.

Award Merit 1986 Wisley and Garden Merit Wisley (NDS) 1994. Available UK: Abacus, National, Oscroft, Tivey.

Neal Gilson
Medium decorative (NDS); bronze exhibition and garden variety; 1.4m (4ft) in height; raised by J. Kidd, UK, in 1985. Available UK: National, Oscroft, P. & L.; elsewhere: Geerlings.

Needles
Collerette (unclassified); white striped red, with similar collar; exhibition variety; height 1.2m (4ft); originated USA in 1956. Available USA: Swan Island.

Nellie Birch
Miniature ball (unclassified); dark red garden plant; 1.1m (3.5ft) in height; unknown raiser.

Nellie Geerlings
Dwarf bedder (single) (NDS); red garden variety; 0.6m (2ft) high; introduced by Cor Geerlings in 1955. Available UK: National; elsewhere: Geerlings, Wirth.

Nenekazi
Fimbriated medium semi-cactus (NDS), small, lacinated (ADS); bronze pink blends (NDS), light blends red and pink (ADS); exhibition and garden variety; 1.2m (4ft) high bush; introduced by Cyril Higgo, South Africa, in 1997. Awarded the Lynn B. Dudley medal, 1996 (ADS). Available UK: Cruikshank, Halls, National, Oscroft, Scotts, Spencer, Station House; USA: Clacks, Connell's, Dahlia Dandies, Elkhorn, SB Gardens; elsewhere: Engelhardt.

NARGOLD

NENEKAZI

NELLIE GEERLINGS

Neon City
Ball (ADS); lavender, exhibition, garden and cut flower variety; 1.2m (4ft) high bush; introduced by Keith Hammett, New Zealand, in 1992. Available USA: Clacks.

Neon Splendor
Medium informal decorative (ADS); flame, garden variety on a 1.2m (4ft) high bush; originated by Swan Island, USA, in 1987. Available USA: Swan Island.

Nepos
Small waterlily (NDS), waterlily (ADS); white and lavender blends, exhibition variety; 0.9m (3ft) high plant, originated by Lombaert, Belgium, in 1958. Available UK: Butterfield, Cruikshank, JRG, National, P. & L., Pratt, Station House; USA: Dahlia Dandies, Dan's Dahlias.

Netterbob
Small, formal decorative (unclassified); pink and yellow blended, cut flower variety, on a 1.2m (4ft) high plant; originated USA in 2001. Available USA: Swan Island.

Nettie
Miniature ball (NDS and ADS); yellow exhibition variety, height 0.9m (3ft); originated by Terry Clarke, UK, in 1966. Sported 'White Nettie' in 1974. Available UK: National; USA: Clacks, Dan's Dahlias, Elkhorn, SB Gardens, Swan Island; Canada: Ferncliff.

Neveric
Large semi-cactus (unclassified); orange yellow blended, exhibition variety; 1.2m (4ft) high plant; raised by Neville Weekes, UK, in 1976. Award Merit 1985 Wisley (NDS).

Newby
Miniature decorative (unclassified); pink cut flower variety; height 1.2m (4ft); raised by Joe Barwise, UK, in 1951. Award Merit Wisley 1954 (NDS); several sports 'Rose Newby'.

Newchurch
Miniature decorative (unclassified); salmon pink cut flower (floral art) variety; 0.9m (3ft) high plant; raised by Joe Barwise, UK, in 1959.

Niagra Baby
Miniature ball (ADS); white; originated by J. Bates, Canada, in 2000.

Nicaro
Small cactus (unclassified); yellow splashed red, exhibition variety on a 1.4m (4.5ft) high bush; originated USA in 1965. Available USA: Swan Island.

Nicola Higgo
Medium lacinated (ADS); light blends white and lavender exhibition variety; introduced by Cyril Higgo, South Africa, in 1988. Available USA: Clacks, Dan's Dahlias, Elkhorn, SB Gardens, Sea-Tac; Canada: Ferncliff.

Nicola Jane
Pompon (NDS and ADS); pink and white blends (NDS), pink (ADS); exhibition and garden variety; 1.1m (3.5ft) in height; originated by Ralph Cook, UK, in 1999. Award Garden Merit, Wisley (NDS). Available UK: Halls, P. & L., Spencer; USA: Clacks.

Nicola Rae
Small, informal decorative (unclassified); pink garden and cut flower variety; long stems on a 1.2m (4ft) high bush; originated by Connell.

Nick's Pick
Small, informal decorative (unclassified); yellow cut flower variety on a 1.2m (4.5ft) high bush; originated USA in 1997. Available USA: Swan Island.

Nicky K
Small lacinated cactus (unclassified); bright red cut flower and exhibition variety; 1.4m (4.5ft) in height; originated USA in 1949. Available USA: Dahlia Dandies, Elkhorn, Swan Island; Canada: Ferncliff.

Nicole C
Medium cactus (ADS); orange variety; originated by Canning, USA, in 1989. Available USA: Dahlia Dandies, SB Gardens; Canada: Ferncliff.

Nicolette
Small cactus (ADS); yellow exhibition variety; strong grower on a 1.5m (5ft) high bush; originated by L. Connell, USA, in 2001. Available USA: Arrowhead, Connell's.

Night Editor
Giant decorative (NDS); purple exhibition variety; 1.2m (4ft) in height; introduced by Hulin, USA, in 1952. Award Merit Wisley 1956 (NDS). Available UK: National; USA: Connell's; elsewhere: Engelhardt.

Night Life
Small cactus (ADS); red garden variety; introduced by Kapler, Australia, in 1983. Available USA: Alpen, Arrowhead, Clacks, Dahlia Dandies, Dan's Dahlias, Elkhorn, SB Gardens.

Nijinkski
Small ball (NDS), ball (ADS); purple exhibition variety; 1.2m (4ft) in height; raised by Geoff Flood, UK, in 1970. Available UK: National, P. & L.; USA: Dahlia Dandies, Dan's Dahlias, Elkhorn, Swan Island; Canada: Ferncliff.

NEPOS

NICOLA JANE

NEON CITY

NICOLA HIGGO

NIGHT EDITOR

Nikki Miner
Small formal decorative (ADS);
bronze exhibition variety;
originated by R. Miner, USA,
in 1999. Available USA:
Arrowhead.

Nina Chester
Small decorative (NDS); white
exhibition and garden variety;
0.9m (3ft) high plant;
originated by G. J. Chester,
UK, in 1974. Award Merit
1977 Wisley (NDS). Available
UK: Abacus, National, P. & L.,
Station House, Taylor, Tivey.

Nita
Medium cactus (ADS);
variegated lavender red
exhibited; originated by Hale,
USA, in 1959. Awarded the
Derrill Hart medal (ADS).
Available USA: Alpen,
Arrowhead, Capistrano, Clacks,
Creekside, Dahlia Dandies,
Elkhorn, SB Gardens; Canada:
Ferncliff.

Noel
Small lacinated (ADS); bicolour
red and white variety;
originated by Bloomfield, USA,
in 2001. Available USA:
Clacks.

Nonette
Small waterlily (NDS),
waterlily (ADS); yellow and red
blends (NDS), orange and red
(ADS); 1.1m (3.5ft) high;
introduced by Ballego,
Holland, in 1956. Available
UK: Abacus, National; USA:
Arrowhead; elsewhere:
Englehardt, Graines.

Noreen
Pompon (NDS and ADS); pink
and purple blends (NDS), or
dark blends dark pink/purple
(ADS); exhibition, garden and
cut flower; height 0.9m (3ft);
introduced by J. Baggs,
Australia, in 1962. Award
Merit Wisley 1966 (NDS).
Available UK: Clark,
Cruikshank, Halls, National,
Oscroft, P. & L., Station
House; USA: Clacks, SB
Gardens, Sea-Tac.

Normandy Adam
Small informal decorative
(ADS); dark red variety;
originated by Schwinck, USA,
in 1999.

Normandy Anna
Small formal decorative (ADS);
dark blends pink and yellow;
variety originated by Schwinck,
USA, in 2002.

Normandy C W
Small semi-cactus (ADS); dark
blends, red and yellow; variety
originated by Schwinck, USA,
in 2000.

Normandy Copper Glow
Medium cactus (ADS); orange
variety; originated by
Schwinck, USA, in 2000.

Normandy Dee Gee
Small formal decorative (ADS);
light blends pink and yellow,
exhibition variety; originated by
Schwinck, USA, in 2001.
Awarded the Derrill Hart medal
(ADS). Available USA: Clacks.

Normandy James
Large, informal decorative
(ADS); red exhibition variety;
originated by Schwinck, USA,
in 1998. Available USA: SB
Gardens.

Normandy Jes-Lee
Waterlily (ADS); orange
variety; originated by
Schwinck, USA, in 2002.

Normandy Lynne
Large, incurved cactus (ADS);
lavender variety; originated by
Schwinck, USA, in 1998.

Normandy Mikey
Star (ADS); bronze variety,
originated by Schwinck, USA,
in 2002.

Normandy Promise
Small, semi-cactus (ADS); pink
exhibition variety; originated
by Schwinck, USA, in 1996.
Awarded the Derrill Hart
medal (ADS). Available USA:
Clacks, Mingus.

Normandy Splendor
Medium lacinated (ADS);
flame, exhibition variety;
originated by Schwinck, USA,
in 1996. Available USA: Sea-
Tac.

Northlake Pride
Large cactus (ADS); red
exhibition variety; height 1.2m
(4ft); originated by Surber,
USA, in 1999. Available USA:
Clacks, Dan's Dahlias, Mingus,
SB Gardens; Canada: Ferncliff.

Northland Primrose
Small cactus (ADS); yellow,
early blooming garden variety
on a 1.2m (4ft) high plant;
introduced by Surber, USA, in
1993. Available USA: Alpen,
Connell's.

Northwest Cosmos
Single (ADS); dark blends,
lavender and purple exhibition
variety; height 1.5m (5ft);
originated by Ellison, USA, in
2001. Awarded the Evie
Gullickson medal (ADS).
Available USA: Clacks, Dan's
Dahlias.

Northwest Star Juliet
Orchid (ADS); light blends,
white and purple variety;
originated by Ellison, USA, in
1998.

Nova Sunset
Small semi-cactus (ADS);
variegated yellow and red
variety; originated by G.
Graham, USA, in 1996.

Nunton Harvest
Small decorative (NDS); orange
blends exhibition variety; a tall
plant, 1.4m (4.5ft) high; raised
by D. Clark, UK, in 1964.
Available UK: Cruikshank,
National, Oscroft, P. & L.,
Pratt, Station House.

Nutley Sunrise
Medium incurved cactus
(ADS); orange garden variety
on a 0.9m (3ft) high bush;
originated by Frey's, USA, in
1957. Available USA: Elkhorn,
Swan Island; Canada: Ferncliff.

NIKKI MINER

NORMANDY SPLENDOR

O

Obsession
Small cactus (unclassified); red
exhibition and cut flower
variety on a 1.2m (4ft) high
bush; originated USA in 1998.
Available USA: Swan Island.

O'Condah
Waterlily (ADS); purple;
originated USA in 1995.
Available USA: Dan's Dahlias.

Odyssey
Miniature ball (ADS); lavender
and white blended exhibition
and cut flower variety; height
1.2m (4ft); originated by K.
Williams, Canada, in 2001.
Available Canada: Ferncliff.

Old Boy
Small ball (NDS); purple
exhibition variety; 1.1m (4ft)
in height; raised by A.T. Hayes,
UK. Available UK: National.

Olson's Folly
Small formal decorative (ADS);
bicolour orange and white
exhibition variety; height 1.5m
(4.5ft); originated USA in
2000. Available USA:
Arrowhead, Clacks, Dan's
Dahlias.

Omnibus
Giant informal decorative
(unclassified); lavender and
purple exhibition variety; 1.2m
(4ft); originated USA.

Omo
Single Lilliput (NDS); white
garden variety, by an unknown
raiser in the UK in 1976;
excellent also for patio pot use,
growing to a height of 45cm
(18in). Award Garden Merit
Wisley (NDS). Available UK:
Abacus, Aylett's, Butterfield,
National, Station House.

Onabrook Mary-Wes
Medium informal decorative
(ADS); white exhibition variety,
height 1.5m (5ft); originated by
D. Jones, Canada, in 2001.
Available Canada: Ferncliff.

Onabrook Reflections
Medium formal decorative
(ADS); light blends pink and
yellow variety; originated by
D. Jones, Canada, in 2000.

Onabrook Rory
Medium formal decorative
(ADS); red variety; originated
by D. Jones, Canada, in 2000.

Opal
Small ball (NDS); pink and
white blends, exhibition
variety; 1.1m (3.5ft) in height;
raised by Alleyn, Australia, in
1961. Available UK: National,
P. & L.

Optic Illusion
Small formal decorative
(unclassified); purple with
white petaloids, exhibition
variety, growing on a 1.4m
(4.5ft) high bush; originated
USA in 1992. Available USA:
Dan's Dahlias, Frey's, SB
Gardens, Swan Island;
elsewhere: Graines.

Orange Cushion
Medium informal decorative
(ADS); orange variety;
introduced in Holland in 1967.
Available USA: Clacks, Frey's.

Orange Hamilton Lillian
Small formal decorative (ADS);
orange sport of Hamilton
Lillian, exhibition variety; 1.4m
(4.5ft) high; originated USA in
2000.

Orange Jewel
Small formal decorative
(unclassified); orange cut flower
variety; 1.2m (4ft) in height;

originated by L. Connell, USA,
in 1975. Available USA:
Connell's.

Orange Julius
Medium formal decorative
(ADS); dark blends,
yellow/orange variety;
originated by Swan Island,
USA, in 1988. Available USA:
Frey's, Hamilton.

Orange Keith's Choice
Medium decorative (NDS),
medium formal decorative
(ADS); orange exhibition
variety; 1.1m (3.5ft) high;
raised by M. Hall, in
1996. Available UK: Halls,
National, P. & L.; USA: Sea-
Tac; elsewhere: Jacks.

Orange Mullet
Dwarf bedder (miniature
decorative) (NDS); orange and
yellow blends; garden variety,
0.6m (2ft) in height; raised in
the UK in 1992. Award Garden
Merit Wisley (NDS). Available
UK: National.

Orange Spice
Small lacinated (ADS); orange
variety; originated by Larkin &
Zydner, USA, in 2001.

Orange Sunset
Ball (ADS); orange exhibition
variety; originated by W.
Almand, USA, in 1997.
Awarded the Derrill Hart
medal (ADS). Available USA:
Clacks.

Orchid Lace
Small incurved cactus (ADS);
light blended white and
lavender cut flower variety on
a tall, vigorous, 1.5m (5ft)
high bush; originated by
Lundgren, USA, in 1961.
Available USA: Capistrano,
Dahlia Dandies, Elkhorn,
Frey's, Sea-Tac, Swan Island.

OMO

ORANGE CUSHION

Oregon Reign
Large informal decorative (unclassified); lavender exhibition variety; sturdy 1.4m (4.5ft) high bush; originated USA in 2000. Available USA: Swan Island.

Orel
Collerette (NDS); purple blends with white collar; exhibition, garden and cut flower; 1.1m (3.5ft) in height; introduced in 1993. Available UK: Abacus, National, Oscroft.

Oreti Candy
Stellar (ADS); white with pink blends, garden and cut flower variety; height 1.2m (4ft); introduced by Walter Jack, New Zealand, in 1994. Available Canada: Ferncliff.

Oreti Chance
Medium formal decorative (ADS); yellow variety, introduced by Walter Jack, New Zealand, in 1992.

Oreti Duke
Pompon (NDS and ADS); purple exhibition variety, 0.9m (3ft) high bush; introduced by Walter Jack, New Zealand, in 1990. Available UK: Halls, JRG, National, Oscroft, P. & L., Pratt, Station House; USA: Clacks, Connell's, SB Gardens; elsewhere: Geerlings.

Oreti Envy
Miniature ball (ADS); purple variety; introduced by Walter Jack, New Zealand, in 1999. Available USA: Creekside.

Oreti Jewel
Small semi-cactus (ADS); dark red variety; introduced by W. Jack, New Zealand, in 1999. Available elsewhere: Jacks.

Oreti Liz
Miniature formal decorative (ADS); purple variety; raised by Walter Jack, New Zealand, in 2001. Available UK: Creekside; elsewhere: Jacks.

Oreti Stacy
Medium lacinated (ADS); light blends, pink and white variety; originated by Walter Jack, New Zealand, in 1996. Available USA: Alpen.

Orfeo
Medium cactus (NDS); purple garden variety, 1.2m (4ft); introduced by dahlia Bruidegom, Holland, in 1951. Available UK: Jager, National; USA: Hamilton; elsewhere: Dgid, Engelhardt.

Originality
Novelty double centre (ADS); dark blends purple and white variety; originated by Ghio, USA, in 2001.

Orkney
Fimbriated medium semi-cactus (NDS), medium lacinated (ADS); yellow, orange blends, 1.2m (4ft) high; introduced by Cyril Higgo, South Africa, in 1996. Available USA: Connell's.

Ornamental Rays
Small incurved cactus (ADS); bronze exhibition variety; introduced by Ballego, Holland, in 1964.

Othello
Medium semi-cactus (NDS); red exhibition variety, 1.2m (4ft) in height; raised by Terry Clarke, UK, in 1968. Award Merit 1981 Wisley (NDS). Available UK: Cruikshank, National.

Otto's Thrill
Large informal decorative (ADS); lavender exhibition variety; originated by Aumiller, USA, in 1956. Available USA: Elkhorn, Hamilton, Mingus; elsewhere: Graines.

P

Pablo
Gallery dahlia (unclassified); rose-orange garden and patio pot variety, height 0.6m (2ft); originated Belgium. Available elsewhere: Graines.

Pacific Corvette
Miniature incurved cactus (ADS); light blends, yellow and bronze garden variety; height 1.2m (4ft); originated by Hulin, USA, in 1966. Available USA: Clacks.

Pacific del Oro
Medium lacinated (ADS); light blends, yellow and red exhibition variety; 1.2m (4ft) high bush; originated by Aird, USA, in 2001.

Pacific R. Sundown
Medium lacinated (ADS); dark blends orange and yellow exhibition variety; 1.2m (4ft) in height; originated by Aird, USA, in 2001.

Pacific Revival
Pompon (NDS and ADS); lavender and white blends (NDS), lavender (ADS); exhibition and garden variety; height 1.1m (3.5ft); introduced by Keith Whittington, New Zealand, in 1997. Available UK: Halls, National, P. & L.; USA: Alpen, Clacks.

Painted Lady
Small, formal decorative (ADS); light blends white and lavender exhibition variety; height 1.5m (5ft); originated by Kempster, Canada, in 1990. Available USA: Clacks, Dan's Dahlias.

Pam
Pompon (ADS); pink exhibition and garden variety; 1.1m (3.5ft) in height; introduced by Blythe, Australia, in 1960. Available USA: Alpen, SB Gardens.

ORETI DUKE

ORKNEY

PABLO

PAINTED LADY

Pamela

Pamela
Waterlily (ADS); bronze garden variety; introduced by Rodgers, New Zealand, in 1970.

Pamela R
Medium formal decorative (ADS); dark pink variety; originated by Hurlbut, USA, in 1989.

Papageno
Giant informal decorative (ADS); light blends pink and yellow, exhibition variety; 1.1m (3.5ft); introduced by Ballego, Holland, in 1972. Available USA: Alpen, Hamilton, Swan Island; Canada: Ferncliff; elsewhere: Engelhardt.

Pape's Pink
Medium semi-cactus (ADS); pink garden variety; originated by Pape, USA, in 1956.

Parakeet
Small formal decorative (ADS); yellow cut flower and exhibition variety; 1.2m (4ft) strong stem; originated by N. Gitts, USA, in 1997. Available USA: Swan Island.

Paritaha Sunrise
Small semi-cactus (unclassified); yellow tipped red cut flower; 1.2m (4ft) high, prolific bush; introduced USA in 1957. Available USA: Frey's, Swan Island.

Park Princess
Dwarf bedder semi-cactus (NDS), small cactus (ADS); pink (NDS), dark pink (ADS); garden and cut flower variety, height 0.6m (2ft); introduced by Maarse, Holland, in 1959. Award Merit Wisley 1960 (NDS). Available UK: Halls, Jager, JRG, National; USA: Dan's Dahlias, Elkhorn, Frey's, SB Gardens, Sea-Tac, Swan Island; Canada: Ferncliff; elsewhere: Dgid, Engelhardt, Geerlings, Graines, Turc.

Parkland Fire
Single (ADS); flame variety, height 1.5m (5ft); originated by Rowse, UK, in 1998.

Parkland Glow
Single (ADS); dark red variety, height 1.5m (5ft); originated by Rowse, USA, in 1999.

Parkland Halo
Single (ADS); purple exhibition variety; originated by Rowse, USA, in 2001. Available USA: Alpen.

Parkland Moonmist
Collarette (ADS); yellow exhibition variety; height 1.2m (4ft); originated by Rowse, USA, in 2001. Evie Gullickson seedling award. Available USA: Alpen.

Parkland Prince
Anemone (ADS); light blends yellow and purple exhibition variety; height 1.2m (4ft); originated by Rowse, USA, in 1999. Available USA: Clacks.

Parkland Roxyann
Collarette (ADS); red with red collar, exhibition variety; originated by Rowse, USA, in 2001. Available USA: Alpen.

Paroa Gillian
Miniature incurved cactus (ADS); flame, cut flower variety; height 1.1m (3.5ft); originated by McCann, New Zealand, in 1981. Available USA: Connell's.

Party Girl
Medium lacinated (ADS); lavender exhibition, early bloomer on a 1.2m (4ft) high bush; originated by Surber, USA, in 1995. Available USA: Connell's, SB Gardens.

Pasodoble
Anemone type (NDS and ADS); provides profuse, long-stemmed, white and yellow-centred blooms for garden purposes. This variety was discovered in a municipal garden park in Germany, and won the John Brown Medal Wisley (UK) in 2000. Available UK: Aylett's, National, Oscroft; elsewhere: Dgid, Englehardt, Turc.

Passion
Medium formal decorative (ADS); purple exhibition variety; 1.1m (3.5ft) in height; originated by Kennedy, USA, in 1968. Available USA: Clacks, Connell's, Dan's Dahlias.

Pat Fearey
Waterlily (unclassified); yellow and red blends, garden and cut flower variety; tall 1.5m (5ft) high bush; prolific bloomer. Originated USA in 1995. Available USA: Connell's; Canada: Ferncliff.

Pat Mark
Medium cactus (unclassified); orange exhibition and cut flower variety; height 1.2m (4ft); raised by W. Mark, UK, in 2001.

Pat 'n' Dee
Small formal decorative (ADS); white, low-growing cut flower variety; 1.1m (3.5ft) bush; originated by Pape, USA, in 1953. Available USA: Connell's, Elkhorn.

Pat O'Neal
Miniature formal decorative (ADS); purple exhibition and garden variety; originated by Kennedy, USA, in 1968.

Patches
Medium formal decorative (ADS); bicolour pink and white garden variety; 1.4m (4.5ft) high bush; originated by Swan Island, USA, in 1986. Available USA: Dan's Dahlias, Frey's, Swan Island.

PASODOBLE

PAT MARK

Patricia
Collarette (ADS); red variety;
originated by G. W. Chambers,
New Zealand, in 1999.

Patriot
Small semi-cactus (ADS);
bicolour red and white,
exhibition variety; height 1.5m
(5ft); originated by Ransell,
USA, in 1998. Available USA:
Clacks.

Patty K
Miniature waterlily
(unclassified); apricot cut
flower (floral art); 1.2m (4ft)
high; originated by Swan
Island, USA, in 1998. Available
elsewhere: Geerlings.

Paul Chester
Small cactus (NDS); orange
yellow blends, exhibition
garden and cut flower variety;
raised by G. J. Chester, UK, in
1966. Available UK: Clarks,
Cruikshank, National.

Paul Critchley
Large cactus (unclassified); dark
pink blooms, garden variety on
strong stems on 1.5m (5ft) high
plant; raised by Paul Critchley,
UK, in 1961. Award Merit
Wisley, 1964 (NDS).

Paul Smith
Ball (ADS); dark red, cut
flower variety on a 1.4m (4.5ft)
high bush; originated by
Palminteri, USA, in 1969.
Available USA: Clacks,
Connell's, Dan's Dahlias,
Mingus, Sea-Tac.

Paul Z
Ball (ADS); dark red exhibition
variety; originated by Larkin &
Zydner, USA, in 2001. Awarded
the Derrill Hart medal (ADS).

Paul's Delight
Small decorative (NDS); white
exhibition, garden and cut
flower variety; raised by
Norman Lewis, UK, in 1984.
Available UK: National,
Oscroft, P. & L., Scotts.

Pazazz
Miniature formal decorative
(unclassified); red, cut flower
variety; compact bush, height
0.9m (3ft); originated USA in
1992. Available USA: Swan
Island.

Peace Pact
Small waterlily (NDS); white
exhibition, garden and cut
flower variety on 1.1m (3.5ft)
high plant; introduced by
Maarse, Holland. Award Merit
1984 Wisley (NDS). Available
UK: Abacus, National, Oscroft;
elsewhere: Graines.

Peach Athalie
Small cactus (NDS); pink
exhibition, garden and cut
flower variety; 1.5m (5ft) in
height; introduced in the UK in
1986. Available UK: National,
P. & L., Scotts.

Peach Cupid
Miniature ball (ADS); pink
blended sport of Wootton
Cupid; excellent for exhibition,
garden and cut flower use;
introduced in 1993. Available
UK: Abacus, Butterfield, Clark,
Cruikshank, Halls, Jones,
National, Oscroft, P. & L.;
USA: Elkhorn.

Peach Star
Orchid (ADS); light blends
pink and yellow; originated by
Sellens, USA, in 2001.
Available USA: Clacks.

Peaches
Medium formal decorative
(unclassified); pink and yellow
blends, cut flower; 1.2m (4ft)
high bush; originated USA in
1991. Available USA: Frey's,
Swan Island.

Peaches & Cream
Waterlily (ADS); light blends,
yellow and pink variety;
originated by Geisert, USA, in
1991.

Peaches-n-Cream
Medium formal decorative
(ADS); light blends, orange and
white exhibition variety;
originated by D. Blue, USA, in
1993. Awarded Lynn B. Dudley
medal (ADS). Available USA:
Alpen, Clacks, Creekside,
Mingus; elsewhere: Jacks.

Peachette
Lilliput miscellaneous (NDS);
pink garden variety, 0.6m (2ft)
high; introduced in the UK in
1976. Award Garden Merit
Wisley 1993 (NDS). Available
UK: Butterfield, National.

Pearl of Heemstede
Small waterlily (NDS); pink
exhibition, garden and cut
flower variety; 0.9m (3ft) high;
introduced by Geerlings,
Holland, in 1990. Award Merit
1989 Wisley, and Award
Garden Merit Wisley 1993
(NDS). Available UK: Aylett's,
Halls, National, P. & L., Tivey;
elsewhere: Geerlings.

Pearson's Ben
Small semi-cactus (ADS); red
exhibition variety; originated
by Pearson, USA, in 1996.
Available USA: Connell's, Dan's
Dahlias, Elkhorn.

Pearson's Michelle
Pompon (ADS); orange variety;
originated by Pearson, USA, in
1997. Available USA: Clacks,
Dan's Dahlias.

Pearson's Patrick
Small cactus (ADS); flame
variety; originated by Pearson,
USA, in 2000. Available USA:
Dan's Dahlias.

Pee Gee
Medium lacinated (ADS); flame
exhibition variety, on strong-
stemmed, 1.1m (3.5ft) high
bush; introduced by Cyril
Higgo, South Africa, in 1997.
Available USA: Clacks,
Connell's, Creekside, Dan's
Dahlias, Elkhorn; elsewhere:
Engelhardt.

PEACH CUPID

PEARL OF HEEMSTEDE

PEE GEE

Peek a Boo
Miniature, formal decorative
(unclassified); lavender, cut
flower; 1.2m (4ft) bush;
originated USA in 1999; sport
of Daniel Edwards. Available
USA: Swan Island.

Peggyann
Small, informal decorative
(ADS); pink variety; originated
by E. Miller, USA, in 1995.

Pembroke Pattie
Pompon (NDS); purple
exhibition variety; 1.2m (4ft)
high, massive bush; raised by
A. G. Davies, UK, in 1996.
Available UK: National, P. &
L., Station House.

Penhill Cream Giant
Giant informal decorative
(ADS); white exhibition variety,
height 1.1m (3.5ft); introduced
by Wallace Maritz, South
Africa, in 1997. Available USA:
Arrowhead, Clacks.

Penhill JB Israelsohn
Large semi-cactus (ADS); dark
pink exhibition variety, 1.4m
(4.5ft) high plant; introduced by
Wallace Maritz, South Africa, in
1991. Available USA: Clacks.

Penhill Miriam McMaster
Large, formal (ADS); lavender
exhibition variety; 1.4m (4.5ft)
high bush; originated by Wallace
Maritz, South Africa, in 2001.

Penhill Moonrise
Giant informal decorative
(ADS); yellow garden variety,
1.1m (3.5ft) high; originated by
Wallace Maritz, South Africa,
in 1994. Available USA: Clacks,
Dan's Dahlias, Mingus.

Penhill Rose Globe
Large, formal decorative
(ADS); lavender exhibition
variety; introduced by Wallace
Maritz, South Africa, in 2001.

Penhill Watermelon
Giant, informal decorative
(ADS); light blends, exhibition
variety, 1.4m (4.5ft) high;
introduced by Wallace Maritz,
South Africa, in 2000.
Available elsewhere: Jacks.

Penns Gift
Giant informal decorative
(ADS); lavender, exhibition
variety, 1.2m (4ft) high bush;
originated by Stanley Johnson,
USA, in 1970. Available USA:
Elkhorn, Frey's; Canada:
Ferncliff.

Pensford Marion
Pompon (NDS and ADS); pink
blends (NDS), red (ADS);
exhibition and garden variety;
height 1.4m (4.5ft); raised by
Frank Newbery, UK, in 1985.
Available UK: Abacus,
Cruikshank, National, P. & L.;
USA: Arrowhead, Clacks.

Periton
Miniature ball (NDS); red
exhibition, garden and cut
flower variety, height 1.2m
(4ft); raised by T. Waddle, UK,
in 1991. Available UK: Aylett's,
National, P. & L.

Perry B
Medium lacinated (ADS);
orange, exhibition variety by
D. Barnes, USA, in 2001.

Persian Monarch
Large semi-cactus (ADS); dark
pink garden variety; introduced
by Bruidegom, Holland, in
1968.

Phill's Pink
Small decorative (unclassified);
pink, garden and cut flower on
a 1.2m (4ft) high, strong-
stemmed plant; raised by Jack
Kinns, UK, in 1970. Award
Garden Merit Wisley, 1995
(NDS).

Phoenix
Medium decorative (NDS),
medium formal decorative
(ADS); purple exhibition
variety; height 1.2m (4ft);
raised by Roger Turrell, UK, in
1989. Available UK: Abacus,
National, P. & L.; USA:
Creekside, Dahlia Dandies,
Dan's Dahlias.

Phyllis F
Small cactus (ADS); pink
variety, originated by Bishop,
USA, in 1996.

Phyllis Mulcahy
Medium informal decorative
(ADS); dark pink variety;
originated by Kurt, USA, in
2001.

Pied Piper
Small ball (NDS); red and
white bicolour, garden and cut
flower variety; 1.1m (3.5ft)
high bush; introduced by
Bruidegom, Holland, in 1976.

Piedmont Rebel
Medium lacinated (ADS); dark
red exhibition variety;
originated by Faust in 1964.
Available USA: Arrowhead.

Pim's Moonlight
(synonymous to **Lauren's
Moonlight**)
Medium semi-cactus (NDS);
yellow exhibition, garden and
cut flower variety; height 1.1m
(3.5ft); raised by Greenaway,
UK, in 1998. Available UK:
National, Porter.

Pineapple Lollipop
Medium formal decorative
(ADS); yellow exhibition and
garden variety; 1.1m (3.5ft) in
height; originated by Phil Traff,
USA, in 1991. Available USA:
Alpen, Clacks, Connell's, Dan's
Dahlias, Elkhorn, Mingus, SB
Gardens, Sea-Tac; Canada:
Ferncliff.

PENHILL MOONRISE

PHOENIX

PIEDMONT REBEL

PERITON

PINEAPPLE LOLLIPOP

Pinelands Flames
Medium lacinated (ADS); flame
exhibition variety, on a 1.2m
(4ft) high bush; introduced by
Cyril Higgo, South Africa, in
2002. Available USA:
Connell's.

Pinelands Pal
Medium lacinated (ADS); light
blends, pink and yellow,
exhibition and garden variety;
1.2m (4ft) in height; introduced
by Cyril Higgo, South Africa, in
1999. Available USA: Connell's.

Pinelands Pam
Medium lacinated (ADS); flame
exhibition and cut flower
variety on a 1.5m (5ft) high
bush; introduced by Cyril
Higgo, South Africa, in 1999.
Awarded the Derrill Hart
medal. Available USA: Alpen,
Connell's, Swan Island.

Pinelands Pixie
Small, lacinated (ADS); red
variety introduced by Cyril
Higgo, South Africa, in 2002.

Pinelands Prickles
Medium lacinated
(unclassified); dark red
exhibition variety, on a 1.1m
(3.5ft) high bush; late bloomer;
introduced Cyril Higgo, South
Africa, in 2002. Available USA:
Connell's.

Pinelands Princess
Medium lacinated (ADS); light
blends, lavender and white
garden variety; introduced by
Cyril Higgo, South Africa, in
1995. Available USA:
Arrowhead, Connell's, Dan's
Dahlias, Elkhorn, SB Gardens,
Swan Island; elsewhere:
Engelhardt.

Pink Beauty
Small cactus (ADS); pink
exhibition variety; originated
by Dykstra, USA, in 2001.

Pink Carol
Pompon (NDS and ADS); pink
(NDS); dark blends, purple and
white (ADS); garden variety;
raised in the UK in 1998.
Available UK: Cruikshank,
National; USA: Clacks:

Pink Connecticut Dancer
Small formal decorative (ADS);
variegated pink and red
exhibition variety; originated
by Sellens, USA, in 2001.
Available USA: Clacks.

Pink Frank Hornsey
Small decorative (NDS); pink,
white blends, exhibition and
garden variety; height 1.2m
(4ft); raised by Terry Clarke,
UK, in 1973. A sport of 'Frank
Hornsey'. Available UK:
National.

Pink Gingham
Small waterlily (ADS); bicolour,
pink and white, cut flower and
floral art variety; 1.4m (4.5ft)
high; originated USA in 2000.
Available USA: Swan Island.

Pink Giraffe
Classified as a 'miscellaneous
double orchid' (NDS), and as a
'novelty double dahlia' (ADS);
pink and bronze blends (NDS),
and pink (ADS); garden variety,
height 0.9m (3ft); introduced
by Burrows, UK, in 1961.
Available UK: National; USA:
Clacks; elsewhere: Dgid.

Pink Honeymoon Dress
Small decorative (unclassified);
pink garden and cut flower
variety on a 0.9m (3ft) high
bush; sport of 'Honeymoon
Dress', introduced to the UK in
1990.

Pink Jupiter
Giant semi-cactus (NDS), or
large semi-cactus (ADS); pink
blends (NDS), light blends,
pink and dark pink (ADS);
exhibition variety; 1.4m (4.5ft)
high, raised by K. Hardham,
UK, in 1981. Award Merit

1984 Wisley (NDS). Available
UK: Clark, Cruikshank, Halls,
National, Oscroft, P. & L.,
Porter, Spencer, Station House;
USA: Clacks, Dahlia Dandies,
Elkhorn, SB Gardens;
elsewhere: Geerlings, Jacks.

Pink Kerkrade
Small cactus (ADS); pink
exhibition variety, 0.9m (3ft)
high bush; raised by Hooper,
UK, in 1987. Sport of
Klankstad Kerkrade. Available
USA: Clacks, Sea-Tac;
elsewhere: Jacks.

Pink Leycett
Giant decorative (NDS); pink
exhibition variety; 1.2m (4ft)
high plant; raised in 1987.
Available UK: National.

Pink Mona
Large informal decorative
(unclassified); lavender and
white exhibition variety; tall, at
1.6m (6ft) in height; plant
introduced to the USA in 1994;
sport of 'Mona Lisa'. Available
USA: Dan's Dahlias.

Pink Parfait
Medium semi-cactus
(unclassified); pink and white
blends, garden variety; a 1.5m
(5ft) tall bush; originated USA
in 1982. Available USA: Frey's,
Swan Island.

Pink Pastelle
Medium semi-cactus (NDS
and ADS); pink (NDS), light
blends pink and white (ADS);
excellent sport of 'Grenidor
Pastelle' for exhibition,
garden and cut flower
purposes; growing to a height
of 1.2m (4ft); raised by Tom
Pashley, UK, in 1991. Award
Garden Merit Wisley (NDS).
Available UK: Abacus, Clark,
Halls, National, Oscroft, P. &
L., Porter, Spencer, Station
House; USA: Alpen, Connell's,
Dahlia Dandies; elsewhere:
Geerlings, Jacks.

PINELANDS PAM

PINK HONEYMOON DRESS

PINK JUPITER

PINELANDS PRINCESS

PINK GIRAFFE

PINK LEYCETT

PINK PASTELLE

Pink Rebel
Single (ADS); light blends, pink and white variety; originated by S. Fry, USA, in 2001. Available USA: Frey's.

Pink Risca Miner
Small ball (NDS); lavender exhibition, garden and cut flower variety; height 1.1m (3.5ft); raised by Terry Clarke, UK, in 1987. Sport of Risca Miner. Available UK: National, P. & L.

Pink Robin Hood
Small decorative (unclassified); pink garden and cut flower variety on a 1.2m (4ft) high bush; sport of Robin Hood; introduced UK in 1992.

Pink Shirley Alliance
Small cactus (NDS), or small incurved cactus (ADS); pink blends (NDS), or dark pink blends (ADS); exhibition and garden variety; 0.9m (3ft) in height; raised by K. Davidson, UK, in 1980. Sport of Shirley Alliance. Available UK: Aylett's, National; USA: Clacks, Frey's, Sea-Tac.

Pink Suffusion
Small decorative (NDS), or small formal decorative (ADS); pink blends (NDS), or light blends pink and yellow (ADS); exhibition, garden and cut flower variety; 0.9m (3ft) in height; raised by C. Pearce, UK, in 1996; sport of Hillcrest Suffusion. Available UK: Aylett's, National; USA: Arrowhead, Creekside, Mingus; elsewhere: Geerlings, Jacks.

Pink Symbol
Medium semi-cactus (NDS); pink bronze blends exhibition, garden and cut flower variety; height 1.2m (4ft); raised by Curnow, UK, in 1975. Sport of 'Symbol'. Available UK: National.

Pink Willo
Pompon (ADS); dark pink, exhibition variety; 0.9m (3ft) high plant; introduced by N. Williams, Australia, in 1971. Sport of 'Pop Willo'.

Piper's Pink
A dwarf bedding semi-cactus (NDS); pink, growing to a height of 45cm (18in); for garden and cut flower use; much used in municipal park displays in the UK; introduced by Pipers, UK, in 1964. Award Garden Merit Wisley 1993 (NDS). Available UK: Aylett's, Cruikshank, National, Station House, Tivey; elsewhere: Dgid.

Pipsqueak
Collerette (unclassified); pink with pink collar, exhibition and garden variety; 1.1m (3.5ft) high bush; originated in the USA in 1998.

Playboy
Giant decorative (NDS); yellow exhibition variety; height 0.9m (3ft); raised by A. T. Hayes, UK, in 1975. Available UK: National, Tivey; USA: Dan's Dahlias, Swan Island.

Plum Pretty
Small cactus (ADS); dark red, garden variety; 1.1m (3.5ft) tall bush; originated by Swan Island, USA, in 1995. Available USA: Swan Island.

Plum Profusion
Medium formal decorative (unclassified); lavender exhibition and garden variety; 1.4m (4.6ft) high bush; originated USA in 2000. Available USA: Clacks.

Plum Surprise
Pompon (NDS); purple exhibition variety; 1.1m (3.5ft) high bush; raised by M. Hall, UK, in 1995. Available USA: Clacks.

Pocrates
Miniature ball (ADS); white, garden variety; compact 1.1m (3.5ft) bush; originated by Phil Traff, USA, in 1991. Available USA: Clacks, Connell's, SB Gardens.

Poetic
Large lacinated (ADS); light blends white and pink; introduced by Bruidegom, Holland, in 1965. Available elsewhere: Wirth.

Polar Sight
Giant cactus (NDS); white, one-time exhibition variety, with huge blooms on 1.2m (4ft) high plant; introduced by dahlia Maarse, Holland, in 1960. Award Merit Wisley 1966 (NDS). Available UK: National; elsewhere: Jacks.

Polly Bergen
Medium formal decorative (ADS); dark pink variety; originated by Dahliadel, USA, in 1959.

PINK RISCA MINER

PINK ROBIN HOOD

PINK SHIRLEY ALLIANCE

PINK SUFFUSION

PINK SYMBOL

PINK WILLO

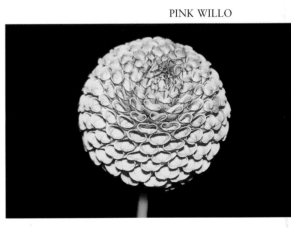

PIPER'S PINK

PLAYBOY

Polventon Supreme
Small ball (NDS), or ball
(ADS); yellow exhibition
variety; height 0.9m (3ft);
raised by Cyril Watkins, UK, in
1992. Available UK: National,
P. & L., Scotts, Station House;
USA: Alpen, Capistrano,
Clacks, Dan's Dahlias,
Elkhorn, SB Gardens; Canada:
Ferncliff; elsewhere: Geerlings.

Polyand
Large decorative (NDS);
lavender blends, exhibition
variety on a 1.4m (4.5ft) high
plant; introduced by T. Young,
Australia, in 1953. Award
Merit 1972 Wisley (NDS).
Available UK: National,
P. & L.; USA: Clacks.

Pontiac
Small, flowered cactus (NDS);
pink/purple blends, garden and
cut flower variety; 1.2m (4ft) in
height; raised by N. J. van
Oostens, Holland, in 1958.
Available UK: National, P. & L.

Pooh
Collarette (ADS); bicolour
orange and yellow, with a
yellow collar; cut flower and
exhibition variety, 1.4m (4.5ft)
high; prolific bloomer;
originated by Swan Island, USA,
in 1998. Available USA: Swan
Island; elsewhere: Geerlings.

Pop Talk
Small, informal decorative
(ADS); variegated lavender and
purple; introduced by
Bruidegom, Holland in 1976.

Pop Willo
Pompon (NDS and ADS);
yellow and orange blends
(NDS), bronze (ADS);
exhibition variety, 0.9m (3ft)
high plant; introduced by N.
Williams, Australia, in 1971.
Available UK: Cruikshank,
National, P. & L., Spencer,
Station House.

Poppers
Small cactus (unclassified);
yellow, splashed red, cut flower

variety; 1.2m (4ft) high bush;
originated USA in 2001. Sport
of Mary Lee McNall. Available
USA: Swan Island.

Poppet
Pompon (ADS); orange garden
and cut flower variety;
introduced by Ballego in 1969.
Available USA: Clacks,
SB Gardens, Sea-Tac;
elsewhere: Geerlings.

Popular Guest
Fimbriated medium semi-cactus
(NDS); lavender, white blends,
garden variety; 1.1m (3.5ft)
high; introduced by dahlia
Bruidegom, Holland, in 1957.
Available UK: National;
elsewhere: Dgid.

Porcelain
Small waterlily (NDS),
waterlily (ADS); white lavender
blends (NDS), white (ADS);
good for garden and cut flower
use; a tall grower at 1.5m (5ft);
blooms borne on long, straight,
strong stems; raised by John
Crutchfield, UK, in 1969.
Award Merit 1971, and
Garden Merit Wisley 1995
(NDS). Available UK:
Butterfield, Halls, National, P.
& L., Tivey; USA: Clacks, SB
Gardens; elsewhere: Geerlings.

Powder Gull
Peony (ADS); pink exhibition
variety; originated by
Gullickson, USA, in 1995.
Awarded the Lynn B. Dudley
medal in 1994 (ADS). Available
USA: Capistrano, Dan's
Dahlias.

Prefect
Medium semi-cactus (NDS);
pink garden and cut flower
variety; 1.2m (4ft) high plant;
raised by Ballego, Holland, in
1961. Available UK: National,
Oscroft, P. & L., Tivey.

Preference
Small semi-cactus (NDS); pink
garden and cut flower variety,
1.1m (3.5ft) in height;
introduced by dahlia

Bruidegom, Holland, in 1995.
Available UK: National;
elsewhere: Dgid.

Preston Park
Dwarf bedder (single) (NDS);
red garden variety with black
foliage; 0.6m (2ft); raised by
John Crutchfield, UK, in 1969.
Named after a park in
Brighton. UK award Garden
Merit Wisley (NDS). Available
UK: Aylett's, Halls, National;
elsewhere: Dgid.

Pretty in Pink
Small cactus (ADS); dark pink,
garden and cut flower variety;
height 1.2m (4ft), strong stems;
brilliant colour; originated by
Wynn, USA, in 2001. Available
Canada: Ferncliff.

Pride of Berlin (original name
Stolze von Berlin)
Miniature ball (unclassified);
lavender, garden and cut
flower, 0.9m (3ft) in height;
introduced by Schwiglowski,
Germany, in 1914.

Pride of Holland
Large cactus (NDS); pink
garden variety, 1.2m (4ft) in
height; introduced by dahlia
Bruidegom, Holland, in 1949.
Available UK: National.

Prime Time
Medium semi-cactus (ADS);
light blends, bronze yellow, cut
flower and exhibition variety;
heavy bloomer at 1.5m (5ft)
high; originated by N. Gitts,
USA, in 1994. Available USA:
Swan Island.

Primrose Diane
Small decorative (NDS), or
small formal decorative (ADS);
yellow exhibition and garden
variety; 1.1m (3.5ft) high bush;
raised by D. Armstrong, UK, in
1900. Available UK: Abacus,
Clark, Cruikshank, Halls,
National, Oscroft,
P. & L., Pratt, Scotts,
Spencer, Taylor; USA: Clacks.

POLVENTON SUPREME

PORCELAIN

PRESTON PARK

PRIMROSE DIANE

Primrose Rustig
Medium decorative (NDS); yellow exhibition variety, 1.2m (4ft) high plant; raised by G. Hoodon, UK, in 1989. Available UK: National, Oscroft.

Prince Valiant
Small formal decorative (ADS); variegated white and dark red, cut flower variety on a 1.2m (4ft) high bush; originated by Rose, USA, in 1971. Available USA: Connell's, Dan's Dahlias, Sea-Tac; elsewhere: Engelhardt, Graines.

Princess Beatrix
Medium decorative (NDS); orange white blends, garden variety; 1.1m (3.5ft) in height; introduced by Ballego, Holland, in 1939. Available UK: National.

Princess Marie Jose
Dwarf bedder (single) (NDS); lavender garden bedding variety; 0.6m (2ft) in height; raised by West, UK, in 1946. Available UK: National.

Princess Megan
Small formal decorative (ADS); dark blends, dark pink and purple, exhibition variety; 1.2m (4ft) high bush; originated by Roger Stevens, USA, in 2001.

Pristine
Medium semi-cactus (NDS), medium cactus (ADS); white exhibition and garden variety; 1.2m (4ft) high bush; introduced by N. Williams, Australia, in 1997. Available UK: National; USA: Clacks.

Procyon
Small decorative (NDS); yellow and red bicolour, garden variety, 1m (3.5ft) high; introduced by dahlia Maarse, Holland, in 1963. Award Merit Wisley 1966 (NDS). Available UK: National, Suttons; elsewhere: Dgid.

Prom Queen
Miniature informal decorative (ADS); light blends, white and lavender variety; originated by Heines, USA, in 1990. Awarded the Derrill Hart medal (ADS). Available USA: Dan's Dahlias, Elkhorn.

Promise
Fimbriated medium semi-cactus (NDS); yellow garden variety, height 1.2m (4ft); introduced by dahlia Bruidegom, Holland, in 1959. Award Merit Wisley 1961 (NDS). Available UK: National; elsewhere: Dgid

Pucker Up
Small semi-cactus (unclassified); yellow cut flower variety, 1.2m (4ft) in height; originated USA in 2002. Available USA: Swan Island.

Puget Sparkle
Miniature formal decorative (ADS); red garden variety, on a 1.2m (4ft) high bush; originated by Harold Miller, USA, in 1984. Available USA: Connell's, Elkhorn.

Puget Sunshine
Small formal decorative (ADS); yellow garden and exhibition variety; originated by Harold Miller, USA, in 1975. Available USA: Dan's Dahlias.

Pugsley
Medium cactus (ADS); orange variety; originated by R. and S. Ambrose, USA, in 1993.

Purbeck Lydia
Large semi-cactus (NDS); flame exhibition variety; 1.2m (4ft) high plant; raised by W. Cann, UK, in 1984, Available UK: National; elsewhere: Jacks.

Purity
Small semi-cactus (NDS); white garden and cut flower variety; 1.1m (3.5ft); introduced by Hoek, Holland, in 1948. Available UK: National.

Purpinka
Dwarf bedder anemone (NDS); purple and purple centre, 0.9m (3ft) garden variety; introduced by T. H. Clemens, Holland, in 1990. Available UK: National; elsewhere: Dgid.

Purple Gem
Small incurved cactus (unclassified); purple exhibition variety, 1.2m (4ft) bush; originated USA in 1960. Available USA: Elkhorn, Frey's, Swan Island; elsewhere: Engelhardt.

Purple Haze
Small incurved cactus (unclassified); pink cut flower variety, 1.2m (4ft) high plant; originated USA in 1999. Available USA: Swan Island.

Purple Imp
Miniature formal decorative (unclassified); purple cut flower, 1.2m (4ft) in height; originated USA in 1991. Available USA: Frey's, Swan Island.

Purple Joy
Medium decorative (NDS); purple exhibition variety, height 1.2m (4ft); introduced by M. Ray, Australia, in 1960. Available UK: National; USA: Clacks; elsewhere: Wirth.

Purple Mist
Small cactus (ADS); bicolour purple and white; variety originated by Willoughby, Canada, in 1996. Available USA: Clacks.

Purple Taiheiyo
Giant informal decorative (unclassified); purple garden variety; 0.9m (3ft) compact bush; originated USA in 1985. Available USA: Elkhorn, Swan Island.

Pwll Coch
Small semi-cactus (unclassified); red garden variety, 0.9m (3ft) in height; raised by Ian Treseder, UK, in 1961. Award Merit Wisley 1965 (NDS).

PRISTINE

PROMISE

PURPLE JOY

Q

Queeny
Small cactus (NDS); pink and yellow blends; exhibition, garden and cut flower; 1.2m (4ft) high; variety introduced by Cor Geerlings, Holland, in 1992. Available USA: Mingus; elsewhere: Jacks.

Quel Diable
Large semi-cactus (NDS); exhibition and garden variety, 1.2m (4ft) in height; introduced by Bruidegom, Holland, in 1968. Award Merit 1973 Wisley (NDS). Available UK: National, Tivey.

Quick Step
Anemone (ADS); yellow; variety originated in USA in 1998.

Quiet Riot
Small semi-cactus (ADS); dark blends yellow, orange and red; introduced by D. Jack, Canada, in 1993. Available USA: Dan's Dahlias.

R

R J R
Miniature formal decorative (ADS); white variety; originated by Rejman in 1994.

Radar
Miniature formal decorative (ADS); bicolour red and white; variety originated by Rejman, USA, in 1995. Available USA: SB Gardens.

Radfo
Small semi-cactus (NDS and ADS); orange blends (NDS), bronze (ADS); exhibition, garden and cut flower variety; raised by B. Fowler, UK, in 1988. Available UK: Abacus, Cruikshank, National, Oscroft, P. & L.; USA: SB Gardens.

Raffles
Small decorative (NDS); pink exhibition and garden variety; raised by Creed. Available UK: Aylett's, National.

Raiser's Pride
Medium cactus (NDS); pink and yellow blends, exhibition variety; 1.2m (4ft) in height; raised by dahlia Maarse, Holland, in 1960. Available UK: Abacus, Halls, National, P. & L., Station House.

Randi Dawn
Waterlily medium (unclassified); lavender exhibition and garden variety, on a 1.4m (4.5ft) high bush; originated USA in 1985. Available USA: Swan Island.

Raspberry Punch
Medium formal decorative (unclassified); red exhibition variety on a 1.4m (4.5ft) high bush; originated in the USA in 2002. Available USA: Swan Island.

Raspberry Splash
Single (ADS); variegated; originated by Knapp, USA, in 1994.

Rare Beauty
Small formal decorative (unclassified); orange exhibition variety on a 1.4m (4.5ft) high bush; originated USA in 1991. Available USA: Connell's.

Ray S
Medium formal decorative (ADS); bronze variety originated by H. Hurley, USA, in 2002.

Raz-Ma-Taz
Miniature formal decorative (ADS); dark blends, yellow and red, exhibition and cut flower variety on a 1.1m (3.5ft) high bush; originated by N. Gitts, USA, in 1993. Available USA:

Dan's Dahlias, Frey's, Swan Island.

Real Gold
Pompon (ADS); bronze exhibition and garden variety; introduced in Australia, 1967. Available USA: Dans' Dahlias.

Rebecca Lynn
Miniature formal decorative (ADS); dark pink, exhibition and cut flower variety, on a 0.9m (3ft) high bush; originated by L. Connell, USA, in 1987. Awarded the Lynn B. Dudley 1986 and the Derrill Hart medals. Available USA: Alpen, Clacks, Elkhorn, Frey's, SB Gardens, Swan Island; elsewhere: Jacks, Konishi.

Red Admiral
Miniature ball (NDS and ADS); red exhibition, garden and cut flower variety; 1.4m (5ft) in height; raised by S. Long, UK, in 1982. Available UK: National; USA: Arrowhead, Dahlia Dandies.

Red Alert
Miniature decorative (NDS); red exhibition, garden and cut flower variety; 1.2m (4ft) high; originated by L. Connell, USA, in 1983. Available UK: National, Tivey.

Red Arrow
Miniature decorative (NDS); red exhibition, garden and cut flower variety; 1.1m (3.5ft); raised by George Brookes, UK, in 1982. Available UK: National.

Red Balloon
Small ball (NDS), ball (ADS); red exhibition and garden variety; height 1.2m (3.5ft); introduced by Geerlings, Holland, in 1996. Available UK: Cruikshank, Halls, National, Oscroft, Scotts, Tivey; elsewhere: Dgid, Geerlings.

QUEENY

QUEL DIABLE

RADFO

RAISER'S PRIDE

RED ADMIRAL

RED BALLOON

Red Carol
Pompon (NDS); red exhibition, garden and cut flower; 1.2m (4ft) high plant; raised by W. Johnson, UK, in 1994. Available UK: National, Oscroft, P. & L., Station House.

Red Dwarf
Lilliput (single) (NDS); red garden variety, 0.6m (2ft) in height; introduced in 1965. Available UK: National.

Red Garnet
Miniature formal decorative (unclassified); cut flower variety; tall grower 1.5m (5ft) in height; originated USA in 1967. Available USA: Swan Island.

Red Mooney
Medium formal decorative (ADS); red variety; originated by Mooney, Canada, in 1997.

Red Pigmy
Small straight cactus (unclassified); cut flower and garden variety; 0.6m (2ft) high bush; originated USA in 1987; prolific bloomer. Available USA: Swan Island; Canada: Ferncliff; elsewhere: Engelhardt, Graines.

Red Riot
Medium lacinated (unclassified); garden and cut flower variety on a 1.2m (4ft) high bush; originated by Connell. Available USA: Connell's.

Red Ruby
Peony (ADS); red exhibition and garden variety; originated by H. Miller, USA, in 1993.

Red Sensation
Medium decorative (NDS); red exhibition variety, 1.2m (4ft) high plant; raised by Alan Dunlop, UK, in 1978. Available UK: National, P. & L.

Red Tide
Miniature formal decorative (ADS); red exhibition variety; height 1.5m (5ft); originated by Sampson, Canada, in 1999. Available Canada: Ferncliff.

Red Umbrella
Star (ADS); red exhibition variety; 1.2m (4ft) in height; originated by Bonneywell, USA, in 2000. Available USA: Alpen.

Red Velvet
Small waterlily (NDS), waterlily (ADS); red and yellow blends (NDS), red (ADS); exhibition, garden and cut flower variety, height 0.9m (3ft); introduced by Clark, Australia, in 1963. Available UK: Aylett's, Cruikshank, National, P. & L., Scotts, Station House; USA: Clacks, Dahlia Dandies, Dan's Dahlias, Mingus, SB Gardens, Sea-Tac; elsewhere: Konishi.

Red Wing
Small semi-cactus (ADS); red garden variety; originated by K. Larkin, USA, in 1997. Available USA: Mingus.

Reddy
Lilliput (single) (NDS), mignon single (ADS); red garden variety; 0.3m (1ft) in height; ideal for containers or garden use; introduced by Topsvoort, Holland, in 1963. Available UK: National; USA: Frey's.

Reedly
Waterlily (ADS); orange garden variety; raised by Joe Barwise, UK, in 1947. Available USA: Clacks, SB Gardens.

Rees' Dream
Giant incurved cactus (ADS); dark pink variety; originated by Rees, USA, in 1989.

Rees Variegated
Large, informal decorative (unclassified); variegated variety, 1.1m (3.5ft) high plant. Available USA: Clacks.

Regal Kerkrade
Small cactus (ADS); light blends, yellow and lavender, exhibition and garden variety; 1.2m (4ft) in height; originated UK in 1983. Available USA: Dahlia Dandies, Dan's Dahlias.

Regal Touch
Large informal decorative (unclassified); purple variety, 1.2m (4ft) high plant. Available USA: Clacks.

Reginald Keene
Large or medium semi-cactus (NDS), medium semi-cactus (ADS); orange flame blends (NDS), light blends, yellow/ bronze (ADS); exhibition variety; height 1.1m (3.5ft); raised by Geoff Flood, UK, in 1974. Award Merit Wisley 1970 (NDS): a variety from which many sports originate. Available UK: Cruikshank, Halls, National, Oscroft, P. & L., Spencer, Station House; elsewhere: Jacks.

Rejman's Candy Corn
Small, formal decorative (ADS); light blends, orange and yellow; originated by Rejman, USA, in 2000.

Rejman's Firecracker
Medium lacinated (ADS); variegated yellow and red, garden variety; tall grower to 1.5m (5ft) in height; originated by Rejman, USA, in 1997. Available USA: Alpen, SB Gardens.

Rejman's Peach
Small, incurved cactus (ADS); light blends; originated by Rejman, USA, in 2000.

RED CAROL

RED VELVET

REES' DREAM

REGINALD KEENE

Rejman's Polish Kid
Miniature formal decorative
(ADS); bicolour, red and white
variety; originated by Rejman,
USA, in 2000. Available USA:
SB Gardens.

Rembrandt
Mignon single (ADS); dark red
exhibition and garden variety,
0.6m (2ft) high; introduced by
Libert, USA, in 1989. Available
UK: Jager, JRG, National;
USA: Alpen, Capistrano,
Clacks, Dahlia Dandies, Dan's
Dahlias; elsewhere: Dgid,
Graines.

Renfrew Jennifer
Medium formal decorative
(unclassified); lavender, garden
and cut flower; height, 1.2m
(4ft); originated by Donaldson,
USA. Available USA: Dahlia
Dandies.

Renfrew Leeza
Medium lacinated (ADS); light
blends; originated by
Donaldson, USA, in 2000.

Requiem
Small decorative (NDS); purple
garden variety, 1.1m (3.5ft) in
height; raised by Raton, UK, in
1952. Available UK: Abacus,
National, Suttons; elsewhere:
Dgid, Engelhardt, Graines.

Respectable
Large semi-cactus
(unclassified); orange blends,
exhibition variety; height 1.2m
(4ft); introduced Holland,
1965. Award Merit Wisley
1967 (NDS). Available USA:
Dan's Dahlias.

Rev P. Holian
Giant semi-cactus (NDS and
ADS); purple exhibition variety,
1.4m (4ft) high; raised by A.
Craven, UK, in 1988. Available
UK: National; Canada:
Ferncliff; elsewhere: Konishi.

Rhonda
Pompon (NDS and ADS);
lavender and white (NDS); light
blends, white and lavender

(ADS); exhibition, garden and
cut flower variety; 0.9m (3ft)
high bush; introduced by
Rumble, Australia, in 1947.
Available UK: Cruikshank,
Halls, National, P. & L., Pratt,
Station House, Tivey; USA:
Clacks.

Rhonda Suzanne
Pompon (NDS); lavender and
purple blends; exhibition,
garden and cut flower variety;
1.2m (4ft) high; raised by B.
Knight, UK, in 1976. Available
UK: National, P.& L., Station
House.

Rhys's Memory
Medium lacinated (ADS); white
variety; originated by
Vandament, Canada, in 1998.

Richard Howells
Miniature ball (ADS); yellow
exhibition and cut flower
variety; height 1.2m (4ft);
originated by Morin, USA, in
1994. Awarded the Lynn B.
Dudley medal 1993 (ADS).
Available USA: Dahlia Dandies.

Richard Marc
Small cactus (NDS); pink and
yellow blends; exhibition,
garden and cut flower variety;
1.2m (4ft) high; raised by G. J.
Chester, UK, in 1968. Available
UK: Butterfield, JRG, National.

Richard Rogers
Large formal decorative
(unclassified); dark red
exhibition variety; 1.1m (3.5ft)
high bush; originated USA in
1966. Available USA:
Connell's, Dan's Dahlias,
Hamilton.

Richard S
Large cactus (ADS); light
blends, yellow and bronze
exhibition variety; originated
by M. Senior, USA, 2001.
Awarded the Lynn B. Dudley
medal (ADS).

Ricky Juul
Collarette (ADS); dark red with
pink collar, exhibition variety;

originated by Juul, USA, in
1983.

Riisa
Miniature ball (NDS and
ADS); red exhibition and
garden variety; 1.2m (4ft) high
bush; originated by L. Connell,
USA, in 1996. Awarded the
Lynn B. Dudley medal in 1995,
and the Derrill Hart medal
(ADS). Available UK: Abacus,
Jones, National; USA: Dan's
Dahlias, SB Gardens.

Ringo
Miniature formal decorative
(ADS); bicolour red and white,
garden and cut flower variety
on a 1.2m (4ft) high bush;
prolific bloomer; originated by
N. Gitts, USA, in 1994.
Available USA: Connell's,
Hamilton, Swan Island;
Canada: Ferncliff.

Rip City
Medium informal decorative
(ADS); dark red exhibition and
cut flower variety on a 1.2m
(4ft) high bush; originated by
N. Gitts, USA, in 1992.
Available USA: Dan's Dahlias,
Frey's, Hamilton, Swan Island;
elsewhere: Engelhardt, Graines.

Ripples
Medium straight cactus
(unclassified); dark purple sport
of Rip City; exhibition and cut
flower variety on a 1.2m (4ft)
high bush; originated by N.
Gitts, USA, in 1999. Available
USA: Swan Island.

Risca Miner
Small ball (NDS); purple
exhibition variety, height 1.1m
(3.5ft); raised by Terry Clarke,
UK, in 1976. Available UK:
Abacus, Cruikshank, National,
P. & L., Porter, Roberts.

Rita Hill
Collerette (NDS); red with
yellow collar; garden and cut
flower variety; height 1.2m
(4ft); raised by Dave Reid, UK,
in 1986. Available UK:
National.

REMBRANDT

RIISA

RISCA MINER

RITA HILL

Rival
Mignon single (ADS); red; originated USA in 1999.

River Road
Medium cactus (ADS); white exhibition variety 0.6m (2ft) high bush; originated by Keith Hammett, New Zealand, in 1991. Available USA: Connell's, Dan's Dahlias, Sea-Tac.

Robann Butterscotch
Small informal decorative (ADS); light blends, dark pink and yellow; originated by Moyahan, USA, in 1999. Available USA: Elkhorn.

Robann Flame
Miniature formal decorative (ADS); flame variety; originated by Moyahan, USA, in 2000.

Robann Regal
Miniature formal decorative (ADS); lavender exhibition variety; tall grower, 1.6m (6ft) high bush; originated by Moyahan, USA, in 1997. Awarded the Derrill Hart medal (ADS). Available USA: Alpen.

Robann Royal
Miniature ball (ADS); red exhibition variety, 1.7m (6ft) in height; originated by Moyahan, USA, in 1991. Awarded the Derrill Hart medal (ADS). Available USA: Clacks, Creekside, Dahlia Dandies, Dan's Dahlias, Elkhorn, Mingus; Canada: Ferncliff.

Robert Lee
Medium formal decorative (unclassified); orange-red sport of Swan's Glory; cut flower variety on a 1.2m (4ft) high bush; originated USA in 2001. Available USA: Swan Island.

Robert Moore
Medium lacinated (ADS); dark pink, exhibition variety; 1.2m (4ft) in height; originated by Steenfott, USA, in 1900. Available USA: Clacks.

Robert Too
Miniature formal decorative (ADS); dark blends, white and purple; cut flower variety, 1.2m (4ft) high; originated by L. Connell, USA, in 1977. Available USA: Connell's, Dan's Dahlias.

Robert Walker
Miniature formal decorative (ADS); dark blends, lavender purple variety; originated by Walker, USA, in 1984. Awarded the Lynn B. Dudley medal in 1983, and the Derrill Hart medal (ADS).

Robin Hood
Small ball (NDS), ball (ADS); orange bronze blends (NDS), dark blends orange and pink (ADS); exhibition, garden and cut flower variety; 1.2m (4ft) in height; raised by Gordon Littlejohn, UK, in 1987. Available UK: Abacus, Jones, National, P. & L.; USA: Creekside, Dan's Dahlias, Elkhorn; elsewhere: Wirth.

Rockabye
Small formal decorative (unclassified); lavender cut flower variety, height 1.2m (4ft); originated USA in 1996. Available USA: Alpen, Capistrano, Clacks, Dahlia Dandies, Swan Island.

Rockcliffe
Miniature decorative (NDS); white and lavender blends; exhibition and cut flower variety; 1.1m (3.5ft) in height; raised by T. Thompson, UK, in 1996. Available UK: Abacus, Jones.

Rocky Mountain High
Small incurved cactus (ADS); light blends, lavender and white; originated by Calvin Cook, USA, in 2001. Available USA: Arrowhead.

Roilyn
Medium semi-cactus (ADS); dark red exhibition variety, 1.2m (4ft) in height; originated by W. Almand, USA, in 1980. Awarded the Derrill Hart medal. Available USA: Clacks, Elkhorn.

Rokesley Mini
Miniature cactus (NDS); white exhibition and garden variety, 0.9m (3ft) in height; raised by Arthur Wood, UK, in 1971. Award Merit 1975 Wisley (NDS). Available UK: National.

Rokewood Opal
Small cactus (ADS); lavender, top exhibition variety; height 1.2m (4ft); early mid-season (USA); originated USA in 1997. Available USA: Capistrano, Clacks; Canada: Ferncliff.

Rolf
Medium semi-cactus (ADS); variegated yellow and red, exhibition variety; 1.2m (4ft) in height; originated by Gregersdal, Denmark, in 1998. Available USA: Clacks; elsewhere: Jacks.

Romance
Miniature straight cactus (unclassified); pink and cream, cut flower variety, on a 1.1m (3.5ft) high bush; originated USA in 1945. Available USA: Dahlia Dandies, Frey's, Swan Island; elsewhere: Turc.

Ron's Dark Ember
Medium lacinated (ADS); dark red, exhibition variety; 1.4m (4.5ft) high bush; originated by Clack, USA, in 1998. Available USA: Clacks, Elkhorn, Mingus.

Ron's R. J.
Miniature ball (unclassified); dark red, garden variety, 1.2m (4ft) in height; originated USA. Available USA: Clacks, Elkhorn.

ROBANN REGAL

ROBIN HOOD

ROCKCLIFFE

ROKEWOOD OPAL

Rosalie
Collerette (NDS); pink with pink collar; exhibition and garden variety, 1.1m (3.5ft) in height; raised by Norman Horton, UK, in 1970. Available UK: National.

Rosario
Miniature formal decorative (ADS); pink variety; originated by Cinquemani, USA, in 2001.

Rose Cupid
Miniature ball (NDS); pink exhibition, garden and cut flower variety; 0.9m (3ft) in height; raised by Morton Hall, UK, in 1990. Available UK: National, P. & L.

Rose Jupiter
Giant semi-cactus (NDS), large semi-cactus (ADS); pink and white blends (NDS), dark blends, white and dark pink (ADS); introduced in the UK in 1986. Available UK: Clark, Cruikshank, Halls, National, P. & L., Porter, Roberts; USA: Elkhorn; elsewhere: Geerlings, Jacks, Konishi.

Rose Toscano
Miniature formal decorative (ADS); orange exhibition variety, 1.2m (4ft) in height; originated by B. and H. Brown, USA, in 1991. Winner of the Lynn B. Dudley 1990 and Stanley Johnson medals. Available USA: Arrowhead, Alpen, Clacks, Dan's Dahlias, Elkhorn, Mingus, Sea-Tac.

Rosemary Webb
Waterlily (unclassified); yellow and pink blends, cut flower variety; 1.2m (4ft) high bush; originated USA in 1966. Available USA: Connell's, Frey's, Sea-Tac.

Rosendale Luke
Small decorative (NDS); pink blended exhibition variety, 1.1m (3.5ft) high; raised by D. Kershaw, UK, in 1996. Available UK: Abacus, Butterfield, Cruikshank, National, Oscroft, P. & L., Spencer, Station House, Taylor.

Rosendale Tara
Miniature decorative (NDS); yellow exhibition variety; 0.9m (3ft) in height; plant raised by D. Kershaw, UK, in 1997. Available UK: Cruikshank, Oscroft, P. & L.

Rosita
Collerette (unclassified); pink with white-collar; 0.6m (2.5ft) high bush; originated USA in 1984. Available: USA: Connell's, Swan Island.

Rosy Morn
Miniature formal decorative (unclassified); pink and white blends, cut flower variety; 1.2m (4ft) high bush; originated USA in 1986. Available USA: Connell's.

Rosy Wings
Collarette (ADS); pink exhibition variety on a 1.2m (4ft) high bush; originated by N. Gitts, USA, in 1990. Available USA: Swan Island.

Rothesay Castle
Dwarf bedder (miniature decorative) (NDS); white blends, garden variety 0.3m (1ft) high; introduced by A. Lister, UK, in 1948. Available UK: National.

Rothesay Herald
Dwarf bedder (small decorative) (NDS); red and white bicolour garden variety, 0.9m (1ft) in height; raised by

A. Lister, UK, in 1960. Available UK: National.

Rothesay Reveller
Medium decorative (NDS); purple and white bicolour, garden and cut flower variety; 1.1m (3.5ft) in height. Raised by A. Lister, UK, in 1954. Available UK: National; USA: Sea-Tac; Canada: Ferncliff.

Rothesay Robin
Small decorative (NDS); pink and bronze blends; exhibition variety; 1.1m (3.5ft) in height; plant raised by A. Lister, UK, in 1968. Available UK: Abacus, Cruikshank, National, P. & L., Station House.

Rothesay Superb
Miniature ball (NDS and ADS); red exhibition, garden and cut flower variety; height 1.2m (4ft); raised by A. Lister, UK, in 1956. Available UK: National; USA: Dan's Dahlias, Swan Island.

Rotterdam
Medium semi-cactus (NDS); red exhibition variety, 1.4m (4.5ft) in height; introduced by Bruidegom, Holland, in 1961. Award Merit Wisley 1964 (NDS). Available UK: National; elsewhere: Jager.

Roundabout
Miniature formal decorative (unclassified); yellow with orange centre, cut flower variety on a 0.9m (3ft) high bush; originated USA in 1988. Available USA: Swan Island.

Rowdy
Collerette (unclassified); orange and red blends with a yellow collar; garden variety on a 1.1m (3.5ft) high bush; originated USA in 1999. Available USA: Swan Island.

ROSALIE

ROSE CUPID

ROSE JUPITER

ROSENDALE LUKE

ROSENDALE TARA

ROTHESAY REVELLER

Royal Globe
Ball (unclassified); variegated garden variety, height 0.9m (3ft); originated USA. Available USA: Clacks.

Rubob's Lady
Small formal decorative (ADS); bicolour, purple and white, height 0.9m (3ft); originated by Lamson, USA, in 1988. Available USA: Clacks.

Rubob's Tessie
Medium formal decorative (unclassified); light blends, 0.9m (3ft); originated USA. Available USA: Clacks.

Ruby Rainbow
Miniature cactus (ADS); red exhibition variety, 1.5m (5ft); originated USA in 2001. Available USA: Clacks.

Ruby Red
Waterlily (unclassified); red cut flower and floral art variety; height 1.2m (4ft); originated by L. Connell, USA, in 1977. Available USA: Connell's.

Ruby Viola
Medium lacinated (ADS); dark pink exhibition variety; originated by Lamour, Canada, in 1997. Available USA: Mingus.

Ruby Wedding
Miniature decorative (NDS); purple exhibition, garden and cut flower variety; 0.9m (3ft) in height; raised by S. Long, UK, in 1981. Available UK: National; USA: Connell's.

Ruddy
Miniature ball (ADS); red exhibition variety; 1.1m (3.5ft) in height; originated by Phil Traff, USA, in 1994. Available USA: Clacks, Elkhorn, SB Gardens.

Rufus
Medium semi-cactus (ADS); flame variety; introduced Gregersdal, Denmark, in 2000.

Ruskin Belle
Medium semi-cactus (NDS); purple exhibition and garden variety; 1.2m (4ft) high plant; raised by Stan Pennington, UK, in 1987. Available UK: National.

Ruskin Charlotte
Medium semi-cactus (NDS); lavender exhibition variety; 1.2m (4ft) high; raised by Stan Pennington, UK, in 1996. Available UK: Abacus, Cruikshank, Halls, JRG, National, Roberts, Station House; elsewhere: Jacks.

Ruskin Diane
Small decorative (NDS), small formal decorative (ADS); yellow (NDS and ADS); exhibition and garden variety; height 1.2m (4ft); raised by Stan Pennington, UK, in 1984. Available UK: Abacus, Butterfield, Clark, Cruikshank, Halls, JRG, National, Oscroft, P. & L., Porter, Pratt, Roberts, Scotts, Spencer, Station House, Taylor; USA: Connell's, Dan's Dahlias, Mingus, SB Gardens, Sea-Tac; elsewhere: Englehardt, Geerlings, Jacks.

Ruskin Gypsy
Ball (ADS); red exhibition and cut flower variety on a 1.4m (4ft) high bush; originated by Stan Pennington, UK, in 1986. Available USA: Elkhorn, Swan Island.

Ruskin Impact
Small formal decorative (ADS); pink exhibition variety; raised S. Pennington, UK, in 2000.

Ruskin Marigold
Small semi-cactus (NDS), small straight cactus (ADS); orange exhibition and garden variety; 1.2m (4ft) high; raised by Stan Pennington, UK, 2001. Available UK: Butterfield, Halls, National, Oscroft, Scotts, Taylor.

Ruskin Myra
Small semi-cactus (unclassified); orange and yellow blended exhibition and garden variety on a 1.2m (4ft) high bush; raised by S. Pennington, UK, 2001. Available UK: Halls, Porter, Spencer, Taylor.

Ruskin Petite
Miniature decorative (NDS); yellow garden variety, 1.1m (3ft) high plant; raised by Stan Pennington, UK. Available UK: National, Tivey.

Ruskin Tangerine
Small ball or miniature ball (NDS), miniature ball (ADS); orange exhibition and garden variety, 1.2m (4ft) in height; raised by Stan Pennington, UK, in 1994. Available UK: National, Spencer; USA: Alpen, Capistrano.

Rustig
Medium decorative (NDS); yellow exhibition and garden variety; height 1.2m (4ft); raised by A. Hindry, South Africa, in 1970. Available UK: Abacus, National, Station House.

Rusty Hope
Miniature decorative (NDS); bronze blends, garden and cut flower variety; raised by Terry Clarke, UK, in 1972. Available UK: National, Tivey.

Rusty Ritchie
Miniature formal decorative (ADS); dark blends, red and yellow; originated by Franklin, USA, in 1997.

Ruth E
Medium semi-cactus (ADS); red exhibition variety; originated by Dickhoff, USA, in 1974. Awarded the Lynn B. Dudley medal 1973 (ADS).

RUDDY

RUSKIN BELLE

RUSKIN CHARLOTTE

RUSKIN DIANE

RUSKIN IMPACT

RUSKIN MARIGOLD

RUSKIN MYRA

RUSKIN TANGERINE

Ruth Elaine
Small lacinated cactus
(unclassified); yellow exhibition
variety; originated by L.
Connell, USA, in 1988.
Available USA: Connell's.

Ruthie G
Waterlily (ADS); light blends,
yellow and pink, garden
variety, 1.2m (4ft) high;
originated by Bateman, USA, in
1978. Available USA: Clacks,
Creekside, Elkhorn, SB
Gardens, Sea-Tac.

Ryan C
Medium formal decorative
(unclassified); bicolour, purple
and white, cut flower variety;
height 1.4m (4.5ft); originated
USA in 1991. Available USA:
Swan Island.

Ryan Fou
Large informal decorative
(unclassified); white with red
and purple stripes and splashes;
garden variety; height 1.2m
(4ft); originated USA in 1962.
Available USA: Swan Island.

Ryan K
Miniature semi-cactus (ADS);
pink exhibition variety; 1.2m
(4ft) in height; originated by
Keiffer, USA, in 1989.

Ryedale Rebecca
Giant semi-cactus (NDS); orange
blends, exhibition variety, 1.2m
(4ft) in height; raised by M.
Hardwick, UK, in 1995.
Available UK: Cruikshank,
National, Oscroft, P. & L.; USA:
Mingus; elsewhere: Jacks.

S

Saanich Lady
Small semi-cactus (ADS);
purple variety; originated by
Iverson, Canada, in 2001.

Saanich Miss
Miniature formal decorative
(ADS); yellow exhibition and
garden variety; 1.2m (4ft) in
height; originated by Iverson,
Canada, in 2000.

Saanich Surprise
Miniature formal decorative
(ADS); bronze exhibition and
garden variety; 1.2m (4ft) in
height; originated by Iverson,
Canada, in 2000.

Safe Shot
Miniature decorative (ADS);
orange blends, garden variety,
1.2m (4ft); introduced
Bruidegom, Holland, in 1964.
Available UK: National;
elsewhere: Dgid.

Sai-Shun
Large semi-cactus (ADS); light
blends; variety introduced by
Kaishi, Japan, in 2000.

Salmon Athalie
Semi-cactus (NDS); pink
exhibition, garden and cut
flower variety; 1.5m (5ft) high;
raised by Otterway, UK, 1986.
Available UK: National; USA:
Elkhorn.

Salmon Keene
Large or medium semi-cactus
(NDS), medium semi-cactus
(ADS); light blends, yellow and

pink exhibition variety, 1.2m
(4ft) in height; raised by Tom
Pashley, UK, in 1978. Award
Merit 1981 Wisley (NDS).
Available UK: Abacus, Clark,
Cruikshank, Hall, Jones,
National, P. & L., Spencer,
Station House; USA: Mingus.

Salmon Rays
Small cactus (NDS), small
incurved cactus (ADS); pink
blends (NDS), bronze (ADS);
garden and cut flower variety;
raised by Dobbie, UK, in 1958.
Award Merit Wisley 1965
(NDS). Available UK: National;
USA: Clacks.

Salmon Symbol
Medium semi-cactus (NDS);
pink blends; exhibition, garden
and cut flower variety, 1.2m
(4ft) high plant; raised by
Harry Cliss, UK, in 1974.
Available UK: Abacus, Station
House.

Salsa
Miniature decorative (NDS);
red garden variety, height 1.2m
(4ft); introduced by Verwer,
Holland, in 1989. Award
Garden Merit Wisley (NDS).
Available elsewhere: Dgid.

Sam Huston
Giant decorative (NDS), giant
formal decorative (ADS);
orange blends (NDS), orange
(ADS); exhibition variety; 1.2m
(4ft) high; originated by Earle
Huston, USA, in 1994.
Available UK: Abacus, Halls,
National, P. & L., Porter; USA:
Alpen, Clacks, Dahlia Dandies,
Dan's Dahlias; elsewhere: Jacks.

RYEDALE REBECCA

SALMON KEENE

SALSA

SAM HUSTON

Sam Wise
Waterlily (unclassified); white and lavender blended, cut flower and garden variety; on a 1.2m (4ft) high bush; originated by Connell, USA. Available USA: Connell's.

San Francisco Sunrise
Small informal decorative (ADS); orange exhibition variety, height 1.2m (4ft); originated by Juul, USA, in 1998. Available USA: Clacks.

Sandia Fancy Dancer
Medium lacinated (ADS); flame variety; originated by Boley, USA, in 2000. Available USA: SB Gardens.

Sandia Shomei
Waterlily (ADS); lavender exhibition variety; originated by Boley, USA, in 2001. Available USA: SB Gardens.

Sandia Showboat
Waterlily (ADS); yellow exhibition variety; originated by Boley, USA, in 2001. Available USA: SB Gardens.

Sandra's Tiffany
Small formal decorative (ADS); red variety; originated by S. Wilson, Canada, in 2000.

Sans Souci
Large incurved cactus (ADS); light blends, pink and yellow exhibition variety; height 1.1m (3.5ft); originated by Simon, USA, in 1994. Available USA: Clacks.

Santa Claus
Small informal decorative (ADS); bicolour, red and white; originated by Harold Miller, USA, in 1983. Available USA: Connell's, Creekside, Dahlia Dandies, Dan's Dahlias, Mingus, SB Gardens; Canada: Candahlia; elsewhere: Konishi.

Santa's Helper
Miniature formal decorative (ADS); red and white bicolour, exhibition and garden variety; 1.1m (3.5ft) in height; originated by Franklin, USA, in 2001

Sara G
Large semi-cactus (NDS); pink blends, exhibition variety, 1.2m (4ft) in height; raised by Tom Mantle, UK, in 1979. Available UK: National, Oscroft, P. & L.

Sarah Jane
Large informal decorative (ADS); orange exhibition variety; originated by Templeman, USA, in 1974.

Sarah Mae
Large incurved cactus (ADS); dark pink, garden variety; height 1.1m (3.5ft); originated by Takeuchi, USA, in 1985. Available USA: Clacks, Dahlia Dandies, Mingus.

Sassy
Miniature formal decorative (ADS); pink, cut flower variety; height 0.9m (3ft); originated by Towell, USA, in 1973. Available USA: Frey's.

Satokagura
Large informal decorative (ADS); light blends, pink and yellow; originated by Konishi, Japan, in 2001.

Scarborough
Brilliant medium incurving cactus (ADS); dark blends, red and pink, garden and cut flower variety; height 1.5m (5ft); originated by Neville Weekes, UK, in 1988. Available USA: Alpen, Arrowhead, Clacks, Connell's, Creekside, Dan's Dahlias, Mingus.

Scarlet Comet
Anemone (ADS); red exhibition and garden variety; 0.9m (3ft) in height; sport of Comet; raised by G. Joyce, UK, in 1959. Award Merit 1975 Wisley (NDS).

Scarlet Kokarde
Miniature decorative (unclassified); red exhibition, garden and cut flower variety; 1.4m (4ft) high sport of Schweitzer's Kokarde; introduced by C. Brown, USA, in 1978. Available UK: Cruikshank, National, P. & L.

Scatter Red
Small informal decorative (ADS); lavender garden and exhibition variety; 1.1m (3.5ft) in height; originated by Paradise, USA, in 1998.

Scaur Swinton
Medium decorative (NDS), medium formal decorative (ADS); pink (NDS), dark pink (ADS); raised by E. Wilson, UK, in 1998. Available UK: Aylett's, Cruikshank, Halls, National, Oscroft, P. & L., Porter.

Schweitzer's Kokarde
Miniature decorative (NDS); yellow and red blends; exhibition, garden and cut flower variety; 1.2m (4ft) in height; introduced by Schweitzer, Germany, in 1963. Award Merit Wisley 1967 (NDS). Available UK: Cruikshank, National.

Scorpion
Large cactus (ADS); orange exhibition and garden variety; height 1.2m (4ft); originated by Wyn, USA, in 2000; early to mid-season (USA). Available USA: SB Gardens; Canada: Ferncliff.

SANTA CLAUS

SARA G

SCARLET COMET

SCAUR SWINTON

SARAH JANE

Scottish Rhapsody (synonym Eileen Denny)
Medium semi-cactus (NDS); white exhibition variety, 1.2m (4ft) high plant; introduced by Dunsholt nursery, UK, in 1981.

Scura
Mignon single (ADS); red exhibition variety; originated USA in 1991. Available USA: Dan's Dahlias.

Sea-Cascabel
Small semi-cactus (ADS); purple variety; originated by Eckhoff, USA, in 2000. Available USA: Sea-Tac.

Sea-Chiquita
Peony (ADS); bronze, cut flower variety; height 0.6m (2ft); Eckhoff, USA, in 1993. Available USA: Frey's, Sea-Tac.

Sea-Electra
Small informal decorative (ADS); purple variety; originated by Eckhoff, USA, in 1992. Available USA: Sea-Tac.

Sea-Fuego
Small semi-cactus (ADS); flame variety; originated by Eckhoff, USA, in 1992. Available USA: Sea-Tac.

Sea-Miss
Miniature ball (ADS); pink, garden variety; 1.1m (3.5ft) in height; originated by Eckhoff, USA, in 1983.

Sean C
Collarette (ADS); purple and white, garden variety; height 0.7m (1.5ft); originated by Fanning, USA, in 1997. Available USA: Alpen.

Sea-Oro
Medium informal decorative (ADS); bronze, garden variety; 1.5m (4.5ft) in height; originated by Eckhoff, USA, in 1988. Available USA: Sea-Tac.

Senior Ball
Ball (ADS); light blends, white and purple/exhibition variety; height 1.1m (3.5ft); originated by Almond, USA, in 1980. Awarded the Derrill Hart medal (ADS). Available USA: Clacks, SB Gardens.

Senzoe Ursula
Small decorative (NDS); lavender and white blends, exhibition and garden variety; 1.2m (4ft) in height; raised by Hans Zoebel, UK, in 1985. Available UK: Cruikshank, Jones, JRG, National, Spencer; USA: Mingus; Canada: Ferncliff; elsewhere: Jacks.

September Moon
Waterlily (ADS); yellow exhibition variety; originated by L. Connell, USA, in 2001. Available USA: Connell's.

September Song
Medium lacinated (ADS); light blends, yellow and pink exhibition variety; originated by Madlyn Geisert, USA, in 1998.

Shadow Cat
Miniature formal decorative (ADS); dark red, exhibition variety; 1.6m (6ft) high bush; originated by L. Connell, USA, in 1986. Available USA: Clacks, Connell's, Dan's Dahlias.

Shandy
Small semi-cactus (NDS); orange and pink blends, garden and cut flower variety; height 1.1m (3.5ft), raised by John Crutchfield, UK, in 1972. Available UK: Aylett's, Halls, National, P. & L.

Sharon Ann
Large semi-cactus (ADS); light blends, pink and white, garden variety; height 1.2m (4ft); originated by Odewwald, USA, in 1986. Available USA: Clacks, Elkhorn, Sea-Tac.

Sheabird
Small lacinated (ADS); light blends, garden variety, 1.2m (4ft) high plant; originated by L. Connell, USA, in 1993. Available USA: Connell's, Dan's Dahlias, Elkhorn.

Shea's Rainbow
Miniature cactus (ADS); variegated pink and yellow exhibition variety; originated by Clacks, USA, in 1999. Available USA: Clacks, Dahlia Dandies.

Sheila Mooney
Giant or large decorative (NDS), large informal decorative (ADS); white exhibition variety; originated by Mooney, Canada, in 1994. Available UK: Cruikshank, P. & L.; USA: Connell's, Dan's Dahlias, Mingus; Canada: Candahlia.

Sherwood Monarch
Giant semi-cactus (NDS); bronze exhibition variety, height 1.4m (4.5ft); raised by R. Marshall, UK. Available UK: National, Tivey.

Sherwood Standard
Medium decorative (NDS), medium informal decorative (ADS); bronze exhibition and garden variety, 1.2m (4ft) in height; raised by R. Marshall, UK, in 1980. Available UK: Abacus, Halls, National.

SCURA

SEAN C

SHANDY

SHEILA MOONEY

SHERWOOD MONARCH

SHERWOOD STANDARD

Sherwood Sunrise
Small decorative (NDS); orange
blends, exhibition and garden
variety, 1.2m (4ft) high plant;
raised by R. Marshall, UK, in
1984. Available UK: National,
Oscroft.

Sherwood Titan
Giant decorative (NDS); orange
exhibition variety; 1.4m (4.5ft)
in height; raised by R.
Marshall, UK, in 1984.
Available UK: National, P. &
L., Tivey.

Shilo Jazzman
Small informal decorative
(ADS); white exhibition
variety; originated by Connell's
in 1989. Available USA: Dan's
Dahlias.

Shiloh Noelle
Giant informal decorative
(ADS); light blends, white and
lavender, exhibition variety;
1.2m (4ft) in height; originated
by Cunningham, USA, in 1986.
Available USA: Clacks, Dan's
Dahlias, Elkhorn; elsewhere:
Graines, Wirth.

Shinkyoku
Novelty double centre (ADS);
purple garden variety, height
1.2m (4ft); introduced Ohta,
Japan, in 1970. Available USA:
Clacks, Dan's Dahlias, Mingus.

Shirley Alliance
Small cactus (NDS), small
incurved cactus (ADS); orange
yellow blends (NDS), orange
(ADS); exhibition, garden and
cut flower variety; height 0.9m
(3ft); raised by W. E. Hall, UK,
in 1977. Available UK: Abacus,
National, Oscroft; USA:
Clacks, Dahlia Dandies, Frey's,
Sea-Tac.

Shirley Jane
Large decorative (NDS), large
informal decorative (ADS);
yellow bronze blends (NDS),
light blends bronze and pink

(ADS); raised by Simpson,
USA, in 1963. Available UK:
National.

Shirley Yeomans
Miniature ball (ADS); lavender
variety, height 1.1m (3.5ft);
originated USA in 2000.
Available USA: Clacks.

Shore Acres
Large semi-cactus (ADS); red
exhibition variety; originated
by Madlyn Geisert, USA, in
1993.

Show Girl
Medium formal decorative
(ADS); pink variety originated
by Shelley, USA, in 2000.

Show 'n' Tell
Large lacinated (ADS); dark
blends, red and yellow;
originated by W. Almand, USA,
in 1985. Awarded the Derrill
Hart medal (ADS). Available
USA: Alpen, Clacks, Connell's,
Dahlia Dandies, Dan's Dahlias,
Swan Island, Elkhorn, Frey's,
SB Gardens, Swan Island;
Canada: Ferncliff.

Show Off
Collerette (unclassified); dark
pink with a white collar;
garden variety; 1.2m (4ft) high
bush; originated USA in 1999.
Available USA: Swan Island.

Showcase Autumn
Large incurved cactus (ADS);
light blends, yellow and pink
variety; originated by T. & D.
Smith, USA, in 2001.

Showcase Sunrise
Large semi-cactus (ADS); light
blends, yellow and bronze
variety; originated by T. & D.
Smith, USA, in 2001.

Shy Princess
Medium cactus (ADS); white
exhibition variety; 1.5m (5ft) in
height; raised by Keith
Fleckney, UK, in 1976.

Siemen Doorenboos
Anemone (ADS); lavender,
garden variety; 0.4m (1.5ft) in
height; originated by Ballego,
Holland, in 1943. Available
USA: Swan Island.

Sierra Glow
Large informal decorative
(ADS); bronze exhibition
variety, 1.2m (4ft) high;
originated USA in 1995.
Available USA: Clacks,
Hamilton, Mingus.

Silhouette
Medium informal decorative
(unclassified); light blends,
yellow and purple, garden
variety, height 1.2m (4ft);
originated USA in 1996.
Available USA: Swan Island.

Silver City
Large decorative (NDS), large
formal decorative (ADS); white
exhibition variety, 1.2m (4ft)
high plant; raised by the
Reverend Brother Simplicius,
UK, in 1967. Award Merit
Wisley 1969 (NDS). Available
UK: Halls, National, P. & L.,
Roberts, Station House;
elsewhere: Geerlings.

Silver Slipper
Small semi-cactus (NDS); white
garden and cut flower variety,
height 1.1m (3.5ft); introduced
by Bruidegom, Holland, in
1975. Available UK: National,
Tivey.

Silver Tips
Pompon (ADS); bicolour
purple and white, height 0.9m
(3ft); introduced in 1959.
Available USA: Clacks,
SB Gardens.

Silverado
Small informal decorative
(unclassified); pink garden and
cut flower variety; 1.4m (4.5ft)
in height; originated USA in
1994. Available USA: Swan
Island.

SHERWOOD TITAN

SHY PRINCESS

SILVER CITY

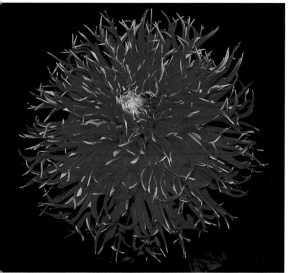

SHOW 'N' TELL

SHOW OFF

Sir Alf Ramsey
Giant decorative (NDS), giant informal decorative (ADS); light blends, lavender and white, exhibition variety; 1.2m (4ft) in height; raised by Peter Cleaver, UK, in 1999. Available UK: Abacus, Cruikshank, Halls, Jones, National, Oscroft, P. & L., Porter, Roberts, Spencer, Station House, Taylor; USA: Clacks, Creekside, Mingus; Canada: Candahlia; elsewhere: Jacks.

Skipley Gloria K
Medium semi-cactus (ADS); light blends, lavender and white, exhibition variety; 1.6m (5.5ft) in height; originated by R.Williams, USA, in 2001. Available USA: Clacks.

Skipley Grande
Large semi-cactus (ADS); light blends, yellow, dark pink exhibition variety; 1.5m (4.5ft) high plant; originated by R. Williams, USA, in 2001. Awarded the Derrill Hart medal (ADS). Available USA: Clacks.

Skipley Lisa
Small formal decorative (ADS); dark pink variety; height 1.5m (4.5ft); originated by R. Williams, USA, in 2000. Available USA: Clacks.

Skipley Night
Small semi-cactus (ADS); dark red exhibition variety; originated by R. Williams, USA, in 1990. Available USA: SB Gardens.

Skipley Select
Small formal decorative (ADS); lavender variety; height 1.2m (4ft); originated by R. Williams, USA, in 1999. Available USA: Clacks.

Skipley Spot
Small decorative (NDS), small formal decorative (ADS); bicolour of striking red and white; garden use; 1.2m (4ft) in height; originated by R. Williams, USA, in 1989. Available UK: National, Oscroft, Tivey; USA: Clacks, SB Gardens; elsewhere: Engelhardt.

Skipley Spot of Gold
Miniature formal decorative (ADS); dark pink, exhibition variety; originated by R. Williams, USA, in 2001. Awarded the Derrill Hart medal (ADS).

Skipley Stripe
Medium semi-cactus (ADS); variegated white and red garden variety, 1.5m (5ft) in height; originated by R. Williams, USA, in 1999. Available USA: Clacks.

Skipley Twyla
Medium incurved cactus (ADS); variegated yellow and red variety; 1.5m (5ft) in height; originated by R. Williams, USA, in 2001. Available USA: Clacks.

Skipley Valentine
Large cactus (ADS); red garden variety, 1.6m (6ft) high plant; originated by R. Williams, USA, in 1993. Available USA: Alpen, Dahlia Dandies.

Sky High
Small decorative (NDS); red exhibition variety, very tall, 1.7m (6ft); raised by John Sharp, UK, in 1974. Available UK: National, Tivey.

Skywalker
Small informal decorative (ADS); red cut flower variety; 1.4m (5ft) high plant; originated by N. Gitts in 1987. Available USA: Frey's, Swan Island.

Small World (synonymous with **Bowen**)
White pompon (NDS); useful for exhibition garden and cut flower; grows to a height of 90cm (2.5ft); raised by Norman Williams, Australia, in 1967. Available UK: Abacus, Aylett's, Clark, Cruikshank, Halls, National, Oscroft, P. & L., Porter, Tivey; USA: SB Gardens; elsewhere: Geerlings, Graines.

Smartypants
Small formal decorative (unclassified); dark red, garden variety, prolific bush, 0.7m (2.5ft) in height; originated USA in 2001.

Smokey Gal
Medium semi-cactus (ADS); lavender, cut flower variety, 1.5m (5ft) in height; originated by L. Connell in 1985. Available USA: Frey's.

Smoots
Small lacinated (ADS); purple exhibition variety; originated by B. Wilson, USA, in 1988. Available USA: Dan's Dahlias, SB Gardens.

Snickerdoodle
Small formal decorative (ADS); orange, cut flower variety, height 1.6m (5.5ft); originated by Swan Island, USA, in 2000. Available USA: Swan Island.

SIR ALF RAMSEY

SKIPLEY SPOT

Snip
Miniature semi-cactus (NDS); bronze blends, garden variety; 1.2m (4ft) in height; raised by A. Bailey, UK, in 1966. Available UK: Abacus, National, Oscroft.

Snoho Beauty
Ball (ADS); light blends, pink and white variety; originated by Bonneywell, USA, in 1985. Available USA: Connell's, Dan's Dahlias.

Snoho Betty
Medium formal decorative (ADS); purple exhibition and cut flower, 1.6m (6ft) tall; variety originated by Bonneywell, USA, in 1994. Available USA: Alpen, Connell's, Dahlia Dandies, Dan's Dahlias, Sea-Tac; Canada: Ferncliff.

Snoho Crown
Small cactus (ADS); orange variety; originated by Bonneywell, USA, in 1998.

Snoho Doris
Ball (ADS); dark blends bronze and red, garden and cut flower variety; 1.5m (5ft) in height; originated by Bonneywell, USA, in 2000. Available USA: Alpen.

Snoho Jo Jo
Ball (ADS); bronze exhibition variety; originated by Bonneywell, USA, in 2000. Awarded the Derrill Hart medal (ADS). Available USA: Dahlia Dandies, Dan's Dahlias, SB Gardens.

Snoho Matthew
Small formal decorative (ADS); dark-red variety; originated by Bonneywell, USA, in 1999.

Snoho Okra
Miniature ball (ADS); bronze exhibition variety; originated

by Bonneywell, USA, in 1994. Available USA: SB Gardens.

Snoho Peggy
Small ball (NDS), ball (ADS); pink and white blends (NDS), dark pink (ADS); exhibition and cut flower variety; 1.5m (5ft) in height; originated by Bonnywell, USA, in 1994. Available UK: Cruikshank, National; USA: Alpen, Clacks, Connell's, Creekside, Dan's Dahlias.

Snoho Skip
Star (ADS); orange exhibition variety; 1.5m (5ft) in height; originated by Bonneywell, USA, in 1998. Available USA: Clacks.

Snoho Splash
Small formal decorative (ADS); dark blends, white and purple; 1.2m (4ft) high; originated by Bonneywell, USA, in 1985. Available USA: Clacks.

Snoho Tammie
Ball (ADS); pink exhibition variety; 1.1m (3.5ft) in height; originated by Bonneywell, USA, in 1986. Available USA: Clacks, SB Gardens.

Snoho Triumph
Large semi-cactus (ADS); dark red exhibition variety; 1.5m (5ft) high bush; originated by Bonneywell, USA, in 1999. Available USA: Alpen, Clacks.

Snow White
Orchid (ADS); white garden and exhibition variety; 1.1m (3.5ft) in height; originated by L. Connell, USA, in 1995.

Snowbound
Large informal decorative (ADS); white exhibition variety; 1.5m (5ft) in height; originated by N. Gitts, USA, in 1997. Awarded the Derrill Hart medal

(ADS). Available USA: Alpen, Capistrano, Clacks, Dahlia Dandies, Swan Island, Dan's Dahlias, Mingus, Swan Island.

Snowflake
Small waterlily (NDS); white garden and cut flower variety; 1.5m (5ft) in height; originated by C. Kennedy, USA, in 1933. Available UK: National; USA: Frey's, Swan Island.

Snowgrandma
Small semi-cactus (ADS); white exhibition variety; originated by Masurat, USA, in 1996. Awarded the Derrill Hart medal (ADS).

Snowy
Miniature ball (NDS); white exhibition and garden variety; 0.9m (3ft) in height; introduced by Cor Geerlings, Holland, in 1997. Available UK: National, Unwin; elsewhere: Dgid, Geerlings.

So Dainty
Miniature semi-cactus (NDS); bronze blends; used for exhibition and cut flower; compact bush growing to a height of 90cm (3ft); raised by E. Richards, UK, in 1971. Award of Merit 1975, Wisley (NDS); award Garden Merit Wisley (NDS). Available UK: Abacus, Aylett's, National, Oscroft; USA: Clacks, Connell's.

Sonny Boy
Small formal decorative (ADS); yellow garden variety, height 1.5m (5ft); originated by L. Connell, in 1997. Available USA: Connell's.

Sophie K
Miniature formal decorative (unclassified); white exhibition and garden variety; 1.2m (4ft) in height; originated by Keiffer, USA, in 1993.

SNOHO PEGGY

SNOHO TAMMIE

SNOWBOUND

SNOWY

SO DAINTY

SONNY BOY

Spartacus
Large decorative (NDS), large informal decorative (ADS); dark red exhibition, garden and cut flower variety; originated by M. Senior, USA, in 1993. Awarded the Lynn B. Dudley medal 1992, and the Derrill Hart and Stanley Johnson medals. Available UK: Jones, National, Oscroft, Spencer, Suttons, Tivey; USA: Alpen, Clacks, Connell's, Creekside, Dahlia Dandies, Dan's Dahlias, Frey's, Mingus, SB Gardens, Sea-Tac; Canada: Ferncliff; elsewhere: Engelhardt, Geerlings, Graines, Jacks, Wirth.

Spectacular
Dwarf bedder (semi-cactus) (NDS); lavender garden variety; 0.6m (2ft) in height; introduced by Bruidegom, Holland, in 1956. Available UK: National.

Speedy
Anemone (ADS); red variety; originated by D. Barnes, USA, in 2001.

Spellbreaker
Miniature formal decorative (ADS); red garden variety; 1.1m (3.5ft) in height; originated by N. Gitts, USA, in 2000. Available USA: Swan Island; elsewhere: Jacks.

Spenser's Angel
Small lacinated (ADS); lavender exhibition variety; height 1.5m (5ft); originated by Clack, USA, in 1998. Available USA: Clacks, Dahlia Dandies, Elkhorn.

Spike
Giant cactus (ADS); white exhibition variety; height 1.5m (5ft); originated by Frasier, USA, in 1967. Available USA: Alpen, Dahlia Dandies, Elkhorn; Canada: Ferncliff.

Square Circle
Medium informal decorative (ADS); white garden variety; 1.2m (4ft) in height; originated by Holicky, USA, in 1986. Available USA: Clacks.

St. Croix
Large informal decorative (ADS); bronze garden variety; originated by Simon, USA, in 1988. Available USA: Elkhorn, Mingus, SB Gardens.

Stacey Rachelle
Small formal decorative (unclassified); lavender cut flower, prolific bush; 1.2m (4ft) in height; originated USA in 1993. Available USA: Dan's Dahlias, Frey's, Swan Island.

Staci Erin
Small formal decorative (ADS); purple exhibition variety; originated by L. Connell, in 1993. Available USA: Dan's Dahlias.

Stanley A
Medium straight cactus (ADS); light blends, yellow and bronze garden variety; originated by Larkins and Zydner, USA, in 1998. Available USA: Arrowhead

Starbrite
Orchid (ADS); orange variety, height 1.2m (4ft); originated by L. Connell, USA, in 1988. Available USA: Clacks, Connell's, Dan's Dahlias.

Starchild
Orchid (ADS); white cut flower variety; height 1.2m (4ft); originated by Vadney, USA, in 1981. Available USA: Frey's, Swan Island.

Starlight Keene
Large or medium semi-cactus (NDS): yellow exhibition variety,

1.2m (4ft) in height; raised by Bassett, UK, in 1994. Available UK: Clark, National, Porter.

Starslady
Dwarf bedder (unclassified); pink, white tipped; garden variety; height 0.6m (2ft); originated USA. Excellent combination with Park Princess. Available Canada: Ferncliff.

Stellyvonne
Fimbriated large semi-cactus (NDS), medium lacinated (ADS); yellow pink blends (NDS), yellow (ADS); exhibition and garden variety; 1.2m (4ft) high; introduced by Cyril Higgo, South Africa, in 1989. Awarded the Derrill Hart medal (ADS). Available UK: National; USA: Alpen, Clacks, Connell's, Dahlia Dandies, Dan's Dahlias, Elkhorn.

Sterling Silver
Medium formal decorative (ADS); white exhibition variety, 1.2m (4ft) in height; originated by Eichman, USA, in 1965. Awarded the Derrill Hart medal (ADS). Available USA: Alpen, Clacks, Connell's, Creekside, Frey's, Mingus, SB Gardens, Sea-Tac, Swan Island.

Stoneleigh Cherry
Pompon (NDS and ADS); red (NDS), dark red (ADS); exhibition, garden and cut flower variety; 1.2m (4ft) in height; raised by Knight, UK, in 1979. Available UK: Aylett's, National; USA: Connell's.

Stoneleigh Joyce
Pompon (ADS); red exhibition variety; 1.1m (3.5ft) in height; originated by Knight, UK, in 1974. Available USA: Clacks, Connell's, Dahlia Dandies, SB Gardens.

SPARTACUS

STARLIGHT KEENE

STELLYVONNE

STERLING SILVER

Stump Cross
Small decorative (NDS); white
garden variety, 1.1m (3.5ft) in
height; raised by Fred Oscroft,
UK, in 1992. Available UK:
National.

Stylemaster
Medium cactus (NDS); yellow
garden and cut flower, 1.2m
(4ft) high plant; raised by dahlia
Maarse, Holland, in 1962.
Available UK: National, Tivey.

Sue Willo
Pompon (NDS); purple
exhibition garden and cut
flower variety, 1.2m (4ft) in
height; introduced by N.
Williams, Australia, in 1964.
Available UK: National.

Suffolk Punch
Medium decorative (NDS),
medium informal decorative
(ADS); purple garden variety,
1.1m (3.5ft) in height; raised
by Geoff Flood, UK, in 1975.
Available UK: Aylett's,
Butterfield, National; USA:
Clacks, Dahlia Dandies,
Elkhorn, Mingus; elsewhere:
Engelhardt, Wirth.

Suffolk Spectacular
Medium decorative (NDS);
white exhibition and garden
variety; 1.2m (4ft) in height;
raised by Geoff Flood, UK, in
1975. Available UK:
Cruikshank, National; USA:
Mingus.

Sugar Cane
Small formal decorative
(unclassified); bicolour, yellow
and white, cut flower variety;
1.2m (4ft) in height. Available
USA: Connell's, Dan's Dahlias,
Mingus, SB Gardens, Swan
Island.

Sugartown Sunrise
Medium formal decorative
(ADS); light blends, lavender
and yellow; originated by S.
Thomas, USA, in 1999.
Available USA: Clacks,
Creekside, Mingus.

Suitzus Julie
Lilliput (miscellaneous) (NDS),
waterlily (ADS); lavender garden
and cut flower variety; 0.3m
(1ft) in height; introduced in
1995. Available UK: National,
Station House; USA: Alpen.

Summer's End
Waterlily (ADS); light blends,
dark pink and yellow,
exhibition variety; height 1.2m
(4ft); originated by N. Gitts,
USA, in 1994. Awarded the
Derrill Hart medal (USA).
Available USA: Clacks,
Connell's, Creekside, Frey's,
Swan Island.

Sunlight Pastelle (synonymous
to **Barbara's Pastelle**)
Medium semi-cactus (NDS and
ADS); yellow blends (NDS),
light blends, yellow and
bronze; originated by James,
USA, in 1996. Available UK:
Clark, Cruikshank, National,
Pratt, Spencer; USA: Dahlia
Dandies, Elkhorn, Mingus;
Canada: Candahlia.

Sunray Glints
Medium semi-cactus (NDS);
yellow and pink blends,
exhibition garden and cut
flower variety; 1.2m (4ft) in
height; raised by R. Barker,
UK, in 1986. Available UK:
Abacus, JRG, National.

Superfine
Small cactus (NDS); yellow
exhibition and garden variety;

1.1m (3.5ft) in height; raised
by Bruidegom, Holland, in
1994. Available UK: Abacus,
National, Tivey; USA: Dan's
Dahlias, Mingus; elsewhere:
Geerlings.

Sure Thing
Medium cactus (NDS); red
exhibition and garden variety;
1.2m (4ft) high plant; raised by
dahlia Bruidegom, Holland, in
1966. Available UK: National;
elsewhere: Dgid.

Surprise
Large semi-cactus
(unclassified); pink exhibition
variety, height 1.2m (4ft);
introduced Holland, 1955.
Award Merit Wisley 1958
(NDS). Available USA: Mingus,
Swan Island.

Survivor
Giant formal decorative (ADS);
lavender exhibition variety;
height 1.2m (4ft); originated
USA in 1970. Available USA:
Clacks, Dahlia Dandies, Frey's,
Hamilton, Mingus.

Swan's Desert Storm
Large informal decorative
(ADS); light blends, lavender
and pink exhibition variety;
0.9m (3ft) in height; originated
by N. Gitts, USA, in 1992.
Available USA: Elkhorn, Sea-
Tac, Swan Island.

Swan's Sunset
Large informal decorative
(ADS); dark blends, red and
orange exhibition variety;
height 1.1m (3.5ft); originated
by N. Gitts, USA, in 1990.
Available USA: Dan's Dahlias,
Elkhorn, Swan Island;
elsewhere: Graines.

SUNLIGHT PASTELLE

SUNRAY GLINTS

STUMP CROSS

SUITZUS JULIE

SUPERFINE

Swanvale
Small decorative (NDS), small formal decorative (ADS); yellow exhibition and garden variety; 1.5m (4.5ft) in height; raised Roger Turrell, UK, in 1989. Available UK: Clark, Cruikshank, National, Station House, Taylor, Tivey; elsewhere: Jacks.

Sweet Content
Small decorative (NDS), small formal decorative (ADS); yellow and bronze blends (NDS), dark blends yellow and dark red (ADS); garden and cut flower; 1.2m (4ft) in height; raised by W. Paterson, UK, in 1970. Available UK: National, Oscroft, P. & L.; USA: Dahlia Dandies.

Sweet Dreams
Medium semi-cactus (ADS); pink exhibition and cut flower variety, 1.5m (4.5ft) in height; originated by N. Gitts, USA, 1993. Available USA: Arrowhead, Clacks, Frey's, Swan Island.

Sweet Sue
Small informal decorative (ADS); purple garden and exhibition variety; originated by Keiffer, USA, in 1989.

Sweetheart
Lilliput single (NDS); pink and white, bicolour garden variety; 0.3m (1ft) in height; raised UK. Available UK: Abacus, National, Station House; elsewhere: Dgid.

Sylvia Craig Hunter
Medium formal decorative (ADS); orange exhibition variety; 1.6m (6ft) in height; originated USA in 2001. Available USA: Clacks, Creekside; elsewhere: Jacks.

Sylvia J
Collarette (ADS); purple with white collar, garden and exhibition variety; height 1.5m (4.5ft); originated by Alley, Canada, in 1997. Available Canada: Ferncliff.

Sylvia's Desire
Small cactus (NDS); pink-orange blends, exhibition variety; 0.9m (3ft) in height; raised by George Ormes, UK, in 1996. Available UK: Halls, National, P. & L., Spencer.

Symbol
Medium semi-cactus (NDS); orange-bronze blends, exhibition, garden and cut flower variety; 1.2m (4ft) high plant; introduced by Bruidegom, Holland, in 1958. Award Merit Wisley 1966 (NDS). Available UK: National, Tivey.

Syringa Elizabeth
Water lily (ADS); pink exhibition and garden variety; 1.4m (4.5ft) in height; originated by Marie Nau, USA, in 2000.

T

T.J.
Medium semi-cactus (ADS); flame variety; originated by Ellison, USA, in 2000.

Tahiti Sunrise
Medium semi-cactus (NDS), or small semi-cactus (ADS); red and yellow blends (NDS), and dark blends yellow and red (ADS); an excellent, striking garden variety, useful for cut flower; grows to a height of 1.2m (4ft); raised by G. Cox, UK, in 1975. Available UK:

National, Oscroft, P. & L.; USA: Connell's, Dan's Dahlias, Sea-Tac, Swan Island.

Tammy Foondle
Small informal decorative (ADS); yellow garden variety; originated by Mauer, USA, in 1970. Available USA: Dan's Dahlias.

Tanjoh
Small cactus (ADS); bicolour white and purple, exhibition and cut flower; height 1.1m (3.5ft); originated by Konishi, Japan, in 1980. Available USA: Swan Island.

Tara Brian
Medium formal decorative (ADS); red exhibition variety; height 1.5m (4.5ft); introduced L. J. Neilson, New Zealand, in 1994. Available USA: Creekside, Dan's Dahlias, Elkhorn; elsewhere: Jacks.

Taranga Jubilee
Medium lacinated (ADS); dark blends, garden variety, height 1.2m (4ft); introduced Elaine Fenton, New Zealand, in 2001. Available USA: Creekside.

Taratahi Lilac
Small semi-cactus (NDS), small incurved cactus (ADS); lavender blooms (NDS), lavender and white (ADS); for exhibition use, growing 1m (3ft) high, blooms on long slender stems; raised by John Frater, New Zealand, in 1994. Winner Stanley Johnson award in 2000. Available UK: Halls, National, P. & L.; USA: Alpen, Arrowhead, Clacks, Creekside, Dahlia Dandies, Geerlings, Mingus, SB Gardens; elsewhere: Jacks.

SWANVALE

SYLVIA'S DESIRE

TARANGA JUBILEE

TARATAHI LILAC

Taratahi Ruby
Small waterlily (NDS),
waterlily (ADS); red exhibition,
garden and cut flower variety;
height 1.5m (4.5ft); introduced
by John Frater, New Zealand,
in 1997. Available UK:
Butterfield, Halls, JRG,
National, Oscroft, P. & L.,
Station House, Taylor; USA:
Alpen, Arrowhead, Clacks,
Connell's, Dahlia Dandies,
Mingus, SB Gardens;
elsewhere: Geerlings.

Taratahi Sunrise
Waterlily (ADS); bicolour,
yellow and orange, exhibition
and cut flower; height 0.7m
(2.5ft); originated by E. & R.
Frater, New Zealand, in 2001.
Awarded the Lynn B. Dudley
medal.

Tartan
Medium decorative (NDS),
medium informal decorative
(ADS); bicolour, dark red and
white, garden variety, 1.2m (4ft);
introduced by H. Johnston, New
Zealand, in 1951. Award Merit
Wisley 1952 (NDS). Available
UK: Jager, National; USA:
Clacks, Sea-Tac; elsewhere:
Engelhardt, Geerlings.

Taum Sauk
Giant semi-cactus (ADS); dark
red exhibition variety, height
1.2m (4ft); strong stems;
originated by Simon, USA, in

1989. Available USA:
Arrowhead, Clacks, Hamilton,
SB Gardens; Canada: Ferncliff.

Taylor Nelson
Small semi-cactus (ADS); dark
red, exhibition variety; 1.2m
(4ft) in height; originated by W.
Almand, USA, in 1994.
Awarded the Derrill Hart
medal (ADS). Available USA:
Dan's Dahlias.

Tea Time
Medium semi-cactus (NDS and
ADS); red and white bicolour
(NDS), dark pink (ADS);
garden and cut flower variety;
height 1.2m (4ft); introduced
by Bruidegom, Holland, in
1970.

Teesbrooke Audrey
Collerette (NDS); lavender, and
lavender with white blends,
collar height, 1.4m (4ft); raised
by Phil Orley, UK, in 2000.
Available UK: Aylett's, Halls.

Television
Medium incurved cactus
(ADS); flame, garden variety,
introduced by Nagel, Belgium,
in 1941.

Temarie Butterscotch
Collarette (ADS); bronze
garden variety, height 1.2m
(4ft); originated in USA in
2000. Available USA: Connell's.

Temptress
Small cactus (NDS); white
blends exhibition and garden
variety; 1.2m (4ft) in height;
introduced by Ludwig,
Holland, in 1958. Available
UK: National.

Tenga
Large, incurved cactus (ADS);
yellow garden variety;
introduced Tokunaga, Japan, in
1972. Available elsewhere:
Konishi.

Thais
Collerette (NDS); red, with
purple collar; exhibition variety,
1.1m (3.5ft); introduced by
dahlia Maarse, Holland, in
1972. Available UK: JRG.

Thames Valley
Medium decorative (NDS);
yellow exhibition variety; 1.2m
(4ft) high plant; introduced by
Bruidegom, Holland, in 1972;
named after a prominent UK
dahlia society. Available UK:
National.

The Baron
Small formal decorative (ADS);
purple exhibition variety;
originated by Beck, USA, in
1982. Awarded the Lynn B.
Dudley 1981 and Derrill Hart
medals (ADS).

TARATAHI RUBY TARTAN

TAYLOR NELSON TEESBROOKE AUDREY

THAIS THE BARON

The Queen
Small semi-cactus (ADS); lavender exhibition variety, height 1.4m (4.5ft); originated by Phillip, USA, in 1973. Awarded the Lynn B. Dudley medal 1972 (ADS). Available USA: Capistrano.

The Shining
Collerette (unclassified); white exhibition variety, height 1.1m (3.5ft); long, straight stems; originated by K. & S. Williams, USA, in 2002. Available Canada: Ferncliff.

Thelma Clements
Large decorative (NDS), giant informal decorative (ADS); orange and white bicolour (NDS), bicolour pink and white (ADS); exhibition, garden and cut flower variety; raised by Les Wright, UK, in 1985. Available UK: National, Tivey; USA: SB Gardens.

Thomas A. Edison
Medium formal decorative (ADS); purple exhibition variety, height 1.1m (3.5ft); originated by Dahliadel in 1929. Available USA: Elkhorn, Swan Island; elsewhere: Engelhardt, Geerlings.

Thomas McNulty
Orchid (ADS); dark red exhibition and garden variety; 0.9m (3ft) in height; originated by McNulty, USA, in 1995. Available USA: Clacks, Dan's Dahlias.

Tinker Bell
Peony (ADS); dark blends lavender, white and purple; garden and exhibition variety; height 0.6m (2ft); originated by Holm, USA, in 1982. Available USA: Dahlia Dandies.

Tiny Tempest
Pompon (ADS); red exhibition variety; originated by Franklin, USA, in 2001.

Tiny Tot
Lilliput (miscellaneous) (NDS); pink, garden variety; 0.4m (1.5ft) high; originated by D. Michaels, USA, in 1944. Available UK: Butterfield, Halls, National.

Tioga Autumn
Medium lacinated (ADS); light blends, yellow and dark pink garden variety, height 1.2m (4ft); originated by Madlyn Geisert, USA, in 1997. Available USA: Arrowhead, Clacks, Dan's Dahlias; elsewhere: Graines.

Tioga Love Song
Large lacinated (ADS); pink exhibition variety, height 1.2m (4ft); originated by Madlyn Geisert, USA, in 1996. Available USA: Dahlia Dandies, Elkhorn, SB Gardens.

Tioga Maiden
Medium lacinated (ADS); dark blends, purple and white, exhibition variety; height 1.4m (4.5ft); originated by Madlyn Geisert, USA, in 1998. Available USA: Clacks.

Tioga Spice
Fimbriated medium semi-cactus (NDS), medium lacinated (ADS); yellow garden and cut flower variety (NDS), flame (ADS); originated by Madlyn Geisert, USA, in 1994. Available UK: Cruikshank, National.

Tip Toe
Small formal decorative (ADS); bicolour, purple and white, exhibition variety; height 1.2m (4ft); originated by W. Almand, USA, in 1972. Awarded the Lynn B. Dudley medal 1971 (ADS). Available USA: Clacks, Elkhorn.

Tohsuikyoh
Double orchid (miscellaneous) (NDS); pink blends, garden and cut flower variety; introduced K. Ohta, Japan, in 1972. Available UK: Abacus, National.

Tom Yano
Large semi-cactus (ADS); dark red exhibition variety; originated by Robert Furrow, USA, in 1983. Awarded the Lynn B. Dudley medal 1982 (ADS). Available USA: Clacks, Connell's, Dahlia Dandies, Hamilton.

Tommy Doc
Small semi-cactus (NDS); pink exhibition variety; height 1.1m (3.5ft); raised by F. Docherty, UK, in 1990. Available UK: Abacus, Halls, National, P. & L.

Tomo
Small formal decorative (ADS); bicolour, purple and white, cut flower variety; height 1.2m (4ft); originated USA in 1988. Available USA: Connell's, Dan's Dahlias; elsewhere: Geerlings, Jacks, Wirth.

Tonja
Giant informal decorative (ADS); bronze exhibition variety; originated USA in 1998. Available USA: Arrowhead.

Tonya
Medium formal decorative (ADS); yellow exhibition and garden variety; height 1.2m (4ft); originated by Hilberg, USA, in 1989. Available USA: Clacks, Elkhorn.

TIOGA AUTUMN

TIOGA SPICE

THE QUEEN

THELMA CLEMENTS

TOM YANO

Top Affair
Medium semi-cactus (NDS);
yellow garden and cut flower
variety, 1.2m (4ft) in height;
introduced by Bruidegom,
Holland, in 1959. Available
UK: National.

Top Choice
Medium semi-cactus (NDS);
flame yellow blends, garden
and cut flower variety; 1.2m
(4ft) in height; introduced by
Bruidegom, Holland, in 1959.
Available UK: Jager, National;
elsewhere: Dgid.

Top Honor
Small lacinated (ADS); dark
pink garden variety, height
1.5m (4.5ft); originated by L.
Connell, USA, in 1994.
Awarded the Derrill Hart
medal (ADS). Available USA:
Connell's, Dahlia Dandies.

Topmix Violetta and
Topmix Yellow
Mignon single (ADS); purple
(violetta), yellow garden
variety; height 0.2m (1ft);
introduced Ballego, Holland:
violetta in 1959, yellow in
1967.

Torrie Lunn
Miniature ball (ADS); yellow
garden and exhibition variety,
1.2m (4ft) in height; originated
by Rodewell, USA, in 1994.

Touch of Class
Medium semi-cactus (ADS);
light blends, lavender and
white, exhibition and cut
flower variety; height 1.5m
(4.5ft); originated by Swan
Island, USA, in 1991. Available
USA: Elkhorn, Swan Island;
elsewhere: Engelhardt, Graines.

Tranquility
Collerette (NDS); white with
white collar; exhibition, garden
and cut flower variety; raised by
Keith Hammett, New Zealand,
in 1999. Available UK: Halls.

Trelawny
Giant decorative (NDS); bronze
and red blends, exhibition
variety, 1.1m (3.5ft) in height;
raised by Dunn, UK, in 1968.
Available UK: Abacus,
Cruikshank, National, P. & L.;
elsewhere: Graines.

Trelyn Kiwi
Small semi-cactus (NDS), small
straight cactus (ADS); white and
pink blends (NDS), white (ADS);
exhibition and garden variety,
height 1.2m (4ft); raised by R.
Tudor, UK, in 1996. Available
UK: Abacus, Clark, Cruikshank,
Halls, JRG, National, Oscroft, P.
& L., Porter, Pratt, Spencer,
Station House, Taylor; USA:
Clacks; Canada: Candahlia;
elsewhere: Geerlings.

Trendy
Small decorative (NDS); yellow
blends, garden variety, 1.1m
(3.5ft) in height; raised by
Terry Clarke, UK, in 1971.
Available UK: National;
elsewhere: Dgid, Engelhardt,
Graines, Wirth.

Trengrove Autumn
Medium decorative (NDS);
bronze exhibition, garden and
cut flower variety, 1.2m (4ft)
high plant; raised by Gerry
Woolcock, UK, in 1990.
Available UK: National, P. &
L., Station House.

Trengrove Jill
Medium decorative (NDS),
small, formal decorative (ADS);
bronze (NDS), orange (ADS);
exhibition, garden and cut
flower variety; height 1.2m

(4ft); raised by Gerry Woolcock,
UK, in 1990. Available UK:
Aylett's, National, Oscroft, P. &
L., Tivey; elsewhere: Jacks.

Trengrove Millennium
Medium decorative
(unclassified); yellow exhibition
variety, height 1.2m (4ft);
raised by Gerry Woolcock, UK,
in 2000. Available UK: Taylor.

Trengrove Summer
Medium decorative (NDS);
yellow exhibition, garden and
cut flower variety; height 1.2m
(4ft); raised by Gerry Woolcock,
UK, in 1990. Available UK:
National, Oscroft, P. & L.,
Tivey; Canada: Ferncliff.

Trengrove Tauranga
Medium decorative (NDS);
bronze exhibition, garden and
cut flower variety; 1.2m (4ft)
high plant; raised by Gerry
Woolcock, UK, in 1990.
Available UK: National, P. &
L.; USA: Clacks, Creekside.

Tribune Judy L
Small, informal, decorative
(ADS); light blends, pink and
yellow exhibition variety;
originated by Lapierre,
Canada, in 2001.

Tribune's Dream Catcher
Large, incurved cactus (ADS);
dark blends, dark pink and
yellow variety; originated by
Lapierre, Canada, in 2001.

Tribune's Mary Moriarty
Large informal decorative
(ADS); white variety;
originated by Lapierre,
Canada, in 2001.

TRANQUILITY

TRELYN KIWI

TRENGROVE AUTUMN

TRENGROVE JILL

TRENGROVE MILLENNIUM

TRENGROVE TAURANGA

Triple Lee D
Small formal decorative (ADS); dark pink exhibition and cut flower variety; 1.5m (5ft) in height; prolific bloomer; good straight stems; originated by Duxbury, Canada, in 1998. Available USA: Alpen, Arrowhead, Mingus; Canada: Candahlia, Ferncliff.

Tropica
Small informal decorative (ADS); flame variety; originated by Ghio, USA, in 1999.

Tui Avis
Small, straight cactus (ADS); pink exhibition and garden variety; introduced Brian Buckley, New Zealand, in 1996. Available USA: Clacks, Connell's, Dan's Dahlias, Elkhorn, Mingus; elsewhere: Jacks.

Tui Christine
Miniature semi-cactus (ADS); red, garden variety; height 1.2m (4ft); introduced by Brian Buckley, New Zealand, in 1988. Available USA: Clacks, Mingus.

Tui Connie
Medium formal decorative (ADS); red cut flower variety; 1.5m (5ft) in height; raised Brian Buckley, New Zealand, in 1996. Available USA: Alpen, Clacks; elsewhere: Jacks.

Tui Orange
Small, semi-cactus (NDS and ADS); flame (NDS), orange (ADS); height 1.1m (3.5ft); introduced by Brian Buckley, New Zealand, in 1990. Available UK: Abacus, Cruikshank, Halls, National, Oscroft, P. & L., Pratt, Scotts, Station House, Taylor; USA: Capistrano, Clacks, Connell's, Dan's Dahlias, Mingus, Sea-Tac; Canada: Ferncliff; elsewhere: Jacks.

Tujay's Nicola
Peony (ADS); light blends, white and dark pink, garden and patio pot plant; 0.2m (1ft) high; raised by Jim Hammond, New Zealand, in 1996. Award Garden Merit, Wisley (NDS). Available USA: Alpen, Dan's Dahlias.

Tu-Tu
Medium semi-cactus (NDS); white, garden variety; height 1.2m (4ft); raised by Walter (pi) Ensum, UK, in 1958. Award Merit Wisley, 1961 (NDS). Available UK: National; USA: Mingus; elsewhere: Dgid, Turc.

Twiggy
Small waterlily (NDS); pink and yellow blends, garden and cut flower variety; 1.1m (3.5ft) in height; raised by Terry Clarke, UK, in 1967. Award Merit Wisley 1968 (NDS). Available UK: National; elsewhere: Geerlings.

Tyler
Medium formal decorative (ADS); bicolour, purple/white exhibition variety; 1.2m (4ft) in height; originated by Simmons, USA, in 1996.

U

Uchuu
Giant decorative (unclassified); red exhibition variety; introduced UK in 1970.

Ukraine
Giant, informal decorative (ADS); yellow exhibition variety, 1.2m (4ft) in height; originated by Marijczuk, USA, in 1991. Awarded the Lynn B. Dudley medal 1990 (ADS).

Ukraine Free
Medium informal decorative (ADS); dark red, exhibition variety; originated by Marijczuk, USA, in 1994.

Umpqua Delight
Large straight cactus (unclassified); yellow exhibition variety; tall, 1.6m (6ft) in height; originated by Olsen, USA. Available USA: Clacks, Elkhorn.

Umpqua Frosty
Miniature formal decorative (ADS); white exhibition variety; 1.2m (4ft) in height; originated by Olsen, USA, in 2000.

Umpqua Magic
Medium lacinated (ADS); flame, exhibition variety; height 1.2m (4ft); originated by Olsen, USA, in 2000. Available USA: Clacks.

Uncle Tom
Large informal decorative (unclassified); bronze exhibition variety; height 1.2m (4ft); originated USA. Available USA: Dan's Dahlias.

Union Gap
Miniature formal decorative (unclassified); purple exhibition, garden and cut flower variety; height 1.2m (4ft); originated USA, in 1992. Available USA: Connell's, Dan's Dahlias.

Urchin
Small lacinated (ADS); dark red, garden variety; originated by Blomfield, USA, in 1995. Available USA: Clacks, Dahlia Dandies, Dan's Dahlias, Elkhorn.

Utmost
Small semi-cactus (unclassified); bicolour, orange and yellow; garden variety 1.5m (4.5ft) in height; originated by L. Connell in 1995. Available USA: Connell's, Mingus; Canada: Ferncliff.

Utrecht
Giant formal decorative (unclassified); bronze, exhibition variety; height 1.2m (4ft).

TUI ORANGE

UCHUU

UKRAINE

V

Valda
Pompon (ADS); purple exhibition variety; 1.2m (4ft) high; originated by W. I. Larson, USA, in 1941.

Valerie's
Miniature formal decorative (ADS); dark blends, lavender and white exhibition variety; originated by Rejman, USA, in 1992. Available USA: SB Gardens.

Valleta
Small incurved (unclassified); light blends, white and lavender exhibition variety; height 1.1m (3.5ft); originated USA. Available USA: Clacks.

Valley CJ
Miniature formal decorative (ADS); dark red, exhibition variety; 1.2m (4ft) in height; originated by D. & L. Smith, USA, in 1998. Available Canada: Ferncliff.

Valley Pop
Miniature formal decorative (ADS); red exhibition variety; originated by D. & L. Smith, USA, in 1997.

Vanquisher
Large semi-cactus (unclassified), lavender and white blends, cut and garden flower; height 1.2m (4ft); originated USA in 1990. Available USA: Dahlia Dandies, Hamilton, Mingus.

Vantage
Giant semi-cactus (unclassified); yellow exhibition; height 1.2m (4ft); originated by Phil Traff, USA, in 1972.

Vazon Bay
Miniature ball (NDS); yellow exhibition dahlia; height 1.2m (4ft); introduced by Norman Flint, UK, in 1989.

Veca Lucia
Medium informal decorative (ADS); blends lavender and white; exhibition variety 1.2m (4ft) in height; originated by Lou Paradise, USA, in 1997. Available USA: Creekside, Elkhorn.

Velda Inez
Miniature formal decorative (unclassified); bicolour white and purple, exhibition variety, 0.9m (3ft); originated USA. Available USA: Clacks, Connell's.

Velvet Night
Miniature formal decorative (ADS); dark red, exhibition and garden variety; introduced Keith Hammett, New Zealand, in 1985. Available elsewhere: Jacks.

Vera May
Medium straight cactus (ADS); flame exhibition variety; originated by Splinter, USA, in 1990. Available USA: Elkhorn.

Vera's Elma
Large, decorative (NDS), large informal decorative (ADS); lavender exhibition variety, 1.2m (4ft) in height; raised by Geoff Gardener, UK, in 1996. Available UK: Halls, National, P. & L.; USA: Arrowhead, Connell's, Creekside; elsewhere: Jacks.

Verda
Large semi-cactus (ADS); white exhibition variety; originated by Maxwell, USA, in 1994. Available USA: Arrowhead, Clacks, Creekside, Dahlia Dandies, Dan's Dahlias, Elkhorn, SB Gardens; Canada: Candahlia; elsewhere: Konishi.

Veritable
Medium semi-cactus (NDS); lavender and white blends, garden variety, 1.1m (3.5ft) high plant; introduced by Ballego, Holland, in 1965. Available elsewhere: Dgid, Engelhardt.

Vermita
Large semi-cactus (unclassified); bronze and yellow blended variety; originated USA. Available USA: Elkhorn.

Vernon Rose
Small formal decorative (ADS); exhibition and garden variety; variegated pink and dark red; height 1.2m (4ft); originated USA in 1977. Awarded the Derrill Hart medal (ADS). Available USA: Connell's, Creekside.

Versa
Miniature formal decorative (ADS); dark blends, lavender purple, cut flower and exhibition variety; height 0.9m (3ft); originated by Madlyn Geisert, USA. Awarded the Derrill Hart medal (ADS). Available USA: Clacks, Dahlia Dandies, Dan's Dahlias, Mingus.

Vets' Love
Small semi-cactus (unclassified); dark red, exhibition variety; height 1.2m (4ft); originated USA. Available USA: Capistrano.

Vicki
Large semi-cactus (ADS); yellow exhibition variety; height 1.6m (6ft); originated by Goss, USA, in 1987. Available USA: Alpen, Arrowhead, Mingus.

VANTAGE

VAZON BAY

VERA'S ELMA

Vicky Crutchfield
Small waterlily (NDS); pink blends, garden and cut flower variety; 1.1m (3.5ft) in height; raised by John Crutchfield, UK, in 1960. Award Merit Wisley 1966 (NDS). Available UK: Butterfield, National, Oscroft, P. & L., Station House.

Vicky Jackson
Small waterlily (NDS); pink blends exhibition, garden and cut flower variety; height 1.1m (3.5ft); raised by N. Jackson, UK, in 1971. Award Merit 1973 Wisley (NDS). Available UK: National; USA: Connell's.

Victor D
Miniature ball (ADS); light blends, pink and yellow, exhibition variety; originated by W. Almand, USA, in 1985.

Vidal Rhapsody
Medium semi-cactus (NDS); pink and white blends, exhibition variety; 1.2m (4ft) in height; raised by H. Wolfgang, UK, in 1983. Available UK: National.

Vidal Tracy
Small semi-cactus (unclassified); pink exhibition variety, height 1.1m (3.5ft); raised by H. Wolfgang, UK, in 1980.

Video
Medium semi-cactus (unclassified); red exhibition variety; height 1.4m (4.5ft); introduced Aartson, Holland, in 1998. Award Garden Merit Wisley (NDS).

Vigor
Small waterlily (NDS); yellow garden and cut flower variety; height 1.2m (4ft); introduced by Bruidegom, Holland, 1963. Available UK: National, Oscroft.

Vincent
Miniature decorative gallery (NDS); orange blends for garden and patio use; 0.9m (3ft); raised by Verweer, Holland, in 1996.

Vincent Paradiso
Miniature semi-cactus (ADS); orange exhibition variety; originated by Lou Paradise, USA, in 1993.

Vino
Pompon (unclassified); dark blends, exhibition variety; height 1.2m (4ft); originated USA. Available USA: Clacks.

Violet Davies
Medium semi-cactus (NDS); yellow garden and cut flower variety; height 1.2m (4ft); raised by George Brookes, UK, in 1978. Available UK: National.

Violetta
Small semi-cactus (unclassified); light blends, white and lavender, exhibition variety; originated by Sea-Tac, USA. Available USA: Sea-Tac.

Vista A-Rod
Small formal decorative (ADS); dark red exhibition variety; originated by Heeringa, USA, in 1999.

Vista Brett
Pompon (ADS); purple exhibition variety; 1.2m (4ft) in height; originated by Heeringa, USA, in 2002.

Vivean B
Small semi-cactus (unclassified); bicolour red and yellow exhibition variety; 1.5m (4.5ft); originated by Connell's, USA, 1977. Available USA: Alpen, Connell's; elsewhere: Jacks.

V J
Small informal decorative (unclassified); yellow exhibition and cut flower variety; 1.2m (4ft); originated by L. Connell, USA, in 1989. Available USA: Connell's.

Volkskanzler
Single (ADS); dark blends, garden variety; originated by Ansorge, Germany, in 1934.

Voodoo
Small formal decorative (unclassified); dark red, cut flower variety; height 1.5m (4.5ft); originated USA in 2000. Available USA: Swan Island.

Vulcan
Large semi-cactus (unclassified); red and yellow bicolour; garden variety; introduced Holland. Available elsewhere: Geerlings.

Vulkan
Medium semi-cactus (unclassified); flame and yellow bicolour, garden variety; originated 1975. Available USA: Swan Island; elsewhere: Engelhardt, Wirth.

Vuurvogel
Medium semi-cactus (NDS); red and yellow bicolour, garden variety; height 1.2m (4ft); introduced by Bruidegom, Holland, in 1962. Available elsewhere: Dgid.

W

Waiva Miner
Miniature formal decorative (ADS); red garden and exhibition variety; originated by R. Miner, USA, in 1996.

Walter Hardisty
Giant decorative (NDS), giant informal decorative (ADS); white exhibition variety, height 1.2m (4ft); originated by Gentile, USA, in 1975. Award of Garden Merit, Wisley, 1993 (NDS); awarded the Lynn B. Dudley 1974 and Stanley Johnson medals (ADS). Available UK: Cruikshank, National, P. & L.; USA: Dahlia Dandies, SB Gardens, Swan Island; Canada: Candahlia, Ferncliff.

Walter Hoppe
Miniature formal decorative (ADS); dark red garden and exhibition variety; originated by R. Miner, USA, in 1993.

VIDAL RHAPSODY

VIDEO

VIVEAN B

WALTER HARDISTY

Walter Huston
Large semi-cactus (ADS); dark pink exhibition variety; height 1.5m (5ft); originated by Earle Huston, Canada, in 1988. Available USA: Clacks; Canada: Ferncliff.

Walt's Wonder
Miniature formal decorative (ADS); pink garden and exhibition variety; originated by W. Taylor, USA, in 1989.

Wanborough Gem
Small ball (NDS); yellow, pink-blended exhibition variety; 1.2m (4ft) in height; raised by Terry Clarke, UK. Available UK: Cruikshank, National, P. & L.

Wanda's Antarctica
Giant decorative (NDS); white exhibition variety; height 1.1m (3.5ft); raised by Les Wright, UK, in 1996. Available UK: P. & L.; Canada: Ferncliff; elsewhere: Jacks.

Wanda's Capella
Giant decorative (NDS), giant informal decorative (ADS); yellow exhibition variety; 1.2m (4ft) high bush; raised Les Wright, UK, in 1986. Available UK: Abacus, Clark, Cruikshank, Halls, National, Oscroft, P. & L.; USA: Dan's Dahlias, Sea-Tac; Canada: Ferncliff; elsewhere: Geerlings.

Wanda's Moonlight
Giant decorative (NDS); yellow exhibition variety, height 1.2m (4ft); raised by Les Wright, UK, in 1986. Available UK: National, Oscroft, P. & L.; USA: Hamilton, Mingus.

Wandy
Pompon (NDS); bronze exhibition, garden and cut flower variety; height 0.9m (3ft); introduced by Cor Geerlings, Holland, in 1988.

Award Garden Merit Wisley (NDS). Available UK: Abacus, National, Oscroft.

Washington County
Mignon single (unclassified); light blends, white and lavender; height 0.2m (1ft) garden and patio pot variety; originated USA. Available USA: Alpen.

Way Pink
Star (ADS); pink exhibition and garden variety; originated by K. Larkin, USA, in 1997.

Wedding Vows
Small lacinated (ADS); white exhibition variety; originated by Ghio, USA, in 2001.

Welcome Guest
Medium semi-cactus (NDS); red garden and cut flower variety; 1.2m (4ft) in height; introduced Bruidegom, Holland, in 1975. Available UK: National, Oscroft, P. & L., Station House, Tivey.

Welsh Beauty
Small ball (NDS); pink blends, garden and cut flower variety; height 1.1m (3.5ft); raised by G. Marsh, UK, in 1990. Available UK: National, P. & L.

Wendy
Miniature ball (NDS); orange blends, exhibition, garden and cut flower variety; height 1.1m (3.5ft); raised by Norman Lewis, UK, in 1991. Available UK: National.

Wendy Miner
Medium semi-cactus (ADS); dark pink garden and exhibition variety; originated by R. Miner, USA, in 1996.

Wendy's Place
Pompon (NDS and ADS); purple exhibition, garden and

cut flower; height 1.2m (4ft); raised by P. Maugham, UK, in 1992. Available UK: Cruikshank, National, P. & L.; USA: Connell's, Dan's Dahlias.

Weston Nugget
Miniature cactus (NDS), miniature semi-cactus (ADS); bronze exhibition and garden variety; height 1.2m (4ft); raised by Tom McLelland, UK, in 1995. Available UK: Abacus, National, Station House.

Weston Pirate
Miniature semi-cactus (NDS), and straight cactus (ADS); red (NDS), dark red (ADS); exhibition and garden variety; height 1.2m (4ft); raised by Tom McLelland, UK, in 1998. Available UK: Oscroft, Porter, Station House, Taylor.

Weston Spanish Dancer
Small or miniature cactus (NDS), or miniature cactus (ADS); red and yellow blends (NDS), or flame (ADS); exhibition, garden and cut flower variety; height 1.2m (4ft); raised by Tom McLelland, UK, in 2000. Winner of the Stredwick medal (NDS). Available UK: Abacus, National, Station House, Tivey; USA: Clacks.

Whale's Rhonda
Pompon (NDS); purple blends, exhibition and garden variety; height 1.2m (4ft); raised by A. Whale, UK, in 1960. Award Merit Wisley 1964 (NDS). Available UK: Abacus, National, Station House, Tivey.

Wheels
Collarette (ADS); red with yellow collar; exhibition variety; 1.2m (4ft) in height; originated by Swan Island, USA, in 1996. Available USA: Clacks, Connell's, Swan Island.

WESTON NUGGET

WANDA'S ANTARCTICA

WANDA'S CAPELLA

WESTON PIRATE

WESTON SPANISH DANCER

WANDA'S MOONLIGHT

WHEELS

White Alvas
Giant decorative (NDS), large formal decorative (ADS); white exhibition variety, sport of 'Alva's Supreme'; raised by Jim Mills, UK, in 1978. Award Garden Merit Wisley (NDS). Available UK: Cruikshank, Halls, National, Oscroft, P. & L., Station House, Tivey; USA: Sea-Tac; elsewhere: Geerlings, Wirth.

White Ballet
Small waterlily (NDS), waterlily (ADS); white garden and cut flower variety, height 0.9m (3ft); introduced Geerlings, Holland, in 1985. Award Garden Merit Wisley (NDS). Available UK: Aylett's, Blooms, Butterfield, Halls, National, Oscroft; USA: Sea-Tac; elsewhere: Dgid, Geerlings.

White Klankstad
Small cactus (NDS and ADS); white exhibition, garden and cut flower variety; 0.9m (3ft) in height; sport of Klankstad Kerkrade, raised by Manson, UK, in 1967. Award Merit Wisley 1969 (NDS). Available: UK: National, Oscroft, Roberts; USA: Dan's Dahlias.

White Knight
Miniature decorative (NDS), miniature formal decorative (ADS); white exhibition and garden variety; height 1.2m (4ft); raised Cleghorn, UK, in 1999. Available UK: Cruikshank, Halls, P. & L., Spencer; elsewhere: Jacks.

White Linda
Small decorative (NDS), small formal decorative (ADS); white exhibition, garden and cut flower variety; height 1.2m (4ft); raised Bill Mark, UK, in 1984. Available UK: Cruikshank, Halls, National, Oscroft, P. & L., Roberts; USA: Dahlia Dandies, Dan's Dahlias, Mingus.

White Moonlight
Medium semi-cactus (NDS); white exhibition, garden and cut flower variety; 1.2m (4ft) in height; sport of 'Eastwood Moonlight'; raised by Len Mace, UK. Available UK: Abacus, Aylett's, Butterfield, Clark, Cruikshank, Halls, National, P. & L., Scotts, Station House, Tivey; USA: Mingus; elsewhere: Jacks.

White Nettie
Miniature ball (ADS); white exhibition variety, height 1.1m (3.5ft); raised in the UK in 1974. Available USA: Connell's, Dan's Dahlias, Frey's, SB Gardens, Swan Island.

White Orchid
Orchid (ADS); white exhibition variety; originated by Knopp, USA, in 2001. Available USA: Clacks.

White Pastelle
Medium semi-cactus (NDS); white exhibition variety, height 1.2m (4ft); sport of 'Grenidor Pastelle'; raised by Deacon, UK, in 1998. Available UK: Abacus, Oscroft, P. & L., Porter, Pratt, Spencer, Station House, Taylor; USA: Sea-Tac.

White Perfection
Giant decorative (NDS); white garden variety; height 1.2m (4ft); sport of 'Lavender Perfection'; introduced van Veelen, Holland, in 1967. Available UK: National, Suttons; USA: Elkhorn; elsewhere: Dgid, Engelhardt.

White Polventon
Small ball (NDS and ADS); white exhibition, garden and cut flower variety; sport of 'Polventon Supreme'; raised Boone, UK, in 1998. Available UK: Halls, National, Oscroft, P. & L., Scotts; Canada: Ferncliff.

White Purity
Small formal decorative (ADS); white exhibition variety; originated by L. Connell, USA, in 1991. Available USA: Mingus.

White Rustig
Medium decorative (NDS); white exhibition variety, 1.2m (4ft) high plant; sport of Rustig; raised by Terry Clarke, UK, in 1979. Available UK: Cruikshank, National; USA: Connell's.

White Shadow
Small formal decorative (ADS); white exhibition variety; originated by Albert, USA, in 2001.

White Swallow
Small semi-cactus (NDS and ADS); white exhibition variety; introduced by dahlia Maarse, Holland, in 1966. Available UK: Halls, P. & L., Roberts; elsewhere: Jacks.

Wicky Woo
Small formal decorative (unclassified); garden and cut flower, bicolour purple and white; height 1.2m (4ft); originated USA in 1960. Available USA: Connell's, Elkhorn, Frey's, Swan Island.

Wiggles
Medium straight cactus (ADS), orange garden variety; introduced Australia in 1964.

Wilbur Seipel
Small incurved cactus (ADS); red exhibition variety; originated by L. Havens, USA, in 2000.

WHITE ALVAS

WHITE BALLET

WHITE KLANKSTAD

WHITE KNIGHT

WHITE MOONLIGHT

WHITE PASTELLE

WHITE POLVENTON

WHITE SWALLOW

Wildcat
Miniature semi-cactus (ADS); dark blends, dark red and yellow, cut flower and garden variety; originated by Swan Island, 1998. Available USA: Frey's, Swan Island.

Wildman
Giant semi-cactus (ADS); red exhibition variety; 1.1m (3.5ft) in height; originated by Phil Traff, USA, in 1984. Available USA: Alpen, Arrowhead, Clacks, Connell's, Dahlia Dandies, Frey's, Hamilton, SB Gardens, Sea-Tac, Swan Island.

Wildwood Glory
Medium semi-cactus (ADS); orange garden variety, 1.2m (4ft) high bush; originated by Papierski, USA, in 1991. Available USA: Elkhorn.

Wildwood Marie
Waterlily (ADS); dark pink exhibition variety, 1.2m (4ft) high plant; originated by Papierski, USA, in 1993. Awarded the Lynn B. Dudley medal 1992 (ADS). Available USA: Alpen, Clacks, Connell's, Creekside, Dahlia Dandies, Dan's Dahlias, Mingus, SB Gardens, Sea-Tac.

Wildwood Swirls
Small incurved cactus (ADS); red exhibition variety, 1.2m (4ft) in height; originated by Papierski, USA, in 1989. Available USA: Elkhorn, Sea-Tac.

William B
Giant decorative (NDS); pink blends, exhibition variety; 1.2m (4ft) in height; raised by Tom Bebbington, UK, in 1980. Available UK: National.

William D
Collarette (ADS); white with white collar; garden variety; height 1.2m (4ft); originated by Dungan, USA, in 2001. Available USA: Alpen.

William John
Pompon (NDS and ADS); orange-red blends (NDS), light blends, yellow and red (ADS); exhibition variety; height 1.1m (3.5ft); introduced Norman Williams, Australia, in 1967. Available UK: Cruikshank, National; USA: Clacks, SB Gardens.

William R
Large semi-cactus (ADS); dark pink exhibition variety; height 1.2m (4ft); originated by Ed Redd, USA, in 1990. Awarded the Derrill Hart medal (ADS). Available USA: Dahlia Dandies.

Willie
Pompon (ADS); light blends, white and pink, exhibition and garden variety; originated by H. Johnston, USA, in 1982.

Willie of Orange
Small semi-cactus (unclassified); orange exhibition variety; height 1.2m (4ft); originated by Ferncliff, Canada, in 2001. Available Canada: Ferncliff.

Willie Willie
Orchid (ADS); light blends, dark red and white; originated USA in 1998.

Willo Fleck
Pompon (NDS and ADS); variegated yellow and red, exhibition and garden variety; 1.2m (4ft) high plant;

introduced by Norman Williams, Australia, in 1966. Available UK: Abacus, National, Tivey.

Willo's Borealis
Pompon (ADS); lavender exhibition variety; 1.2m (4ft) in height; introduced by Norman Williams, Australia, in 1980. Available USA: Clacks, Connell's, SB Gardens.

Willo's Surprise
Pompon (ADS and NDS); dark red exhibition variety; height 90cm (3ft), blooms on long stems; raised by Norman Williams in 1964. Available UK: Cruikshank, Halls, National, P. & L., Station House, Tivey; USA: Clacks.

Willo's Violet (synonymous to **Birchwood Minx**)
Pompon (ADS); purple exhibition and garden variety; height 1.1m (3.5ft); introduced by Norman Williams, Australia, in 1937. Available UK: Abacus, Clarks, Cruikshank, Jones, JRG, National, Oscroft, P. & L., Roberts, Spencer, Station House, Tivey; USA: Dan's Dahlias, Frey's.

Willo's Night
Pompon (NDS); red exhibition variety; height 0.9m (3ft); raised by Stuart Ogg, UK, in 1960. Available UK: National.

Willowfield Mick
Large, decorative (NDS); orange and pink blends, exhibition variety; 1.2m (4ft) high plant; raised by Powley, UK, in 1999. Available UK: Abacus, Halls, National, Oscroft, P. & L., Porter, Roberts.

WILDWOOD MARIE

WILLIAM B

WILLO'S VIOLET

WILLOWFIELD MICK

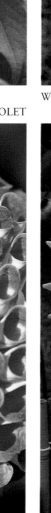

Will's Starburst
Large, formal decorative (ADS); dark pink, exhibition variety; originated by Dufresne, USA, in 2000.

Windhaven Blush
Large semi-cactus (ADS); yellow exhibition variety; originated by Romano, USA, in 2001. Awarded the Lynn B. Dudley medal (ADS).

Windhaven Copper
Miniature formal decorative (ADS); orange garden and exhibition variety; originated by Romano, USA, in 2000.

Windhaven Highlight
Medium incurved cactus (ADS); yellow exhibition variety; height 1.5m (5ft); originated by Romano, USA, in 2000. Awarded the Lynn B. Dudley medal, 1999 (ADS). Available USA: Alpen, Arrowhead, Clacks, Mingus.

Windhaven Premier
Large straight cactus (ADS); white exhibition variety; height 1.5m (5ft); originated by Romano, USA, in 1998. Awarded the Lynn B. Dudley medal, 1997 (ADS). Available USA: Alpen, Clacks, Dahlia Dandies, Elkhorn.

Wine & Roses
Waterlily (ADS); dark blends, white and purple, exhibition variety; 1.2m (4ft) high plant; originated in the USA in 1981. Available USA: Clacks, Connell's, Dan's Dahlias, Elkhorn, SB Gardens; Canada: Ferncliff.

Wine Frost
Orchid (ADS); dark red, originated by L. Connell, USA, in 1989. Awarded the Lynn B. Dudley medal, 1988 (ADS). Available USA: Dan's Dahlias.

Winkie Colonel
Giant decorative (NDS), giant informal decorative (ADS); red exhibition variety, 1.2m (4ft) high; introduced by Menzel, Australia, in 1996. Available UK: Cruikshank, Halls, National, P. & L., Spencer; USA: Alpen, Clacks, Sea-Tac; Canada: Ferncliff; elsewhere: Jacks.

Winter Dawn
Small waterlily (NDS); yellow garden and cut flower; height 1.1m (3.5ft); raised by John Crutchfield, UK, in 1981. Award Merit 1987 Wisley (NDS). Available UK: National.

Wisemark
Medium semi-cactus (unclassified); yellow exhibition, garden and cut flower; height 1.2m (4ft); raised by W. Mark, UK, in 1994.

Witteman's Superba
Medium semi-cactus (NDS and ADS); red, garden variety, height 1.1m (3.5ft); introduced by L. Berbee, Holland, in 1991. Award Garden Merit Wisley (NDS). Available UK: Aylett's, Halls, National, P. & L.; USA: Clacks; elsewhere: Jacks.

Woodland's Accolade
Miniature formal decorative (ADS); lavender variety; originated by Mishler, USA, in 2001. Available USA: Mingus.

Woodland's Autumn
Small semi-cactus (ADS); orange variety; originated by Mishler, USA, in 2001. Available USA: Mingus.

Woodland's Donna
Small semi-cactus (ADS); light blend, lavender and yellow; originated by Mishler, USA, in 1999. Available USA: Elkhorn, Mingus.

Woodland's Dufus
Miniature ball (ADS); purple garden and exhibition variety; originated by Mishler, USA, in 2001.

Woodland's Little China
Small formal decorative (ADS); dark red variety; originated by Mishler, USA, in 2000. Available USA: Mingus.

Woodland's Naomi
Miniature formal decorative (ADS); lavender exhibition and garden variety; originated by Mishler, USA, in 2001.

Woodland's Sparkle
Large lacinated (ADS); white variety; originated by Mishler, USA, in 1999. Available USA: Mingus.

Woodland's Sweet
Large, informal decorative (ADS); light blends, pink and yellow, garden and exhibition variety; originated by Mishler, USA, in 2001.

WINDHAVEN PREMIER

WINE & ROSES

WISEMARK

WITTEMAN'S SUPERBA

WINKIE COLONEL

Woodland's Uptown Girl
Miniature formal decorative (ADS); red exhibition and garden variety; height 1.5m (5ft); originated by Mishler, USA, in 1998. Awarded the Derrill Hart medal (ADS). Available USA: Clacks, Mingus.

Woodland's Wildthing
Medium semi-cactus (ADS); orange exhibition variety, 1.2m (4ft) high plant; originated by Mishler, USA, in 2000. Available USA: Clacks, Dahlia Dandies, Mingus.

Woody Woodpecker
Collerette (unclassified); red with yellow collar, garden and cut flower variety; height 1.1m (3.5ft); originated USA in 1993.

Wootton Cupid
Miniature ball (NDS), ball (ADS); pink (NDS), dark pink (ADS); exhibition, garden and cut flower variety; 0.9m (3ft) high plant; raised Les Jones, UK, 1980. Award Merit 1981 Wisley (NDS). Available UK: Abacus, Butterfield, Clark, Cruikshank, Halls, National, Oscroft, P. & L., Robert, Scotts, Station House, Tivey; elsewhere: Graines, Wirth.

Wootton Impact
Medium semi-cactus (NDS and ADS); bronze blends, exhibition variety; 1.2m (4ft) high plant; raised by Les Jones, UK, in 1982. Award Merit 1981 Wisley (NDS). Available UK: Butterfield, Clark, Cruikshank, Oscroft, P. & L., Station House, Tivey; elsewhere: Geerlings, Jacks.

Worton Blue Streak
Small semi-cactus (ADS); lavender exhibition and cut flower variety; 0.9m (3ft) in

height; originated by Ivor Lewis, UK, in 1975. Available USA: Clacks, Dan's Dahlias, Elkhorn, Mingus, SB Gardens, Swan Island; Canada: Ferncliff; elsewhere: Graines, Jacks.

Wowie
Collarette (ADS); red with white collar; garden variety; originated USA in 1998. Available USA: Clacks, Swan Island.

X

Xmas Carol
Collerette (unclassified); dark red with white collar; garden variety; 1.1m (3.5ft) in height.

Y

Yara Falls
Large informal decorative (ADS); bicolour dark/red and white, exhibition variety; height 1.1m (3.5ft); introduced Australia in 1992.

Yellow Baby
Pompon (ADS); yellow exhibition variety, height 1.2m (4ft); originated by Impiccichi, USA, in 1960. Available USA: Alpen, Clacks, Dan's Dahlias, SB Gardens.

Yellow Bird
Collarette (ADS); yellow garden variety; height 1.2m (4ft); originated 1995. Available USA: Connell's, Dan's Dahlias, Swan Island.

Yellow Button
Medium formal decorative (unclassified); yellow garden variety. Available USA: Elkhorn.

Yellow C
Small straight cactus (unclassified); cut flower variety; 1.2m (4ft) in height; originated USA. Available USA: Frey's.

Yellow Climax
Small formal decorative (unclassified); yellow cut flower and garden variety; height 1.2m (4ft); originated USA in 1969. Available USA: Swan Island.

Yellow Corvette
Medium incurved cactus (ADS); yellow exhibition variety, height 1.1m (3.5ft); originated by Gill, USA, in 1982. Available USA: SB Gardens.

Yellow Frank Hornsey
Small decorative (NDS); yellow bronze blends, exhibition, garden and cut flower variety; 1.2m (4ft) in height; raised by Ivor Lewis, UK, in 1977. Available UK: Abacus, National.

Yellow Hammer
Dwarf bedder (NDS); garden variety, height 0.6m (2ft); introduced 1966. Award Garden Merit Wisley (NDS). Available UK: Aylett's, Halls, National; elsewhere: Wirth.

Yellow Harlequin
Medium informal decorative (ADS); variegated yellow and red exhibition variety; originated by Gregersdal, USA, in 1998.

Yellow Impact
Medium semi-cactus (NDS); yellow exhibition, garden and cut flower variety; sport of 'Wootton Impact'; height 1.2m (4ft); raised by David Reid, UK, in 1991. Available UK: Cruikshank.

WOODLAND'S UPTOWN GIRL

WOODY WOODPECKER

WOOTTON CUPID

WOOTTON IMPACT

XMAS CAROL

YELLOW HAMMER

YELLOW IMPACT

Yellow Linda's Chester
Small cactus (NDS); yellow
exhibition variety, height 0.9m
(3ft); sport of 'Linda's Chester';
raised by Bob Porter, UK, in
1995. Available UK: National,
P. & L.

Yellow Spiky
Medium semi-cactus (NDS);
yellow orange blends,
exhibition, garden and cut
flower variety; height 1.2m (4ft);
sport of 'Spiky Symbol'; raised
by Terry Clarke, UK, in 1967.
Award Merit 1976 Wisley
(NDS). Available UK: National.

Yellow Star
Small semi-cactus (ADS);
yellow exhibition and garden
variety; originated by de
Ruyter, Holland, in 1952.
Available USA: Elkhorn.

Yellow Submarine
Miniature formal decorative
(ADS); yellow exhibition
variety; originated by Sampson,
Canada, in 2000.

Yellow Symbol
Medium semi-cactus (NDS);
garden variety, 1.2m (4ft) in
height; sport of 'Symbol';
raised by R. F. Howes, UK, in
1977. Available UK:
Butterfield, National.

Yelno Enchantment
Small waterlily (NDS); pink
blends, garden and cut flower

variety; height 1.2m (4ft); raised
by John Sharpe, UK. Available
UK: Aylett's, National.

Yelno Firelight
Small waterlily (NDS); orange
blends, garden and cut flower
variety; 1.2m (4ft) high plant;
raised by John Sharpe, UK.
Available UK: National.

Yelno Harmony
Small waterlily (NDS); purple
garden and cut flower variety;
1.2m (4ft) in height; raised by
John Sharpe, UK, in 1986.
Award Garden Merit Wisley
(NDS). Available UK:
Butterfield, National;
elsewhere: Dgid, Engelhardt.

Yelno Velvena
Small waterlily (NDS); red
garden and cut flower variety;
height 1.2m (4ft); raised by
John Sharpe, UK. Available
UK: Aylett's.

YMA Sumac
Medium semi-cactus
(unclassified); yellow garden
and exhibition variety; height
1.5m (4.5ft); raised by G.
Brookes, UK, in 1976. Award
Merit 1977 Wisley (NDS).

Yorkie
Medium semi-cactus (NDS);
white exhibition, garden and
cut flower variety; height 1.2m
(4ft); raised by Fred Oscroft,
UK. Available UK: Abacus,

National, Scotts, Station
House, Tivey.

Yoro Kobi
Waterlily (unclassified);
red/white garden variety; height
0.9m (3ft). Available USA:
Hamilton, Swan Island.

Yunioh
Large informal decorative
(unclassified); bicolour, dark
red and white garden variety;
height 1.2m (4ft). Available
USA: Clacks; elsewhere: Jacks.

Yuukyu
Medium informal decorative
(ADS); white exhibition variety,
height 1.6m (5ft); originated by
Tokunnaga, Japan, in 1974.
Available USA: Creekside,
Dan's Dahlias, SB Gardens.

Yvonne
Small waterlily (NDS),
waterlily (ADS); pink garden
and cut flower variety; height
1.2m (4ft); introduced
Geerlings, Holland, in 1991.
Available UK: Abacus,
National, P.& L.; USA:
Connell's, Dan's Dahlias,
Mingus, SB Gardens; Canada:
Ferncliff; elsewhere: Dgid,
Geerlings.

YELNO ENCHANTMENT

YORKIE

YELLOW LINDA'S CHESTER

YELLOW SYMBOL

YVONNE

Z

Zachary
Waterlily (ADS); variegated lavender and red exhibition variety; originated by McClaren, USA, in 1980.

Zakuro Hime
Medium formal decorative (unclassified); bicolour red and white, garden variety. Available USA: Dan's Dahlias, Sea-Tac.

Zalu
Small cactus (unclassified); garden variety on a 1.2m (4ft) high bush; originated by Connell, USA. Available USA: Connell's.

Zanny
Small formal decorative (ADS); dark red exhibition variety; originated by Goff, USA, in 2001. Available USA: Elkhorn, SB Gardens.

Zapf's Desert Storm
Small semi-cactus (ADS), dark red exhibition variety; originated by Zapf, USA, in 1992. Available USA: Arrowhead, Elkhorn, Mingus.

Zeal
Medium formal decorative (unclassified); lavender and purple blends, garden variety. Available USA: Dan's Dahlias.

Zelda
Large informal decorative (unclassified); dark red garden variety. Available USA: Dan's Dahlias, Elkhorn, Mingus, SB Gardens.

Zenith
Medium semi-cactus (unclassified); lavender garden and cut flower variety; 1.2m (4ft) in height.

Zeus
Small straight cactus (unclassified); purple garden variety. Awarded the Lynn B. Dudley medal 1966 (ADS). Available USA: Elkhorn.

Zing
Large semi-cactus (unclassified); white and pink, garden variety. Available USA: Dan's Dahlias.

Zodiac
Medium lacinated (unclassified); purple garden variety; height 1.2m (4ft); originated USA. Available Canada: Ferncliff.

Zonnegoud
Miniature ball (NDS); yellow and orange blends, garden and cut flower variety; height 1.2m (4ft); introduced C. Geerlings, Holland, in 1950.

Zorro
Giant decorative (NDS), giant informal decorative (ADS); red (NDS), dark red (ADS); exhibition variety, originated by Madlyn Geisert, USA. In 1987 awarded the Lynn B. Dudley, in 1986 the Derrill Hart and Stanley Johnson medals. Available UK: Abacus, Cruikshank, Halls, National, Oscroft, P. & L., Station House, Tivey; USA: Arrowhead, Clacks, Connell's, Dahlia Dandies, Dan's Dahlias, Frey's, Hamilton, Mingus, SB Gardens, Sea-Tac, Swan Island; Canada: Candahlia, Ferncliff; elsewhere: Geerlings, Jacks.

Zufall's Gold
Large formal decorative (ADS); yellow exhibition variety; originated by Zufall, USA, in 1978.

Zurich
Medium semi-cactus (unclassified); orange garden variety, 1.2m (4ft) in height; introduced Cor Geerlings.

ZELDA

ZENITH

ZORRO

ZURICH

Suppliers

United Kingdom

Abacus
Abacus Nurseries, Drummau Road,
Skewen, Neath SA10 6NW, Wales
Tel: 01792 817994

Aylett's
Aylett Nurseries Ltd, North Orbital Road,
St Albans AL2 1DH
Tel: 01727 822255

Blooms
Blooms Bulbs Ltd, Primrose Nursery,
Sharnbrook MK44 1LW
Tel: 01234 782424

Butterfield
Ian Butterfield, The Nursery, Harvest Hill,
Bourne End SL8 5JJ
Tel: 01628 525455

Clark
J. Clark (Dahlias), 15 Elm Grove, South
Shields NE34 6AZ
Tel: 01914 558116

Cruikshank
J. & I. Cruikshank, Ridgeview Nursery,
Longridge EH47 9AB, Scotland
Tel: 01501 71144

Halls
Halls of Heddon, Heddon on the Wall,
Newcastle upon Tyne NE15 0JS
Tel: 01661 852445

Jager
P. de Jager & Sons Ltd, Staplehurst Road,
Marden, Kent TN12 9PT
Tel: 01622 831235

Jones
Hywel Jones, Or-Dawe Cwmdu, Llandeilo,
Carmarthenshire SA19 7DY, Wales
Tel: 01558 685423

JRG
Mrs J. Gott, 22 Summerville Road,
Milnethorpe LA7 7DF
Tel: 01539 562691

National
National Collection, Varfell Farm, Long
Rock, Penzance, Cornwall TR20 8AQ
Tel: 01736 851033

Oscroft
Oscroft Nurseries, Sprotboro Road,
Doncaster, South Yorkshire DN5 8BE
Tel: 01302 785026

P. & L.
P. & L. Nursery, 58 Cambridge Street,
St Neots PE19 1PH
Tel: 01480 391087

Porter
Mrs R. Porter, Willowbrook, 58 Stanley
Road, Halstead, Essex CO9 1LA
Tel: 01817 476690

Pratt
Neil Pratt's Dahlias, 75 Bruce Glazier
Terrace, Shotton Colliery, Durham
DH6 2PN
Tel: 0191 517 3694

Proculture
Proculture Plants Ltd,
Knowle Hill, Badsey, Evesham WR11 5EN
Tel: 01386 832839

Roberts
E. Roberts, Fellin Nursery, Dolwyddelan,
Gwynedd LL25 0EQ
Tel: 01690 750319

Scotts
Scotts Nurseries, Capri, Old Denaby,
Doncaster DN12 4LD
Tel: 01709 589906

Spencer
D. Spencer, Fieldview, High Road, Fobbing,
Essex SS17 9HG
Tel: 01268 558260

Station House
Station House Nurseries, Station House
Road, South Wirral CH64 5SD
Tel: 01513 530022

Surrey
Surrey Dahlias, 48 Vickers Road, Ash Vale,
Surrey GU12 5SE
Tel: 01252 693003

Suttons
Suttons Seeds, Woodview Road, Paignton,
Devon TQ4 7NG
Tel: 01803 696366

Taylor
F. Taylor, 12 Shawbury Grove, Sale,
Cheshire M33 4DS
Tel: 01619 737178

Tivey
P. Tivey, 28 Wanlip Road, Syston, Leicester
LE7 8PA
Tel: 01162 692968

Unwin
Unwin Seeds Ltd, Hyston, Cambridge
CB4 4ZZ
Tel: 01945 588522

United States of America

Alpen
Alpen Gardens, 29477 SW Ladd Hill
Road, Sherwood, OR97140
Tel: 503 625 3327
Tel: 360 3181405

Arrowhead
Arrowhead Dahlias, Calvin Cook 10567,
Road 37, Fort Lupton CO86021
Tel: 303 5364384

Capistrano
Capistrano Dahlia Gallery,
547 Capistrano Drive, Kalispell MT59901
Tel: 406 7524371

Clacks
Clacks Dahlia Patch, 5585 North Myrtle
Road, Myrtle Creek OR97457
Tel: 541 8634501

Connell's
Connell's Dahlias, 10616 Waller Road
East, Tacoma WA98446
Tel: 253 5310292

Creekside
Creekside Dahlia Farm, 3447 Whitepath
Road, Ellijay, GA30540
Tel: 1-706 2761405

Dahlia Dandies
Dahlia Dandies, 1717 South Woodland
Drive, MT59901
Tel: 406 7552735

Dan's Dahlias
Dan's Dahlias, 994 South Bank Road,
Oakville, WA98568
Tel: 360 4822406

Elkhorn
Elkhorn Gardens, PO Box 1149, Carmel,
CA93921
Tel: 1-831 7612280

Frey's
Frey's Dahlias, 12054 Brick Road, Turner,
OR97392
Tel: 503 7433910

Hamilton
Hamilton Dahlia Farm, 4710 South Street,
Hamilton, MI49419
Tel: 616 7512981

Juul
Gerda and Erik Juul
1674 44th Avenue, San Francisco,
CA94122

Mingus
Mingus Dahlias, 7407 N.E. 139th Street,
Vancouver, WA98662
Tel: 360 5732983

SB Gardens
SB Gardens, 12027 62nd Avenue South,
Seattle, WA98178

Sea-Tac
Sea-Tac Gardens, 20020 Des Moines
Memorial Drive, Seattle WA98198
Tel: 206 8243846

Swan Island
Swan Island Dahlias, PO Box 700-CDS,
Canby, OR97013
Tel: 1-800 4106540

Suppliers

Canada

Candahlia
Candahlia Gardens, 82 Clifton Downs Road, Hamilton, Ontario L9C2P3
Tel: 905 3885595

Ferncliff
Ferncliff Gardens, 8502 McTaggart Street, Mission BC V2V 6S6
Tel: 604 8262447

Elsewhere

Dgid
Dahliagid, Dutch CNB, Handelscentrum Lisse, Holland
Tel: 0031 252431169

Engelhardt
Engelhardt, 01809 Heidenau bei Dresden, Guterbahnhafstrade 53
Tel: 03529 512069

Geerlings
Geerlings Dahlias, Kadjik 38 2104 AA Heemstede, Holland
Fax: 0031 235284075

Graines
Graines Baumax, B.P. 100, 54062 Nancy Cedex France
Tel: 0383 158686

Jacks
Belle Fleur Gardens, W. & K. Jack, Drain Road, Northope RD4, Invercargill, New Zealand
Tel: (03) 236 8523

Konishi
Yusaku Konishi, 455 Chibadera Chuo-ku Chiba-shi Japan Trade Only
Tel: 043 2645450

Turc
Ernest Turc, 4980000 Brain sur l'Authion, Angers, France
Tel: 33 241660101

Wirth
Gerhard Wirth, 1180 Wien Leschetitzkygasse 11, Germany
Tel: 479 5383